English/Japanese Edition

The New Oxford Picture Dictionary

E. C. Parnwell

Translated by Akito Miyamoto

Illustrations by:
Ray Burns
Bob Giuliani
Laura Hartman
Pamela Johnson
Melodye Rosales
Raymond Skibinski
Joel Snyder

Oxford University Press

Oxford University Press

200 Madison Avenue
New York, NY 10016 USA

Walton Street
Oxford OX2 6DP England

OXFORD is a trademark of Oxford University Press.

ISBN 0-19-434356-1

Associate Editor: Mary Lynne Nielsen
Assistant Editor: Mary Sutherland
Art Director: Lynn Luchetti
Production Coordinator: Claire Nicholl
The publishers would like to thank the following agents for their cooperation:
Carol Bancroft and Friends, representing Bob Giuliani,
Laura Hartman, and Melodye Rosales.

Publishers Graphics Inc., representing Ray Burns,
Pamela Johnson, and Joel Snyder.

Cover illustration by Laura Hartman.

Printing (last digit): 9 8 7 6 5 4
Printed in Hong Kong.

The New Oxford Picture Dictionary contextually illustrates over 2,400 words. The book is a unique language learning tool for students of English. It provides students with a glance at American lifestyle, as well as a compendium of useful vocabulary.

The *Dictionary* is organized thematically, beginning with topics that are most useful for the "survival" needs of students in an English-speaking country. However, pages may be used at random, depending on the students' particular needs. The book need not be taught in order.

The New Oxford Picture Dictionary contextualizes vocabulary whenever possible. Verbs have been included on separate pages, but within a topic area where they are most likely to occur. However, this does not imply that these verbs only appear within these contexts.

Articles are shown only with irregular nouns. Regional variations of the primary translation are listed following a slash (/). A complete index with pronunciation guide in English is in the Appendix.

For further ideas on using *The New Oxford Picture Dictionary*, see the *Teacher's Guide* and the two workbooks: *Beginner's* and *Intermediate* levels. Also available in the program are a complete set of *Cassettes*, offering a reading of all of the words in the *Dictionary*; *Vocabulary Playing Cards*, featuring 40 words and the corresponding pictures on 80 cards, with ideas for many games; and sets of *Wall Charts*, available in one complete package or in three smaller packages. All of these items are available in English only.

　英語を学ぶものはだれしも語彙を増やしたいと願うものですが、(辞書のページを次々に食べてしまったというような武勇伝があるにもかかわらず) 単語をその意味と共にアルファベット順に暗記するのは大抵徒労に終わります。その最大の理由は、覚えるべき単語の配列に確かな根拠がないことです。覚えやすくするには、関連しあった語をグループにまとめる、意味に関して強い印象を残すようにする、などの工夫が必要です。

　この小辞典に収めた2400語はこの2点を考慮して選んだものです。収録単語は、現代アメリカ人の生活様式を一瞥できるように、主題別・場面別に示してあります。英語圏での滞在にまず必要となる生活語から次第に社会・自然を対象とするより一般的な語へ至るように配列してありますが、学習の都合や自分の興味によっては、どのページから始めても差し支えありません。大事なことは、単語と絵をしっかりと結び付け、必要に応じて日本語の相当語を参照しながら、場面全体の中でその語のイメージを頭に焼きつけることです。

　日本語の相当語のうち、読みの難しい漢字には振仮名を振ってあります。またいわゆる当て字は [角括弧] の中にいれて示してあります。1つの対象に対して2つ以上の英語表現が考えられる場合は、現代のアメリカで最も普通に使われる基本語を1つだけ掲げてあります。他の表現や地方による語彙の違いなどは、別売の Teacher's Guide に詳しく解説してあります。

　本書を教室で使用する場合には、単に単語集としてではなく、与えられた場面を中心にアメリカの生活・文化に関する質疑応答やゲームの資料として役立てることもできます。その他、使い方のアイデアについては、Teacher's Guide および Beginner's と Intermediate レベルの2冊のワークブックが役立ちます。また、本書に収録した全ての英単語を録音したカセットと、教室用のウォールチャート、単語カードも用意してあります。これらの材料が少しでも語彙増強に励む学習者の助けとなれば幸いです。

　フルカラーのイラストを使った日米語小辞典は故清水克祐文教大学女子短期大学部教授の発案になるもので、本書の初版も先生の手によるものです。今回の改訂を担当するに当たって、先生の生前のご指導に厚く御礼申し上げる次第です。

1989年6月　　　　　　　　　　　　　　　　　　　　　　　　　　宮 本 明 人

iv Contents
目　次

	Page
People and Relationships　家族の成長	2
The Family　親族関係	3
The Human Body　人体各部	4-5
Vegetables　野菜類	6-7
Fruits　果実類	8-9
Meat, Poultry, and Seafood　獣肉、家禽肉および魚貝類	10-11
Containers, Quantities, and Money　容器、量および貨幣の単位	12-13
The Supermarket　スーパーマーケット	14-15
Family Restaurant and Cocktail Lounge　ファミリーレストランおよびカクテルラウンジ	16
Restaurant Verbs　食事に関する動作	17
Common Prepared Foods　調理済み食品	18
Outdoor Clothes　外出着	19
Everyday Clothes　普段着	20-21
Underwear and Sleepwear　下着および夜着	22
Jewelry and Cosmetics　装身具および化粧品	23
Describing Clothes　衣服に関する表現	24
Describing the Weather　天候に関する表現	25
Seasonal Verbs　四季に関する動作	26
Houses　住居	27
The Living Room　居間/居室	28
The Dining Room　食堂/食事室	29
The Kitchen　台所/厨房	30
Kitchen Verbs　料理に関する動作	31
The Bedroom　寝室	32
The Baby's Room　育児室	33
The Bathroom　浴室兼手洗い	34
The Utility Room　家事室	35
A Workshop　工作場	36-37
Housework and Repair Verbs　家事と修繕に関する動作	38
Medical and Dental Care　医療および歯科医療	39
Ailments and Injuries　痛みおよび傷病	40
Treatments and Remedies　療養および治療法	41
Firefighting and Rescue　消火および救出活動	42
Crime and Punishment　犯罪および刑罰	43
The City　市中の景観	44-45
The U.S. Postal System　郵便制度	46
The Public Library　公共図書館	47
The Armed Forces　軍隊	48
Trucks　運搬車	49
Cars　乗用車	50-51
Bikes　二輪車	52
Highway Travel　高速道路	53
Public Transportation　公共輸送	54-55

Contents v

目　次

	Page
Air Travel　空の旅	56
Aircraft　航空機	57
In Port　港湾施設	58
Pleasure Boating　行楽用船舶	59
Plants and Trees　草花および樹木	60-61
Simple Animals　下等動物	62
Insects　昆虫類	63
Birds　鳥類	64
Fish and Reptiles　魚類および爬行動物	65
Mammals I　哺乳動物 I	66-67
Mammals II　哺乳動物 II	68-69
Map of the World　世界地図	70-71
The United States of America　アメリカ合衆国	72-73
The Universe　大宇宙	74
The Space Program　宇宙開発	75
A Classroom　教室	76
School Verbs　学校での動作	77
A Science Lab　理科実験室	78
Math　数学	79
Energy　エネルギー	80
Farming and Ranching　農耕および牧畜	81
Construction　建設工事	82
An Office　事務所	83
Occupations I: Main Street USA　職業 I：アメリカの典型的本通り	84
Occupations II　職業 II	85
Occupations III　職業 III	86
Neighborhood Parks　地域住民の公園	87
Outdoor Activities　野外活動	88-89
At the Beach　海辺の光景	90-91
Team Sports　チームスポーツ	92
Ballfields　球技場	93
Individual Sports　個人スポーツ	94
Fields and Courses　野外競技場	95
Sports Verbs　スポーツに関する動作	96-97
Musical Instruments　楽器	98
Music, Dance and Theater　音楽、舞踊および観劇	99
Electronics and Photography　電子技術および写真術	100
Handicrafts　手芸	101
Prepositions of Description　場所を表わす前置詞	102
Prepositions of Motion　動きを表わす前置詞	103
Appendix　付録	104
Index　索引	105

家族の成長

女性	**1.** woman	赤子/赤児/赤ん坊	**5.** baby	女の子	**9.** girl
男性	**2.** man	両親/父母	**6.** parents	祖父母	**10.** grandparents
夫	**3.** husband	子供たち	**7.** children	孫娘	**11.** granddaughter
妻	**4.** wife	男の子	**8.** boy	孫息子	**12.** grandson

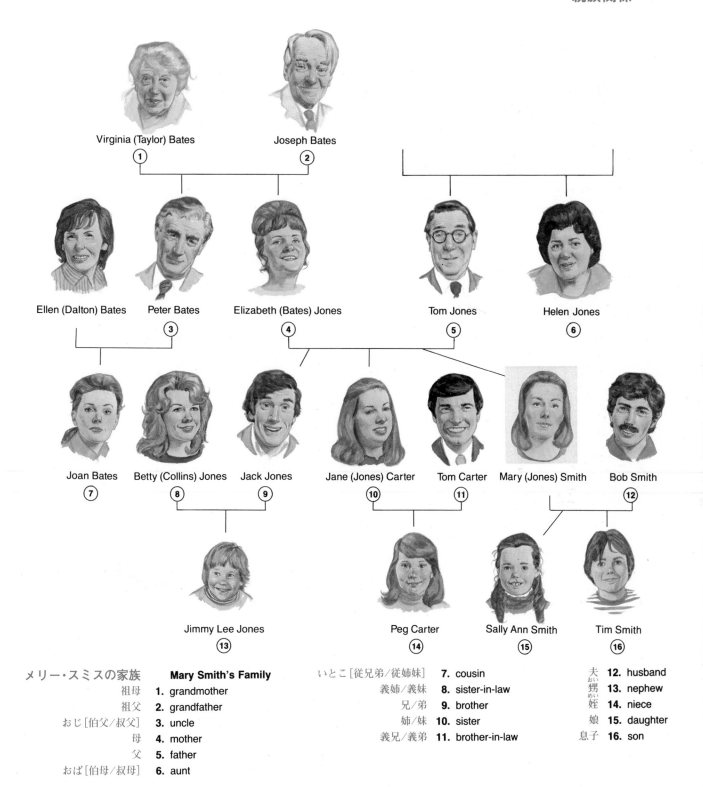

Virginia (Taylor) Bates ①
Joseph Bates ②

Ellen (Dalton) Bates
Peter Bates ③
Elizabeth (Bates) Jones ④
Tom Jones ⑤
Helen Jones ⑥

Joan Bates ⑦
Betty (Collins) Jones ⑧
Jack Jones ⑨
Jane (Jones) Carter ⑩
Tom Carter ⑪
Mary (Jones) Smith
Bob Smith ⑫

Jimmy Lee Jones ⑬
Peg Carter ⑭
Sally Ann Smith ⑮
Tim Smith ⑯

メリー・スミスの家族	**Mary Smith's Family**	いとこ［従兄弟／従姉妹］	**7.** cousin	夫	**12.** husband
祖母	**1.** grandmother	義姉／義妹	**8.** sister-in-law	甥	**13.** nephew
祖父	**2.** grandfather	兄／弟	**9.** brother	姪	**14.** niece
おじ［伯父／叔父］	**3.** uncle	姉／妹	**10.** sister	娘	**15.** daughter
母	**4.** mother	義兄／義弟	**11.** brother-in-law	息子	**16.** son
父	**5.** father				
おば［伯母／叔母］	**6.** aunt				

人体各部

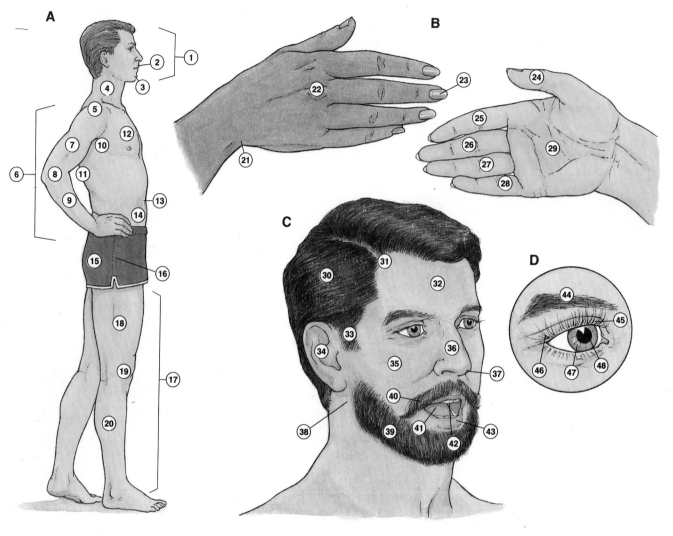

身体	**A. The Body**	尻の側面／ヒップ	**16.** hip	頭部	**C. The Head**
顔	**1.** face	脚／下肢	**17.** leg	髪／髪の毛／頭髪	**30.** hair
口	**2.** mouth	腿／太腿／大腿	**18.** thigh	分け目	**31.** part
顎先	**3.** chin	膝	**19.** knee	額／おでこ	**32.** forehead
首	**4.** neck	脹ら脛	**20.** calf	揉上	**33.** sideburn
肩	**5.** shoulder			耳	**34.** ear
腕／上肢	**6.** arm	手	**B. The Hand**	頬	**35.** cheek
上腕／二の腕	**7.** upper arm	手首	**21.** wrist	鼻	**36.** nose
肘／肱	**8.** elbow	節／関節	**22.** knuckle	鼻の穴／鼻孔	**37.** nostril
前腕	**9.** forearm	(手指の)爪	**23.** fingernail	顎(全体)	**38.** jaw
腋(の下)	**10.** armpit	親指／拇指	**24.** thumb	顎鬚	**39.** beard
背(中)	**11.** back	人差し指／食指	**25.** (index) finger	口髭	**40.** mustache
胸	**12.** chest	中指／高高指	**26.** middle finger	舌	**41.** tongue
腰(の括れ)／ウエスト	**13.** waist	薬指／無名指／名無し指／紅差し指	**27.** ring finger	歯	**42.** tooth
腹	**14.** abdomen	小指	**28.** little finger	唇／脣	**43.** lip
尻／臀部	**15.** buttocks	掌	**29.** palm		

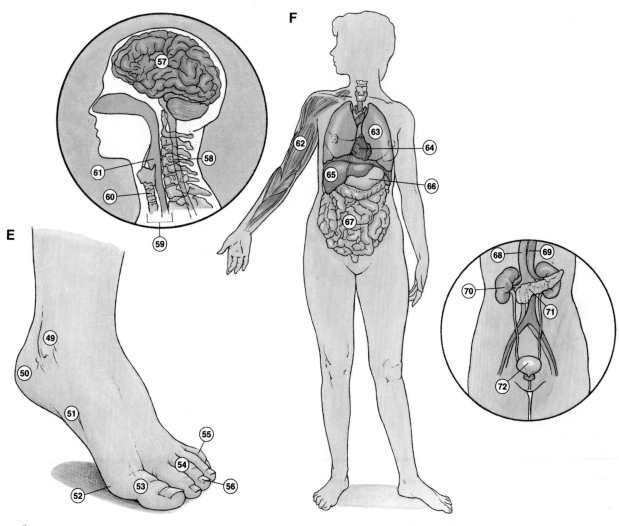

E

F

<table>
<tr><td>

目/眼
_め
眉/眉毛
_{まゆ　まゆげ}
瞼
_{まぶた}
睫
_{まつげ}
虹彩
_{こうさい}
眸/瞳孔
_{ひとみ　どうこう}

</td><td>

D. The Eye

44. eyebrow
45. eyelid
46. eyelashes
47. iris
48. pupil

</td></tr>
</table>

足
_{あし}

踝
_{くるぶし}

踵
_{かかと}

足の甲
_{あし　こう}

(足の)拇指球
_{あし　ぼしきゅう}

足親指/足の拇指
_{あしおやゆび　あし　ぼし}

足指/爪先
_{あしゆび　つまさき}

足小指
_{あしこゆび}

足の爪
_{あし　つめ}

E. The Foot

49. ankle
50. heel
51. instep
52. ball
53. big toe
54. toe
55. little toe
56. toenail

内部器官/臓器
_{ないぶきかん　ぞうき}

脳
_{のう}

脊髄
_{せきずい}

喉/咽
_{のど　のど}

気管
_{きかん}

食道
_{しょくどう}

筋肉
_{きんにく}

肺(臓)
_{はい ぞう}

心臓
_{しんぞう}

肝臓
_{かんぞう}

胃(袋)
_{い ぶくろ}

小腸
_{しょうちょう}

静脈
_{じょうみゃく}

動脈
_{どうみゃく}

腎臓
_{じんぞう}

膵臓
_{すいぞう}

膀胱
_{ぼうこう}

F. The Internal Organs

57. brain
58. spinal cord
59. throat
60. windpipe
61. esophagus
62. muscle
63. lung
64. heart
65. liver
66. stomach
67. intestines
68. vein
69. artery
70. kidney
71. pancreas
72. bladder

野菜類

カリフラワー/花椰菜 1. (head of) cauliflower

ブロッコリ 2. broccoli

キャベツ/甘藍/玉菜 3. cabbage

芽キャベツ/子持ち玉菜 4. brussels sprouts

オランダ芥子 5. watercress

レタス/ちさ/ちしゃ[萵苣] 6. lettuce

菊ぢしゃ[萵苣] 7. escarole

ほうれんそう[菠薐草] 8. spinach

ハーブ/薬草 9. herb(s)

セロリ/オランダ三葉 10. celery

朝鮮薊 11. artichoke

(とう)もろこし[(玉)蜀黍]/
唐黍 12. (ear of) corn

穂軸 a. cob

隠元(豆)/鶉豆 13. kidney bean(s)

黒豆 14. black bean(s)

莢隠元 15. string bean(s)

リラ豆 16. lima bean(s)

豌豆/莢 17. pea(s)

a. pod

アスパラガス 18. asparagus

トマト／赤なす［茄子］ **19.** tomato(es)
きゅうり［胡瓜］ **20.** cucumber(s)
なす(び)［茄子］ **21.** eggplant
唐辛子／唐芥子［蕃椒］ **22.** pepper(s)
じゃがいも／馬鈴薯 **23.** potato(es)
薩摩芋 **24.** yam

葫［大蒜］ **25.** garlic
小球根／かけら **a.** clove
かぼちゃ［南瓜］／ **26.** pumpkin
唐なす［茄子］
ズッキーニ **27.** zucchini
団栗形かぼちゃ［南瓜］ **28.** acorn squash
二十日大根／西洋大根 **29.** radish(es)

マッシュルーム／西洋松茸／ **30.** mushroom(s)
シャンピニオン
葱／根深 **31.** onion(s)
人参 **32.** carrot(s)
ビート／甜菜／火炎菜 **33.** beet(s)
蕪［蕪菁］ **34.** turnip

葡萄(一房)	1. (a bunch of) grapes	柑橘類	**Citrus Fruits**	ベリー類	**Berries**
林檎	2. apple	グレープフルーツ	7. grapefruit	グーズベリー／西洋酸塊／丸酸塊	11. gooseberries
軸／柄	a. stem	オレンジ	8. orange	ブラックベリー	12. blackberries
芯／核	b. core	袋	a. section	クランベリー／つるこけ桃	13. cranberries
ココナッツ／ココ椰子	3. coconut	(厚)皮	b. rind	ブルーベリー	14. blueberries
パイナップル	4. pineapple	種	c. seed	苺／莓／ストロベリー	15. strawberry
マンゴー	5. mango	レモン[檸檬]	9. lemon	木苺／ラズベリー	16. raspberries
パパイヤ	6. papaya	ライム	10. lime	すばい桃／ネクタリン	17. nectarine
				西洋梨	18. pear

桜ん坊[桜桃]	**19.** cherries	杏(子)	**25.** apricot	アボカド	**33.** avocado
バナナ(一房)	**20.** (a bunch of) bananas	西瓜/水瓜	**26.** watermelon	プラム/西洋李	**34.** plum
皮	**a.** peel			甘露メロン	**35.** honeydew melon
		木の実	**Nuts**	カンタループメロン	**36.** cantaloupe
乾燥果実	**Dried Fruits**	カシューナッツ	**27.** cashew(s)	桃	**37.** peach
いちじく[無花果]	**21.** fig	ピーナッツ/落花生/南京豆	**28.** peanut(s)	芯/核	**a.** pit
プルーン/李	**22.** prune	くるみ[胡桃]	**29.** walnut(s)	(薄)皮	**b.** skin
棗椰子	**23.** date	榛の実	**30.** hazelnut(s)		
乾し葡萄/干し葡萄	**24.** raisin(s)	アーモンド/扁桃	**31.** almond(s)		
		栗	**32.** chestnuts		

獣肉、家禽肉および魚貝類

A

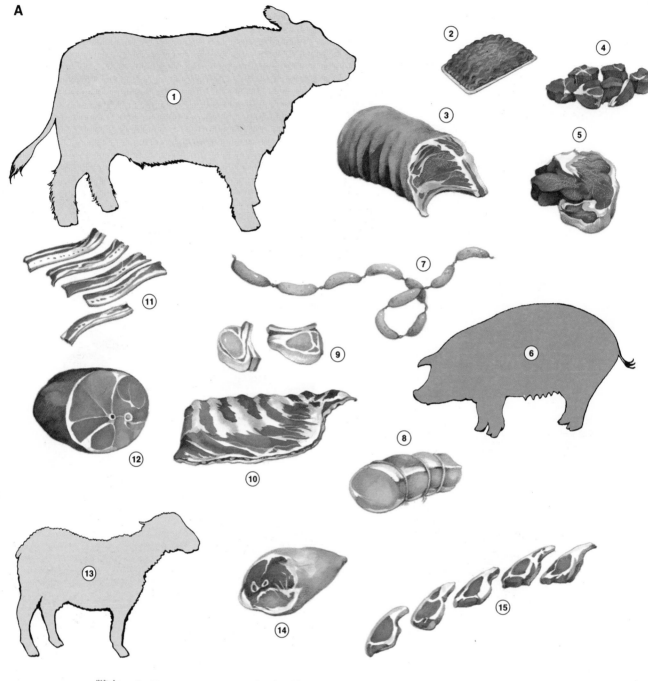

獣肉	**A. Meat**	ソーセージ／	**7.** sausage	ベーコン	**11.** bacon
牛肉	**1.** beef	腸詰め		ハム／	**12.** ham
牛挽肉	**2.** ground beef	炙焼用肉／	**8.** roast	腿肉の塩漬け薫製	
炙焼用肉／肩肉・背中肉	**3.** roast	肩肉・背中肉		子羊肉	**13.** lamb
シチュー用肉	**4.** stewing meat	厚切り	**9.** chops	脚肉	**14.** leg
ステーキ用肉	**5.** steak	スペアリブ／	**10.** spare ribs	厚切り	**15.** chops
豚肉	**6.** pork	骨つき肋肉			

獣肉、<ruby>家禽<rt>かきん</rt></ruby>肉および魚貝類

B

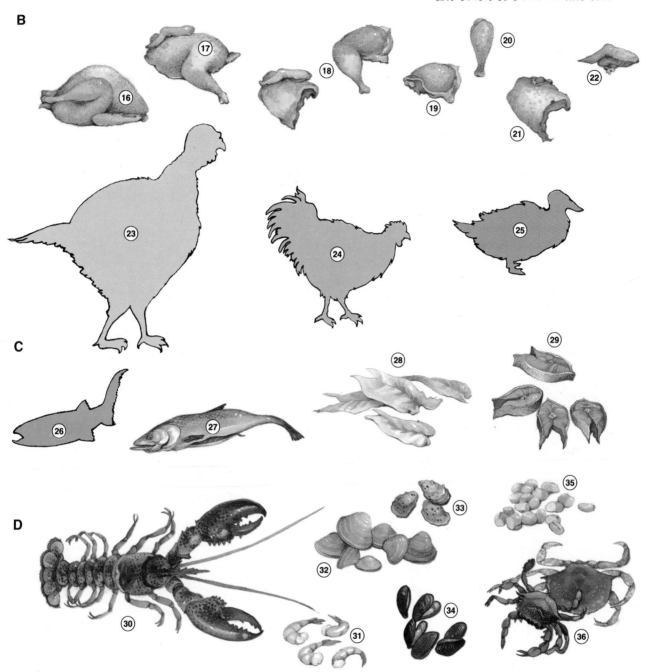

C

D

<ruby>家禽<rt>かきん</rt></ruby>肉	**B. Poultry**		<ruby>鶏<rt>とり</rt></ruby>肉	**24.** chicken		貝類と甲殻類	**D. Shellfish**
(鶏肉)一羽／丸ごと	**16.** whole (chicken)	<ruby>鴨<rt>かも</rt></ruby>肉／あひる［家鴨］の肉		**25.** duck	伊勢えび［海老］／鎌倉えび／	**30.** lobster
半身	**17.** split				大型海ざりがに［蝲蛄］	
四分の一	**18.** quarter		**魚貝類**	**C. Seafood**	小蝦／舼［海老］	**31.** shrimp
<ruby>腿<rt>もも</rt></ruby>肉	**19.** thigh	魚		**26.** fish	<ruby>蛤<rt>はまぐり</rt></ruby>	**32.** clam(s)
脚肉／チューリップ	**20.** leg	一匹／一尾／丸ごと		**27.** whole	かき［牡蠣］	**33.** oyster(s)
胸肉	**21.** breast	切り身／開き身		**28.** filet	<ruby>貽貝<rt>い</rt></ruby>／姫貝	**34.** mussel(s)
手羽肉	**22.** wing	厚切り		**29.** steak	帆立貝［海扇］(の柱)	**35.** scallop(s)
七面鳥(の肉)	**23.** turkey				<ruby>蟹<rt>かに</rt></ruby>	**36.** crab(s)

紙箱／ボール箱	**1.** carton	（棒状の）塊	**5.** stick	広口瓶	**9.** jar
器／入れ物	**2.** container	鉢／桶／壺	**6.** tub	缶詰	**10.** can
瓶／壜	**3.** bottle	（山状の）塊	**7.** loaf	巻き	**11.** roll
包装	**4.** package	袋	**8.** bag		

箱	**12.** box	カップ	**19.** cup	貨幣	**Money**	
半ダース／六缶入り	**13.** six-pack	コップ／グラス	**20.** glass	ドル紙幣	**25.** dollar bills	
ポンプ	**14.** pump	薄切り	**21.** slice	硬貨	**26.** coins	
チューブ／絞り出し容器	**15.** tube	区画／ひと切れ	**22.** piece	1 セント貨	**27.** penny	
小箱	**16.** pack	ボール／深皿	**23.** bowl	5 セント貨	**28.** nickel	
綴じ／綴り／冊子	**17.** book	スプレー／噴霧器	**24.** spray can	10セント貨	**29.** dime	
（板状の）塊	**18.** bar			25セント貨	**30.** quarter	

スーパーマーケット

そうざい 惣菜売場/調製食品売場	1. deli counter	陳列棚	6. shelf	練り焼き製品/固め焼き製品	11. baked goods
冷凍食品	2. frozen foods	計量器/秤	7. scale	食パン	12. bread
冷凍庫	3. freezer	店内籠	8. shopping basket	缶詰	13. canned goods
乳製品	4. dairy products	農産物	9. produce	飲み物	14. beverages
牛乳	5. milk	通路	10. aisle		

FISH MEAT POULTRY

家庭用品	**15.** household items	レシート／受け取り／	**20.** receipt	食料品	**24.** groceries
陳列冷蔵庫	**16.** bin	領収書		紙袋	**25.** bag
買物客	**17.** customer	レジ／金銭登録機	**21.** cash register	レジカウンター	**26.** checkout counter
菓子類／お抓み／お八	**18.** snacks	レジ係	**22.** cashier	小切手	**27.** check
買物（用手押）車	**19.** shopping cart	移動ベルト	**23.** conveyor belt		

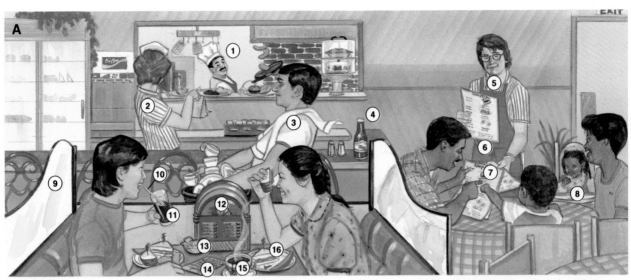

ファミリーレストラン	**A. Family Restaurant**	ジュークボックス	12. jukebox	（蒸留）酒（瓶）	22. liquor (bottle)
コック／料理人／シェフ	**1.** cook	（袋入り）砂糖	13. sugar (packet)	ビール／麦酒	23. beer
ウエートレス／女給	**2.** waitress	勘定書き／会計伝票	14. check	カウンター	24. bar
雑用係	**3.** busboy	紅茶	15. tea	カウンター椅子／腰掛け	25. bar stool
ケチャップ	**4.** ketchup	サンドイッチ	16. sandwich	パイプ	26. pipe
ウエーター／給仕	**5.** waiter			コースター／敷き皿	27. coaster
エプロン／前掛け	**6.** apron	**カクテルラウンジ**	**B. Cocktail Lounge**	紙マッチ	28. (book of) matches
メニュー／品書き	**7.** menu	（コルク）栓抜き	17. corkscrew	灰皿	29. ashtray
子供椅子	**8.** high chair	コルク栓	18. cork	ライター	30. lighter
区画／仕切り席	**9.** booth	ワイン／果実酒	19. wine	（紙巻き）莨［煙草］	31. cigarette
ストロー	**10.** straw	サイホン／樽の栓	20. tap	ウエートレス	32. cocktail waitress
清涼飲料	**11.** soft drink	バーテン	21. bartender	盆	33. tray

食事に関する動作

食べる	**1.** eat	片付ける	**6.** clear	延ばす/広げる	**11.** spread
飲む	**2.** drink	支払う	**7.** pay	手に持つ	**12.** hold
出す/給仕する	**3.** serve	(テーブルの上を)整える	**8.** set (the table)	明かりを点ける/灯す	**13.** light
煮る/加熱する	**4.** cook	渡す	**9.** give	やけど[火傷]する	**14.** burn
注文する	**5.** order	取る/返してもらう	**10.** take		

（西洋）芥子	**1.** mustard	野菜サラダ	**13.** tossed salad	春巻き	**25.** egg roll
ホットドッグ	**2.** hot dog	ビーフシチュー	**14.** beef stew	苺のショートケーキ	**26.** strawberry shortcake
煮込み隠元（豆）／鶉豆	**3.** baked beans	ポークチャップ／	**15.** pork chops	マフィン／スコーン	**27.** biscuit
ポテトチップ	**4.** potato chips	豚肉の厚切り		ポテトフライ	**28.** french fries
ホットケーキ／パンケーキ	**5.** pancakes	野菜ミックス	**16.** mixed vegetables	フライドチキン	**29.** fried chicken
シロップ	**6.** syrup	マッシュポテト	**17.** mashed potatoes	ピザ	**30.** pizza
（ハンバーガー用）パン	**7.** bun	バター	**18.** butter	ゼリー	**31.** jelly
ピクルス	**8.** pickle	ロールパン	**19.** roll	玉子（の目玉焼き）	**32.** (sunnyside-up) egg
ハンバーガー（の肉）	**9.** hamburger	じゃがいもの	**20.** baked potato	ベーコン	**33.** bacon
スパゲッティー	**10.** spaghetti	ホイル焼き		トースト	**34.** toast
ミートボール	**11.** meatballs	ステーキ	**21.** steak	コーヒー	**35.** coffee
ドレッシング	**12.** salad dressing	クッキー	**22.** cookie	アイスクリームコーン	**36.** ice cream cone
		クリームサンデー	**23.** sundae		
		タコス	**24.** taco		

手袋	**1.** gloves
帽子	**2.** cap
ネルのシャツ	**3.** flannel shirt
リュックサック	**4.** backpack
ウインドブレーカー／ スポーツ用ジャンパー	**5.** windbreaker
（ブルー）ジーンズ／ デニムのズボン	**6.** (blue) jeans
丸首セーター	**7.** (crewneck) sweater
頭巾つきコート	**8.** parka
登山靴	**9.** hiking boots

耳当て	**10.** earmuffs
二股手袋／ミトン	**11.** mittens
ダウンベスト／ 羽毛チョッキ	**12.** down vest
（とっくり［徳利］ 襟の）セーター	**13.** (turtleneck) sweater
タイツ	**14.** tights
スケート靴	**15.** ice skates
スキー帽	**16.** ski cap
ジャンパー／ブルゾン	**17.** jacket
（鍔つき）帽子	**18.** hat

襟巻き／スカーフ／ マフラー	**19.** scarf
オーバー／外套	**20.** overcoat
ブーツ／深靴	**21.** boots
ベレー帽	**22.** beret
（Vネックの） セーター	**23.** (V-neck) sweater
コート／長上着	**24.** coat
レーンシューズ／ 雨靴	**25.** rain boots

ふだんぎ
普段着

折り襟	**1.** lapel	トレーナーズボン	**10.** sweatpants	買物籠	**18.** shopping bag
ブレザー	**2.** blazer	運動靴	**11.** sneakers	サンダル	**19.** sandal
ボタン	**3.** button	鉢巻き／スエットバンド	**12.** sweatband	襟／カラー	**20.** collar
ズボン	**4.** slacks	ランニング	**13.** tank top	半袖／三分袖	**21.** short sleeve
踵	**5.** heel	半ズボン／短パン	**14.** shorts	ワンピース（ドレス）	**22.** dress
靴底	**6.** sole	長袖	**15.** long sleeve	ハンドバッグ	**23.** purse
靴紐	**7.** shoelace	ベルト	**16.** belt	傘／こうもり［蝙蝠］（傘）／洋傘	**24.** umbrella
トレーナー（の上着）	**8.** sweatshirt	ベルトの留め金／バックル	**17.** buckle	ハイヒール	**25.** (high) heels
札入れ／財布	**9.** wallet				

カーデガン	**26.** cardigan	ショルダーバッグ	**35.** (shoulder) bag	突っ掛け靴	**42.** loafer
（コール天の）ズボン	**27.** (corduroy) pants	スカート	**36.** skirt	制帽	**43.** cap
安全帽／ヘルメット	**28.** hard hat	書類鞄	**37.** briefcase	眼鏡	**44.** glasses
ティーシャツ	**29.** T-shirt	レーンコート／	**38.** raincoat	制服	**45.** uniform
作業ズボン／繋ぎ	**30.** overalls	トレンチコート		ワイシャツ	**46.** shirt
弁当箱	**31.** lunch box	チョッキ／ベスト	**39.** vest	ネクタイ	**47.** tie
作業靴	**32.** (construction) boots	三揃（スーツ）	**40.** three-piece suit	新聞	**48.** newspaper
上着	**33.** jacket	ポケット	**41.** pocket	靴	**49.** shoe
ブラウス	**34.** blouse				

下着および夜着

肌着	**1.** undershirt	ウエストスリップ	**8.** half slip	ガードル	**15.** girdle
半ズボン	**2.** boxer shorts	カミソール/スリマー	**9.** camisole	ハイソックス	**16.** knee socks
(男子用)パンツ	**3.** underpants	スリップ/シュミーズ/	**10.** full slip	ソックス/靴下	**17.** socks
サポーター	**4.** athletic supporter	シミーズ		部屋履き/室内履き	**18.** slippers
パンティーストッキング	**5.** pantyhose	(ビキニ)パンティー	**11.** (bikini) panties	パジャマ/寝巻き	**19.** pajamas
(ナイロン製)靴下	**6.** stockings	ブリーフ/パンツ	**12.** briefs	バスローブ/湯上がり着	**20.** bathrobe
防寒用下着	**7.** long johns	ブラジャー	**13.** bra(ssiere)	ネグリジェ/部屋着	**21.** nightgown
		ガーターベルト/	**14.** garter belt		
		靴下留めつきベルト			

装身具	**A. Jewelry**	（差し込み式）ネクタイピン	**13.** tie pin	かみそり［剃刀］の刃	**23.** razor blades
イヤリング／耳飾り	**1.** earrings	ネクタイピン／ネクタイ留め	**14.** tie clip	爪鑢	**24.** emery board
指輪	**2.** ring(s)	挟み式イヤリング	**15.** clip-on earring	マニキュア	**25.** nail polish
婚約指輪	**3.** engagement ring	ピアス	**16.** pierced earring	眉書き／眉墨	**26.** eyebrow pencil
結婚指輪	**4.** wedding ring	留め金	**17.** clasp	香水	**27.** perfume
鎖／鏈	**5.** chain	（ピアスの）差し針	**18.** post	マスカラ	**28.** mascara
ネックレス／首飾り	**6.** necklace	（ピアスの）受け具	**19.** back	口紅	**29.** lipstick
ビーズ（紐）	**7.** (strand of) beads			アイシャドー	**30.** eye shadow
ピン／ブローチ	**8.** pin	**洗面用品と化粧品**	**B. Toiletries and Makeup**	爪切り	**31.** nail clippers
ブレスレット／腕輪	**9.** bracelet	かみそり［剃刀］	**20.** razor	頬紅	**32.** blush
（腕）時計	**10.** watch	アフターシェーブローション／	**21.** after-shave lotion	アイライン入れ	**33.** eyeliner
時計のベルト	**11.** watchband	ひげ剃り後化粧水			
カフスボタン	**12.** cuff links	ひげ剃りクリーム	**22.** shaving cream		

衣服に関する表現

短い	**1.** short		淡い／薄い	**9.** light		閉じた	**16.** closed
長い	**2.** long		濃い	**10.** dark		縞模様の	**17.** striped
きつい／窮屈な	**3.** tight		高い	**11.** high		市松模様の	**18.** checked
緩い	**4.** loose		低い	**12.** low		水玉模様の	**19.** polka dot
汚れた	**5.** dirty		新しい	**13.** new		無地の	**20.** solid
洗った／清潔な	**6.** clean		古い	**14.** old		プリント柄の	**21.** print
小さい	**7.** small		開いた	**15.** open		格子縞の	**22.** plaid
大きい	**8.** big						

雨の降る	**1.** rainy	暑い	**7.** hot	霧の立籠めた	**12.** foggy
曇った	**2.** cloudy	暖かい	**8.** warm	風の強い	**13.** windy
雪の降る	**3.** snowy	涼しい	**9.** cool	乾いた	**14.** dry
晴天の	**4.** sunny	寒い	**10.** cold	濡れた	**15.** wet
寒暖計／温度計	**5.** thermometer	氷点	**11.** freezing	凍った	**16.** icy
気温／温度	**6.** temperature				

四季に関する動作

春	Spring	夏	Summer	秋	Fall	冬	Winter
ペンキを塗る	1. paint	水を遣る	5. water	詰める	9. fill	掬う	13. shovel
綺麗にする	2. clean	草刈りをする	6. mow	熊手を掛ける	10. rake	砂を撒く	14. sand
穴を掘る	3. dig	摘む	7. pick	薪を割る	11. chop	(雪を)掻き落とす	15. scrape
植える	4. plant	刈り込む/切り揃える	8. trim	押す	12. push	運ぶ	16. carry

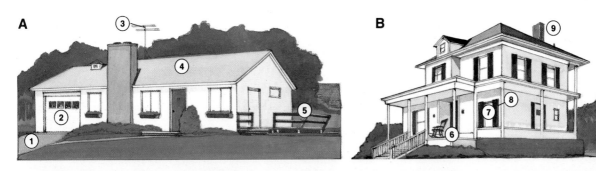

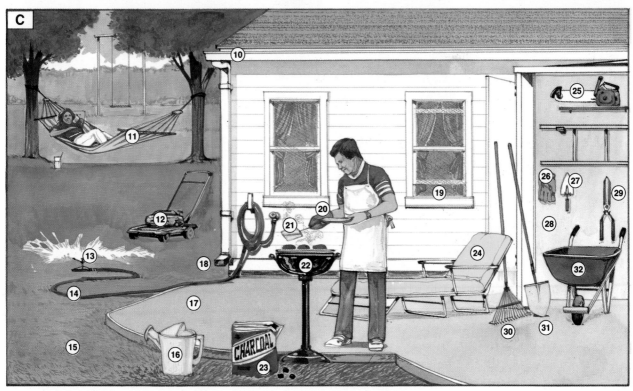

農家	**A. Ranch House**	裏庭	**C. The Backyard**	鏝／返し	**21.** spatula
車輛出入道	**1.** driveway	樋	**10.** gutter	グリル／網焼き器	**22.** grill
車庫	**2.** garage	ハンモック／吊り床	**11.** hammock	炭団／固形燃料	**23.** charcoal briquettes
テレビアンテナ	**3.** TV antenna	芝刈り機	**12.** lawn mower		
屋根	**4.** roof	撒水器	**13.** sprinkler	休憩椅子	**24.** lounge chair
ベランダ	**5.** deck	庭園用ホース	**14.** garden hose	チェーンソー／電動鋸	**25.** power saw
		芝生	**15.** grass		
コロニアル様式の家屋	**B. Colonial-style House**	撒水バケツ[馬穴]／如雨露	**16.** watering can	作業手袋	**26.** work gloves
ポーチ／前ベランダ	**6.** porch			移植鏝	**27.** trowel
窓	**7.** window	パチオ／屋外テラス	**17.** patio	物置き／道具置き場	**28.** toolshed
日除け／目隠し	**8.** shutter	排水管／縦樋	**18.** drainpipe	刈り込み鋏／剪定鋏	**29.** hedge clippers
煙突	**9.** chimney	網戸	**19.** screen	熊手	**30.** rake
		ミット	**20.** mitt	シャベル／スコップ	**31.** shovel
				手押し一輪車	**32.** wheelbarrow

居間/居室

天井扇風機	1. ceiling fan	手摺	11. banister	スピーカー	21. speaker
天井	2. ceiling	階段(の枠)	12. staircase	書棚/本箱	22. bookcase
壁	3. wall	(階段の)段	13. step	(厚手の)カーテン	23. drapes
額縁	4. frame	机	14. desk	クッション	24. cushion
絵/絵画	5. painting	床に敷きつめたカーペット	15. wall-to-wall carpeting	ソファー	25. sofa
花瓶	6. vase	凭れ椅子	16. recliner	低テーブル	26. coffee table
マントルピース/炉棚	7. mantel	リモコン/遠隔操作器	17. remote control	(電灯の)傘	27. lampshade
暖炉	8. fireplace	テレビ(受像機)	18. television	電気スタンド	28. lamp
(炉で燃える)火	9. fire	壁面飾り棚	19. wall unit	サイドテーブル	29. end table
薪	10. log	ステレオ/立体音響装置	20. stereo system		

瀬戸物/食器	**1.** china	パン用小皿	**11.** bread and butter plate	受け皿	**21.** saucer
食器戸棚	**2.** china closet	フォーク	**12.** fork	ナイフ・フォーク・スプーン類/	**22.** silverware
シャンデリア	**3.** chandelier	大皿	**13.** plate	食卓用刃物	
水差し	**4.** pitcher	ナプキン	**14.** napkin	砂糖入れ	**23.** sugar bowl
ワイングラス	**5.** wine glass	ナイフ	**15.** knife	クリーマー/ミルク入れ	**24.** creamer
水グラス	**6.** water glass	テーブルクロス	**16.** tablecloth	サラダボール	**25.** salad bowl
食卓	**7.** table	食卓椅子	**17.** chair	炎/焔	**26.** flame
スプーン/小匙	**8.** spoon	コーヒーポット	**18.** coffeepot	蝋燭	**27.** candle
胡椒入れ	**9.** pepper shaker	ティーポット	**19.** teapot	燭台	**28.** candlestick
食塩入れ	**10.** salt shaker	カップ/茶碗	**20.** cup	サイドボード	**29.** buffet

台所 / 厨房
ちゅうぼう

食器洗い機	1. dishwasher	深鍋 なべ	13. pot	(混ぜ物) ボール	24. mixing bowl
水切り	2. dish drainer	蒸し焼き鍋 なべ	14. casserole dish	麺棒 めん	25. rolling pin
蒸し器	3. steamer	密閉容器	15. canister	俎板/真魚板 まな まな	26. cutting board
缶切り	4. can opener	トースター	16. toaster	調理台	27. counter
フライパン	5. frying pan	炙皿 あぶり	17. roasting pan	薬罐/薬鑵 やかん やかん	28. teakettle
栓抜き	6. bottle opener	食器用布巾 ふきん	18. dish towel	バーナー/燃焼部	29. burner
濾し器 こ	7. colander	冷蔵庫	19. refrigerator	コンロ/レンジ	30. stove
シチュー鍋 なべ	8. saucepan	冷凍庫	20. freezer	コーヒーメーカー	31. coffeemaker
蓋 ふた	9. lid	製氷皿	21. ice tray	オーブン/天火	32. oven
食器用洗剤	10. dishwashing liquid	食器戸棚	22. cabinet	(焼肉用) 直焼炉 じか	33. broiler
磨きたわし[束子]	11. scouring pad	電子レンジ	23. microwave oven	鍋摑み なべつか	34. pot holder
ミキサー	12. blender				

料理に関する動作

掻き回す	**1.** stir	割る	**7.** break	蒸す	**12.** steam
下ろす	**2.** grate	攪拌する	**8.** beat	直火で焼く	**13.** broil
開ける	**3.** open	切る	**9.** cut	(天火で)固め焼きする	**14.** bake
注ぐ	**4.** pour	薄切りにする	**10.** slice	炒める/揚げる	**15.** fry
皮を剥く	**5.** peel	刻む	**11.** chop	茹でる	**16.** boil
切り分ける	**6.** carve				

寝室

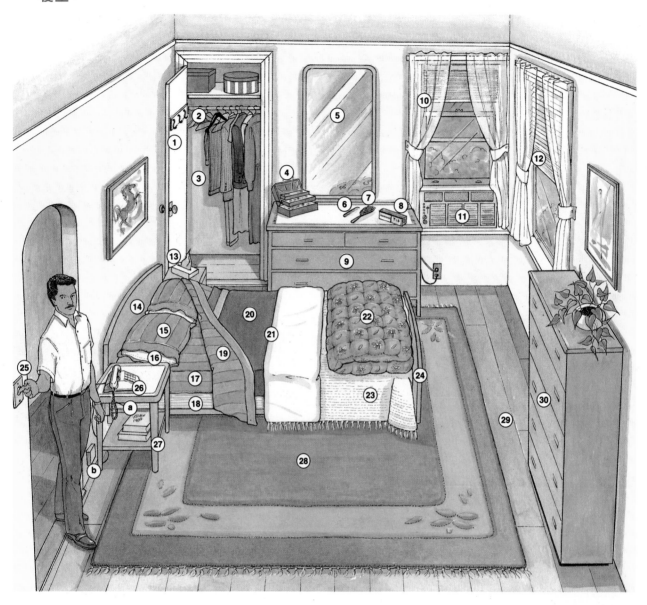

物掛け	**1.**	hook	ブラインド／日除け／目隠し	**12.**	blinds	ベッドカバー	**23.**	bedspread
ハンガー／洋服掛け／衣紋掛け	**2.**	hanger	ティッシュペーパー	**13.**	tissues	（寝台の）足板	**24.**	footboard
押し入れ／収納庫	**3.**	closet	（寝台の）頭板	**14.**	headboard	（電灯の）スイッチ	**25.**	light switch
宝石箱	**4.**	jewelry box	枕カバー	**15.**	pillowcase	電話器	**26.**	phone
鏡	**5.**	mirror	枕	**16.**	pillow	コード	**a.**	cord
櫛	**6.**	comb	マットレス	**17.**	mattress	差し込み／コンセント	**b.**	jack
ヘアブラシ	**7.**	hairbrush	スプリングマットレス	**18.**	box spring	サイドテーブル	**27.**	night table
目覚まし時計	**8.**	alarm clock	シーツ／敷布	**19.**	(flat) sheet	敷物／絨毯／絨緞	**28.**	rug
（引き出し［抽斗］つき）鏡台	**9.**	bureau	毛布	**20.**	blanket	床	**29.**	floor
（薄手の）カーテン	**10.**	curtain	ベッド／寝台	**21.**	bed	箪笥	**30.**	chest of drawers
空（気）調（製）機／エアコン	**11.**	air conditioner	掛け布団	**22.**	comforter			

ブラインド／日除け／目隠し	**1.** shade	使い捨て紙おむつ	**12.** disposable diaper	歩行器	**23.** walker
モビール	**2.** mobile	［紙褓褓］		自動ぶらんこ［鞦韆］	**24.** swing
熊の人形	**3.** teddy bear	布おむつ［御褓褓］	**13.** cloth diaper	人形の家	**25.** doll house
幼児用ベッド	**4.** crib	（折り畳み式）乳母車／	**14.** stroller	揺り籃	**26.** cradle
緩衝材	**5.** bumper	ベビーカー		縫包の動物人形	**27.** stuffed animal
ベビーローション／	**6.** baby lotion	煙感知器	**15.** smoke detector	人形	**28.** doll
小児用洗浄剤		ロッキングチェアー	**16.** rocking chair	おもちゃ［玩具］箱	**29.** toy chest
ベビーパウダー／天花粉	**7.** baby powder	哺乳瓶	**17.** bottle	遊戯用囲い／	**30.** playpen
小児用ウエットティッシュー	**8.** baby wipes	（哺乳瓶の）乳首	**18.** nipple	ベビーサークル	
着せ替え台	**9.** changing table	伸縮性繋／ロンパス	**19.** stretchie	（ジグソー）パズル	**31.** puzzle
綿棒	**10.** cotton swab	涎掛け	**20.** bib	積み木	**32.** block
安全ピン	**11.** safety pin	がらがら	**21.** rattle	おまる［御虎子］	**33.** potty
		おしゃぶり	**22.** pacifier		

浴室兼手洗い

カーテンレール	**1.** curtain rod	バスマット	**12.** bath mat	顔拭きタオル／	**23.** hand towel
カーテンリング	**2.** curtain rings	塵箱	**13.** wastepaper basket	手拭きタオル	
シャワー用キャップ	**3.** shower cap	薬品戸棚	**14.** medicine chest	バスタオル	**24.** bath towel
シャワーノズル	**4.** shower head	石鹸	**15.** soap	タオル掛け	**25.** towel rack
シャワーカーテン	**5.** shower curtain	練り歯磨き	**16.** toothpaste	ヘアドライヤー	**26.** hair dryer
石鹸台	**6.** soap dish	湯栓	**17.** hot water faucet	タイル	**27.** tile
スポンジ	**7.** sponge	水栓	**18.** cold water faucet	洗濯物入れ	**28.** hamper
シャンプー	**8.** shampoo	洗面用シンク	**19.** sink	便器	**29.** toilet
排水孔	**9.** drain	爪ブラシ	**20.** nailbrush	トイレットペーパー	**30.** toilet paper
栓	**10.** stopper	歯ブラシ	**21.** toothbrush	トイレブラシ	**31.** toilet brush
浴槽／湯舟	**11.** bathtub	浴用タオル	**22.** washcloth	体重計／秤	**32.** scale

脚立／脚榻／踏み台	**1.** stepladder		アイロン	**12.** iron	紙タオル	**23.** paper towels
塵叩き	**2.** feather duster		アイロン台	**13.** ironing board	乾燥機	**24.** dryer
懐中電灯	**3.** flashlight		吸引棒／ラバーカップ	**14.** plunger	洗濯用洗剤	**25.** laundry detergent
布切れ	**4.** rags		バケツ［馬穴］	**15.** bucket	漂白剤	**26.** bleach
ブレーカー	**5.** circuit breaker		（電気）掃除機	**16.** vacuum cleaner	ソフト仕上げ剤	**27.** fabric softener
（スポンジ）モップ	**6.** (sponge) mop		取り付け部品	**17.** attachments	洗濯物	**28.** laundry
帚／箒	**7.** broom		水道管	**18.** pipe	洗濯籠	**29.** laundry basket
塵取り	**8.** dustpan		物干し紐	**19.** clothesline	（電気）洗濯機	**30.** washing machine
清浄剤／磨き粉	**9.** cleanser		洗濯挟み	**20.** clothespins	芥容器	**31.** garbage can
窓用洗剤	**10.** window cleaner		洗濯糊	**21.** spray starch	鼠取り器	**32.** mousetrap
予備モップ	**11.** (mop) refill		電球	**22.** lightbulb		

折り尺	**1.** carpenter's rule	（ドリルの）曲がり柄	**9.** brace	手斧	**17.** hatchet
C字形締め具	**2.** C-clamp	スパナ	**10.** wrench	金鋸	**18.** hacksaw
機械糸鋸	**3.** jigsaw	木槌	**11.** mallet	ペンチ/鋏	**19.** pliers
木材	**4.** wood	モンキーレンチ/自在スパナ	**12.** monkey wrench	丸鋸	**20.** circular saw
延長コード	**5.** extension cord	金鎚	**13.** hammer	巻き尺	**21.** tape measure
コンセント/差し込み	**6.** outlet	剥ぎ取り器	**14.** scraper	作業台	**22.** workbench
アースつきプラグ	**7.** grounding plug	釘差し盤	**15.** pegboard	道具箱	**23.** toolbox
鋸	**8.** saw	掛け鉤	**16.** hook		

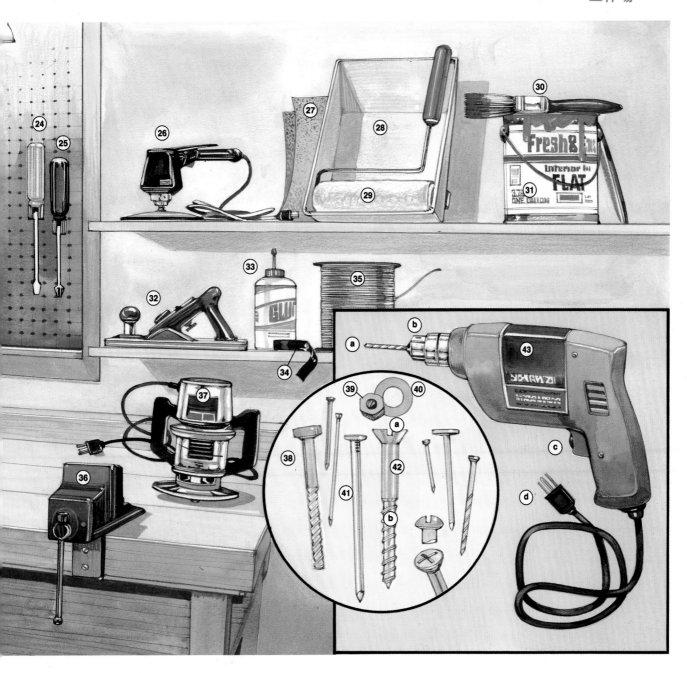

ドライバー／ねじ［螺子／捻子／捩子］回し	**24.** screwdriver	絶縁テープ	**34.** electrical tape	ねじ［螺子／捻子／捩子］釘	**42.** screw	
十字ドライバー	**25.** Phillips screwdriver	針金	**35.** wire			
電動研磨機	**26.** power sander	万力	**36.** vise	頭	**a.** head	
サンドペーパー／研磨紙／紙鑢	**27.** sandpaper	刳り鉋	**37.** router	ねじ［螺子／捻子／捩子］山	**b.** thread	
平槽／ペンキ皿	**28.** pan	ボルト／締め釘	**38.** bolt			
ペンキローラー	**29.** roller	ナット／留めねじ［螺子／捻子／捩子］	**39.** nut	電気ドリル	**43.** electric drill	
ペンキ刷毛	**30.** paintbrush			穂先／ビット	**a.** bit	
ペンキ／塗料	**31.** paint	ワッシャー／座金	**40.** washer	柄	**b.** shank	
（木材用）鉋	**32.** wood plane	釘	**41.** nail	スイッチ	**c.** switch	
接着剤／糊	**33.** glue			プラグ	**d.** plug	

家事と修繕に関する動作

折る	**1.** fold	掃く	**7.** sweep	注油する／油を点す	**12.** oil
擦る	**2.** scrub	（ベッドを）整える	**8.** make (the bed)	（シーツを）取り替える	**13.** change (the sheets)
磨く	**3.** polish	拭く	**9.** dry	掃除機を掛ける	**14.** vacuum
締め（付け）る	**4.** tighten	修理する	**10.** repair	埃を払う	**15.** dust
拭き取る／拭う	**5.** wipe	アイロンを掛ける	**11.** iron	洗う／洗濯する	**16.** wash
吊す	**6.** hang				

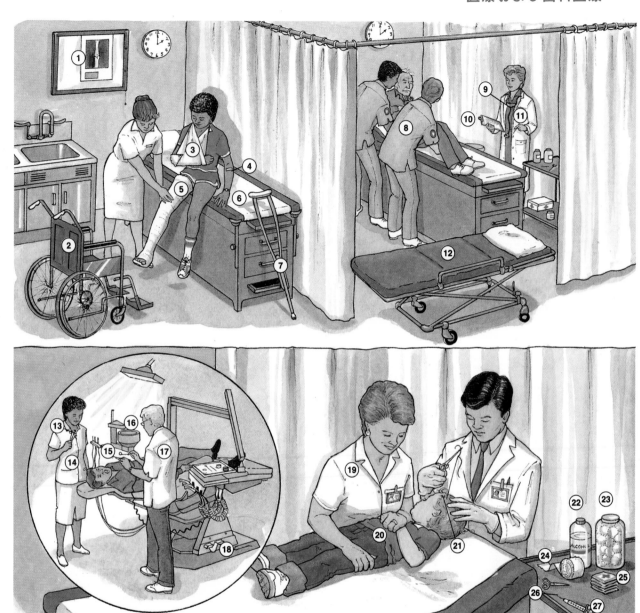

レントゲン写真	**1.** X-ray	カルテ	**10.** chart	看護婦/看護士	**19.** nurse
車椅子	**2.** wheelchair	医師/医者	**11.** doctor	患者	**20.** patient
三角巾/吊包帯	**3.** sling	担架	**12.** stretcher	縫合部	**21.** stitches
バンドエイド	**4.** Band-Aid	器具	**13.** instruments	アルコール	**22.** alcohol
ギプス/ギブス	**5.** cast	口腔衛生士	**14.** oral hygienist	綿玉	**23.** cotton balls
診察台	**6.** examining table	ドリル	**15.** drill	（ガーゼの)包帯	**24.** (gauze) bandage
松葉杖	**7.** crutch	スピットン/唾吐き	**16.** basin	ガーゼの傷当て	**25.** gauze pads
介添え人	**8.** attendant	歯科医/歯医者	**17.** dentist	注射針	**26.** needle
聴診器	**9.** stethoscope	ペダル	**18.** pedal	注射器	**27.** syringe

痛みおよび傷病

発疹 <small>はっしん・はっしん</small>	**1.** rash	腹痛	**7.** stomachache	捻挫 <small>ねんざ</small>	**13.** sprain
熱	**2.** fever	背中の痛み	**8.** backache	伸縮性包帯	**a.** stretch bandage
虫螫され <small>さ</small>	**3.** insect bite	歯痛	**9.** toothache	化膿 <small>のう</small>	**14.** infection
悪寒/寒け <small>あさ</small>	**4.** chills	高血圧	**10.** high blood pressure	骨折	**15.** broken bone
目の回りの痣	**5.** black eye	風邪	**11.** cold	切り傷 <small>あさ</small>	**16.** cut
頭痛	**6.** headache	喉の痛み <small>のど</small>	**12.** sore throat	打ち身/青痣 <small>あさ</small>	**17.** bruise
		舌圧子/スパチュラ	**a.** tongue depressor	やけど[火傷]	**18.** burn

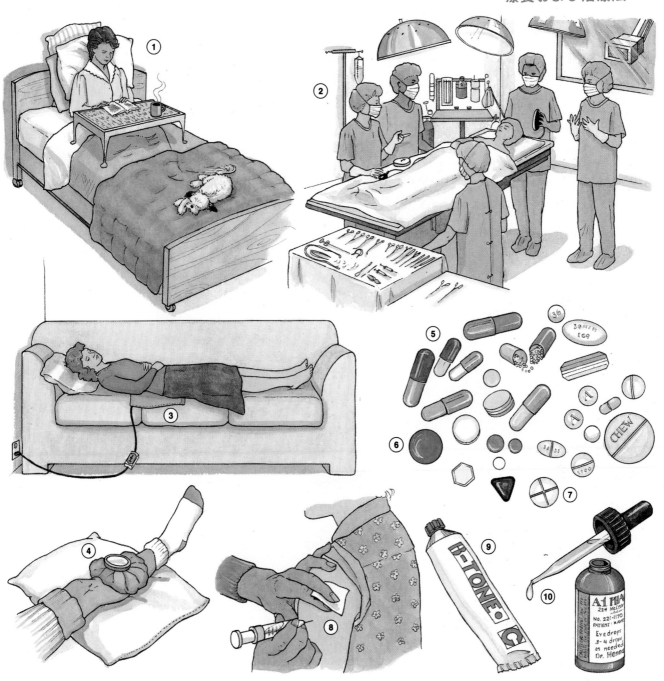

安静	**1.** bed rest	医薬品	**Medicine**	注射	**8.** injection
外科手術	**2.** surgery	カプセル	**5.** capsule	軟膏	**9.** ointment
電気座布団	**3.** heating pad	錠剤	**6.** tablet	目薬	**10.** eye drops
氷嚢	**4.** ice pack	丸薬	**7.** pill		

消火および救出活動

<ruby>梯子<rt>はしご</rt></ruby>	**1.** ladder	診療補助者/救護員	**7.** paramedic	防火服	**13.** coat
ポンプ車	**2.** fire engine	ホース	**8.** hose	<ruby>斧<rt>おの</rt></ruby>	**14.** ax
消防車	**3.** fire truck	消火栓	**9.** fire hydrant	煙/噴煙	**15.** smoke
避難階段	**4.** fire escape	消防士	**10.** fire fighter	水	**16.** water
火事/火災	**5.** fire	消化器	**11.** fire extinguisher	ノズル/筒先	**17.** nozzle
救急車	**6.** ambulance	ヘルメット/消防<ruby>兜<rt>かぶと</rt></ruby>	**12.** helmet		

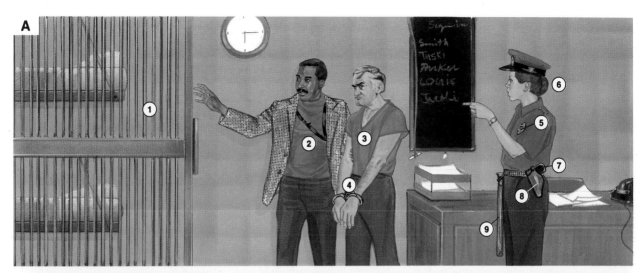

警察署	**A. Police Station**	法廷/裁判所	**B. Court**	証人台	**18.** witness stand
留置場	**1.** jail	判事／裁判官	**10.** judge	法廷吏	**19.** court officer
刑事	**2.** detective	法衣／法服	**11.** robes	陪審員席	**20.** jury box
被疑者	**3.** suspect	小槌	**12.** gavel	陪審員団	**21.** jury
手錠	**4.** handcuffs	証人	**13.** witness	被告側弁護士／弁護官	**22.** defense attorney
バッジ／徽章	**5.** badge	法廷速記者	**14.** court reporter	被告人	**23.** defendant
警察官	**6.** police officer	速記録	**15.** transcript	指紋	**24.** fingerprints
短銃／拳銃／ピストル	**7.** gun	判事席／裁判官席	**16.** bench		
ホルスター／拳銃サック	**8.** holster	地方検事／検察官	**17.** prosecuting attorney		
警棒	**9.** nightstick				

市中の景観

オフィスビル	**1.** office building	公衆電話器	**7.** public telephone	歩行者	**12.** pedestrian
ロビー	**2.** lobby	街路標識	**8.** street sign	バス停留所	**13.** bus stop
角	**3.** corner	郵便局	**9.** post office	ベンチ/長椅子	**14.** bench
横断歩道	**4.** crosswalk	交通巡査	**10.** traffic cop	屑籠	**15.** trash basket
デパート/百貨店	**5.** department store	交差点/交叉点	**11.** intersection	地下鉄駅	**16.** subway station
パン屋	**6.** bakery				

市中の景観

エレベーター／昇降機	**17.** elevator	アパート／	**23.** apartment house	青果店／青果市場	**28.** fruit and vegetable market
書店／本屋	**18.** bookstore	マンション／		街灯	**29.** streetlight
駐車場	**19.** parking garage	集合住宅		新聞売店	**30.** newsstand
パーキングメーター	**20.** parking meter	住居標示	**24.** building number	通り／街路	**31.** street
交通信号	**21.** traffic light	歩道	**25.** sidewalk	マンホール	**32.** manhole
薬屋／雑貨屋	**22.** drugstore	縁石	**26.** curb		
		乳母車	**27.** baby carriage		

郵便制度

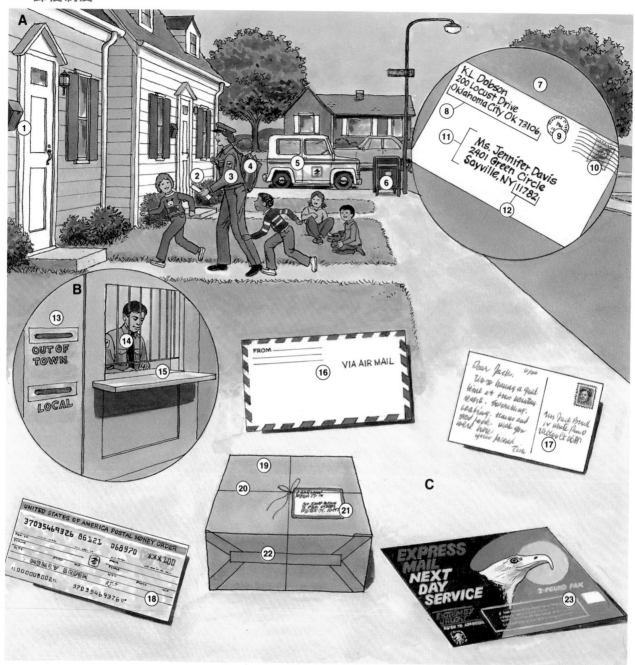

郵便配達	**A. Delivering Mail**	消し印	**9.** postmark	郵便物の種別	**C. Types of Mail**
郵便受け	**1.** mailbox	切手	**10.** stamp	（航空郵便用）封筒	**16.** (airmail) envelope
郵便物	**2.** mail	宛先	**11.** address	絵葉書	**17.** postcard
郵便集配員	**3.** letter carrier	郵便番号	**12.** zip code	郵便為替	**18.** money order
郵便袋／郵袋	**4.** mailbag			小包	**19.** package
郵便車	**5.** mail truck	郵便局	**B. The Post Office**	紐	**20.** string
郵便ポスト	**6.** U.S. mailbox	投函口	**13.** mail slot	貼り付け紙／ラベル	**21.** label
手紙／封書	**7.** letter	郵便局員	**14.** postal worker	ガムテープ	**22.** tape
返送用住所／	**8.** return address	窓口	**15.** window	速達便（小包）	**23.** Express Mail
差出人住所氏名					(package)

図書館員	**1.** library clerk	件名	**10.** subject	地球儀	**19.** globe
貸し出し口	**2.** checkout desk	書架	**11.** row	地図帳	**20.** atlas
貸し出しカード	**3.** library card	閲覧請求票	**12.** call slip	参考図書部	**21.** reference section
索引カード類	**4.** card catalog	マイクロフィルム	**13.** microfilm	案内所	**22.** information desk
索引カード箱	**5.** drawer	マクロフィルムリーダー	**14.** microfilm reader	(参考図書)司書	**23.** (reference) librarian
検索カード	**6.** call card	定期刊行物部	**15.** periodicals section	辞書/辞典	**24.** dictionary
分類番号	**7.** call number	雑誌	**16.** magazine	百科事典	**25.** encyclopedia
著者名	**8.** author	陳列棚	**17.** rack	棚	**26.** shelf
書名	**9.** title	コピー機/複写機	**18.** photocopy machine		

軍隊

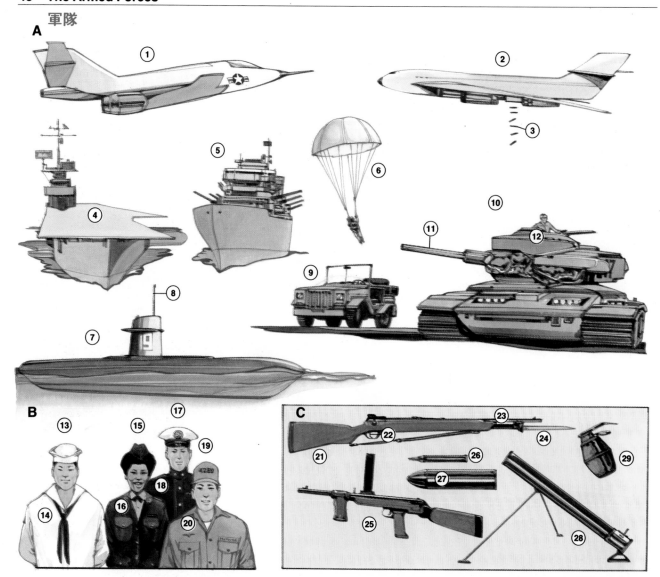

車輌と装備	**A. Vehicles and Equipment**	人員/部隊	**B. Personnel**	武器と弾薬	**C. Weapons and Ammunition**
戦闘機	**1.** fighter plane	海軍	**13.** Navy	施条銃/ライフル	**21.** rifle
爆撃機	**2.** bomber	海軍兵/水兵	**14.** sailor	引き金	**22.** trigger
爆弾	**3.** bomb	陸軍	**15.** Army	銃身	**23.** barrel
航空母艦	**4.** aircraft carrier	陸軍兵	**16.** soldier	銃剣	**24.** bayonet
戦艦	**5.** battleship	海軍隊	**17.** Marines	機関銃	**25.** machine gun
落下傘/パラシュート	**6.** parachute	海兵隊員	**18.** marine	銃弾	**26.** bullet
潜水艦/潜水艇	**7.** submarine	空軍	**19.** Air Force	砲弾	**27.** shell
潜望鏡	**8.** periscope	空軍兵/航空兵	**20.** airman	臼砲	**28.** mortar
ジープ	**9.** jeep			手榴弾/手投げ弾/擲弾	**29.** hand grenade
戦車	**10.** tank				
大砲/戦車砲	**11.** cannon				
砲塔/銃座	**12.** gun turret				

運搬車

道路清掃車	**1.** street cleaner	清掃（局）員	**7.** sanitation worker	セメント車／	**13.** cement truck
牽引車／レッカー車	**2.** tow truck	軽食販売車	**8.** lunch truck	コンクリートミキサー	
燃料運搬車／	**3.** fuel truck	小型有蓋車／	**9.** panel truck	ダンプカー	**14.** dump truck
タンクローリー		ワゴン車／バン		トレーラー車	**15.** tractor trailer
小型貨物乗用車	**4.** pickup truck	運送員	**10.** delivery person	トラック運転士	**16.** truck driver
除雪車	**5.** snow plow	引っ越し専用車	**11.** moving van	自動車運搬車	**17.** transporter
芥収集車／芥集車	**6.** garbage truck	引っ越し業者	**12.** mover	平台トラック	**18.** flatbed

乗用車

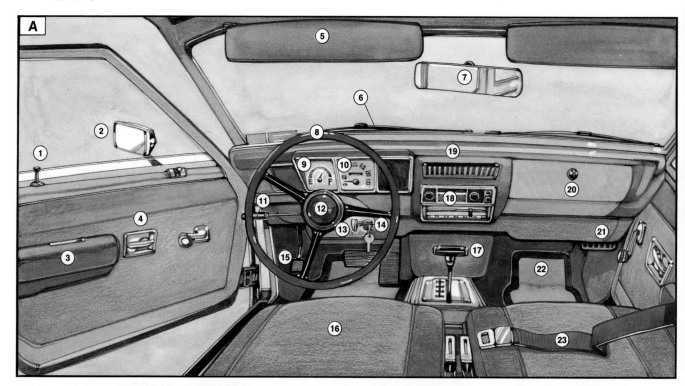

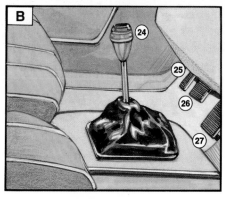

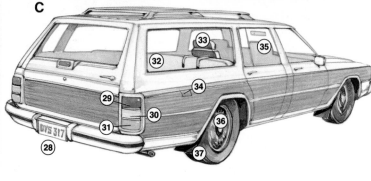

自動変速伝動装置	**A. Automatic Transmission**	点火スイッチ／イグニッション	14. ignition	クラッチペダル	25. clutch
ドアロック	1. door lock	非常ブレーキ	15. emergency brake	ブレーキペダル	26. brake
サイドミラー	2. side mirror	バケットシート	16. bucket seat	アクセル／加速ペダル	27. accelerator
肘掛け	3. armrest	ギヤシフト／変速レバー	17. gearshift		
ドア把手	4. door handle	カーラジオ	18. radio	**ライトバン／ワゴン車**	**C. Station Wagon**
日除け	5. visor	ダッシュボード／計器盤	19. dashboard	ナンバープレート	28. license plate
ワイパー	6. windshield wiper	小物入れ	20. glove compartment	ブレーキランプ／制動灯	29. brake light
バックミラー	7. rearview mirror			バックライト	30. backup light
ハンドル	8. steering wheel	空気吹き出し口／通風孔	21. vent	テールランプ／尾灯	31. taillight
燃料計／ガソリンメーター	9. gas gauge	ゴムマット	22. mat	後部座席	32. backseat
		シートベルト	23. seat belt	子供用座席	33. child's seat
速度計／スピードメーター	10. speedometer			ガソリンタンク	34. gas tank
方向指示器レバー	11. turn signal lever	**手動変速伝動装置**	**B. Manual Transmission**	ヘッドレスト／頭支え／頭受け	35. headrest
クラクション／警笛	12. horn	フロアシフト／変速レバー	24. stick shift	ホイールキャップ	36. hubcap
コラムシャフト	13. column			タイヤ	37. tire

D

F

E

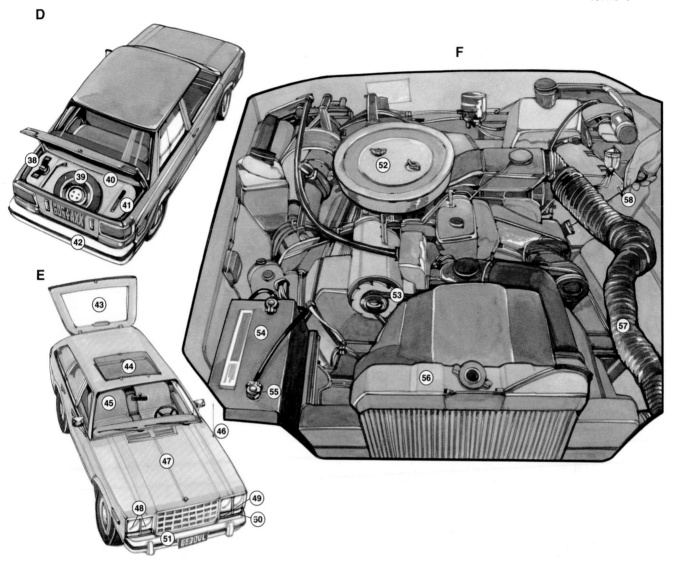

ツードアセダン車	**D. (Two-door) Sedan**	ファイブドア	**E. Four-door Hatchback**	エンジン	**F. Engine**
ジャッキ	**38.** jack	ハッチバック	**43.** hatchback	空気フィルター/	**52.** air filter
スペアタイヤ/	**39.** spare tire	サンルーフ	**44.** sunroof	空気濾過器	
予備タイヤ		フロントガラス	**45.** windshield	ファンベルト	**53.** fan belt
トランク/荷物室	**40.** trunk	カーラジオアンテナ	**46.** antenna	バッテリー/蓄電池	**54.** battery
照明筒	**41.** flare	ボンネット	**47.** hood	電極/端子	**55.** terminal
後部バンパー	**42.** rear bumper	ヘッドライト/前照灯	**48.** headlights	ラジエーター/	**56.** radiator
		駐車灯	**49.** parking lights	冷却器	
		方向指示灯/	**50.** turn signal (lights)	ホース	**57.** hose
		ウインカー		油面ゲージ/計量棒	**58.** dipstick
		前部バンパー	**51.** front bumper		

二輪車

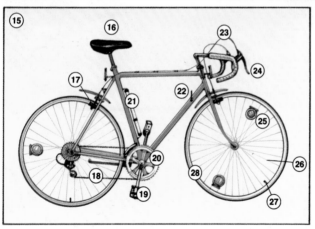

補助輪	**1.** training wheels	ツーリングハンドル	**12.** touring handlebars	手動ブレーキ	**24.** hand brake
ドロップハンドル	**2.** (racing) handlebars	錠(前)	**13.** lock	反射板	**25.** reflector
女子用車体	**3.** girl's frame	自転車立て	**14.** bike stand	スポーク	**26.** spoke
車輪	**4.** wheel	自転車	**15.** bicycle	空気弁	**27.** valve
喇叭／警笛	**5.** horn	サドル	**16.** seat	タイヤ	**28.** tire
三輪車	**6.** tricycle	ブレーキ	**17.** brake	スクーター	**29.** motor scooter
ヘルメット	**7.** helmet	チェーン	**18.** chain	オートバイ／バイク／	**30.** motorcycle
悪路用自転車／	**8.** dirt bike	ペダル	**19.** pedal	自動二輪車／単車	
モトクロス用自転車		鎖歯車／鏈歯車	**20.** sprocket	緩衝器	**31.** shock absorbers
（キック）スタンド	**9.** kickstand	空気入れ	**21.** pump	エンジン	**32.** engine
泥除け	**10.** fender	チェンジレバー	**22.** gear changer	排気管	**33.** exhaust pipe
男子用車体	**11.** boy's frame	ワイヤー	**23.** cable		

州間高速道路	**1.** interstate highway	サービスエリア	**11.** service area	（長距離）バス	**20.** bus
出口/退出傾斜路/ランプウエー	**2.** exit ramp	従業員	**12.** attendant	入口/進入傾斜路	**21.** entrance ramp
高路交差/高路交叉/高架路	**3.** overpass	空気ポンプ	**13.** air pump	路肩	**22.** shoulder
立体交差十字路/立体交叉十字路	**4.** cloverleaf	ガソリンポンプ	**14.** gas pump	道路標識	**23.** road sign
左（追い越し）車線	**5.** left lane	乗用車	**15.** passenger car	出口標示板	**24.** exit sign
中央（走行）車線	**6.** center lane	キャンピングカー	**16.** camper	トラック/貨物運搬車	**25.** truck
右（出口専用）車線	**7.** right lane	スポーツカー	**17.** sports car	バン/貨物自動車	**26.** van
速度制限標識	**8.** speed limit sign	中央分離壁	**18.** center divider	料金（徴集）所	**27.** tollbooth
ヒッチハイカー	**9.** hitchhiker	オートバイ/バイク/	**19.** motorcycle		
トレーラーハウス/付随車	**10.** trailer	自動二輪車/単車			

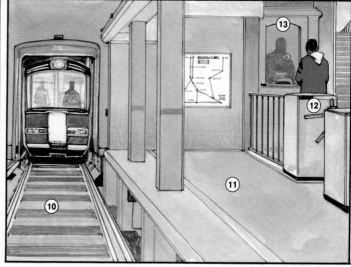

バス	**A. Bus**	地下鉄	**B. Subway**	プラットホーム	**11.** platform
停車合図紐	**1.** cord	車掌/検札係	**7.** conductor	回転式改札口	**12.** turnstile
座席/シート	**2.** seat	吊革	**8.** strap	コイン売り場	**13.** token booth
バス運転士	**3.** bus driver	車輛	**9.** car		
乗り換え切符	**4.** transfer	線路	**10.** track		
料金箱	**5.** fare box				
乗客	**6.** rider				

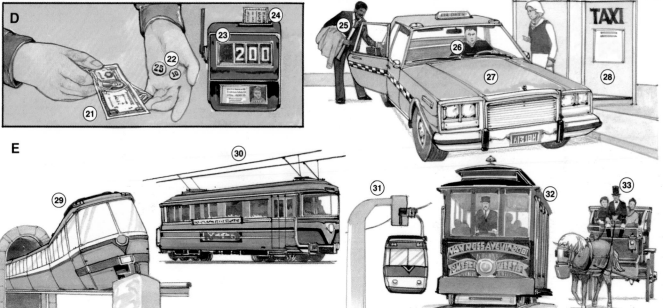

列車	**C. Train**		タクシー	**D. Taxi**		その他の輸送手段	**E. Other Forms of**
							Transportation
通勤列車	**14.** commuter train		料金	**21.** fare		モノレール	**29.** monorail
機関士/運転士	**15.** engineer		チップ/心付け	**22.** tip		市内電車/路面電車	**30.** streetcar
切符/乗車券	**16.** ticket		(料金表示)メーター	**23.** meter		ロープウエー	**31.** aerial tramway
通勤客	**17.** commuter		レシート/受け取り/領収書	**24.** receipt		ケーブルカー	**32.** cable car
駅	**18.** station		乗客	**25.** passenger		馬車	**33.** horse-drawn carriage
切符売り場/出札口	**19.** ticket window		タクシー運転士	**26.** cab driver			
時刻表	**20.** timetable		タクシー	**27.** taxicab			
			タクシー乗り場	**28.** taxi stand			

空の旅

チェックイン/ 搭乗手続き	**Airport Check-In**	手荷物検査	**Security**	副操縦士	**16.** copilot
折り畳みスーツケース	**1.** garment bag	(安全)検査官	**9.** security guard	航空機関士	**17.** flight engineer
機内持ち込み手荷物	**2.** carry-on bag	金属探知機	**10.** metal detector	搭乗カード	**18.** boarding pass
旅行者/搭乗客	**3.** traveler	X線看視装置	**11.** X-ray screener	客室	**19.** cabin
切符/航空券	**4.** ticket	移動ベルト	**12.** conveyor belt	客室乗務員/	**20.** flight attendant
赤帽	**5.** porter			スチュワード	
簡易カート	**6.** dolly	搭乗	**Boarding**	荷物棚	**21.** luggage
スーツケース	**7.** suitcase	コックピット/操縦室	**13.** cockpit		compartment
手荷物	**8.** baggage	計器	**14.** instruments	折り畳み式テーブル	**22.** tray table
		操縦士/機長	**15.** pilot	通路	**23.** aisle

A

B

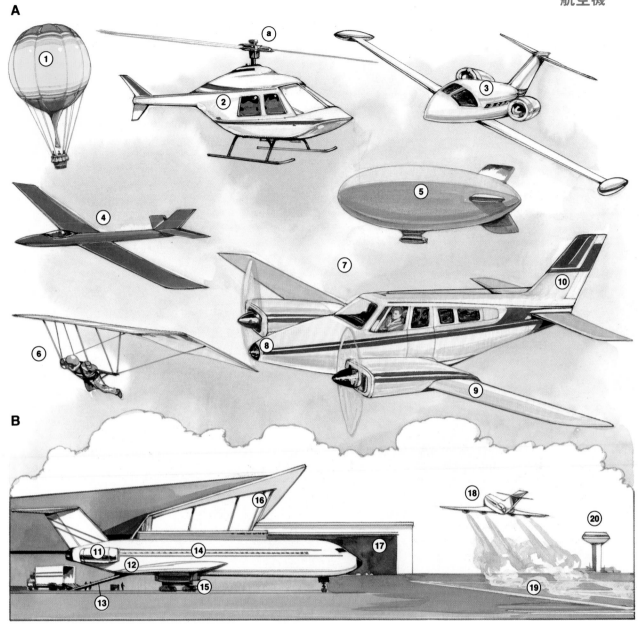

航空機の種類	**A. Aircraft Types**	機首	**8.** nose	機体／胴体	**14.** fuselage
熱気球	**1.** hot air balloon	翼／主翼	**9.** wing	車輪	**15.** landing gear
ヘリコプター	**2.** helicopter	尾部／垂直安定板	**10.** tail	ターミナルビル	**16.** terminal building
回転翼	**a.** rotor			格納庫	**17.** hangar
小型ジェット機	**3.** private jet	離陸	**B. Takeoff**	ジェット機／	**18.** (jet) plane
グライダー／滑空機	**4.** glider	ジェットエンジン／	**11.** jet engine	噴射式推進機	
小型飛行船	**5.** blimp	噴射式エンジン		滑走路	**19.** runway
ハンググライダー	**6.** hang glider	貨物室	**12.** cargo area	管制塔	**20.** control tower
プロペラ機	**7.** propeller plane	貨物搬入口	**13.** cargo door		

港湾施設

漁船	**1.** fishing boat	平底荷船	**12.** barge	舷窓/丸窓	**21.** porthole
漁船員	**2.** fisherman	タグボート/	**13.** tugboat	甲板/デッキ	**22.** deck
埠頭/波止場/船着き場	**3.** pier	曳　船/曳航船		巻き揚げ機	**23.** windlass
フォークリフト	**4.** forklift	灯台	**14.** lighthouse	錨	**24.** anchor
船首/　軸　/軸先	**5.** bow	タンカー/石油輸送船	**15.** tanker	繋船縄/舫綱	**25.** line
クレーン/起重機	**6.** crane	ブイ/浮標	**16.** buoy	繋船柱/ボラード	**26.** bollard
コンテナ/貨物容器	**7.** container	フェリー/連絡船	**17.** ferry	外洋航路船/遠洋定期船	**27.** ocean liner
船倉	**8.** hold	煙突	**18.** smokestack	埠頭/波止場/船着き場	**28.** dock
（コンテナ）船/貨物船	**9.** (container)ship	救命ボート	**19.** lifeboat	乗船待合所	**29.** terminal
積み荷/船荷	**10.** cargo	タラップ/搭乗桟橋	**20.** gangway		
船尾/　艫	**11.** stern				

救命胴衣	**1.** life jacket	帆	**9.** sail	居室つきモーターボート／巡航艇	**16.** cabin cruiser
カヌー／丸木船	**2.** canoe	水上スキーをしている人	**10.** water-skier	カヤック	**17.** kayak
櫂	**3.** paddle	引き綱	**11.** towrope	小型ボート	**18.** dinghy
帆船／ヨット	**4.** sailboat	船外エンジン	**12.** outboard motor	繋留場	**19.** mooring
舵	**5.** rudder	モーターボート／発動機船	**13.** motorboat	膨脹式ゴムボート	**20.** inflatable raft
垂下竜骨	**6.** centerboard	ウインドサーファー	**14.** windsurfer	オール留め	**21.** oarlock
ブーム／帆底材	**7.** boom	帆つきボード／	**15.** sailboard	オール	**22.** oar
マスト／帆柱	**8.** mast	ウインドサーフボード		ボート／漕ぎ船	**23.** rowboat

草花および樹木

花	**Flowers**	ヒヤシンス［風信子］	**10.** hyacinth
チューリップ／鬱金香	**1.** tulip	（花）あやめ／花菖蒲／	**11.** iris
茎	**a.** stem	かきつばた［杜若／燕子花］	
パンジー／三色菫	**2.** pansy	蘭	**12.** orchid
ゆり［百合］	**3.** lily	百日草	**13.** zinnia
菊	**4.** (chrysanthe)mum	くちなし［梔子／山梔］	**14.** gardenia
デージー／雛菊	**5.** daisy	ポインセチヤ／掌状木菫	**15.** poinsettia
マリーゴールド／	**6.** marigold		**16.** violet
金盞花／長春花		金鳳花［毛茛］	**17.** buttercup
ペチュニア／	**7.** petunia	ばら［薔薇］	**18.** rose
衝羽根朝顔		蕾／莟	**a.** bud
喇叭水仙	**8.** daffodil		**b.** petal
球根	**a.** bulb	花弁	
クロッカス／	**9.** crocus	棘／荊／茨／刺	**c.** thorn
花サフラン［泊夫藍］		ひまわり［向日葵］	**19.** sunflower

稲科植物と穀類	**Grasses and Grains**
砂糖黍	**20.** sugarcane
稲／米	**21.** rice
小麦	**22.** wheat
オート麦／燕麦／烏麦	**23.** oats
（とう）もろこし［（玉）蜀黍］／唐黍	**24.** corn

高木／喬木	**Trees**	松	**34.** pine	その他の植物	**Other Plants**
赤杉／アメリカ杉	**25.** redwood	針状葉	**a.** needle	室内用鉢植え	**39.** house plants
（ココ）椰子	**26.** palm	球果／毬果／	**b.** cone	サボテン／	**40.** cactus
ユーカリ［有加利］（樹）	**27.** eucalyptus	松笠／松毬／		シャボテン	
花水木	**28.** dogwood	松ふぐり［陰囊］		［仙人掌／覇王樹］	
木蓮／泰山木	**29.** magnolia	高木／喬木	**35.** tree	低木／灌木	**41.** bushes
ポプラ／西洋箱柳／白楊	**30.** poplar	枝	**a.** branch	蔓状植物	**42.** vine
柳	**31.** willow	幹	**b.** trunk		
樺／白樺	**32.** birch	樹皮	**c.** bark	有毒植物	**Poisonous Plants**
撫／楢／樫／槲／椎	**33.** oak	根	**d.** root	毒オーク	**43.** poison oak
小枝	**a.** twig	楡	**36.** elm	毒漆／櫨	**44.** poison sumac
団栗／橡	**b.** acorn	葉	**a.** leaf	（黄）櫨漆	
		西洋柊	**37.** holly	（アメリカ）蔦漆	**45.** poison ivy
		楓	**38.** maple		

下等動物

かたつむり[蝸牛]	**1.** snail	槍いか[烏賊]／	**5.** squid	みみず[蚯蚓]／蠕虫	**11.** worm
貝殻／介殻／外殻	**a.** shell	剣先いか[烏賊]／鞘長		くらげ[水母／海月]	**12.** jellyfish
頭触角	**b.** antenna	蛸	**6.** octopus	触手	**a.** tentacle
かき[牡蠣]	**2.** oyster	ひとで[海星]	**7.** starfish	伊勢えび[海老]／鎌倉えび／	**13.** lobster
胎貝／姫貝	**3.** mussel	小蝦／鰕[海老]	**8.** shrimp	大型海ざりがに [蝲蛄]	
なめくじ(ら／り)[蛞蝓]	**4.** slug	蟹	**9.** crab	螯	**a.** claw
		帆立貝[海扇]	**10.** scallop		

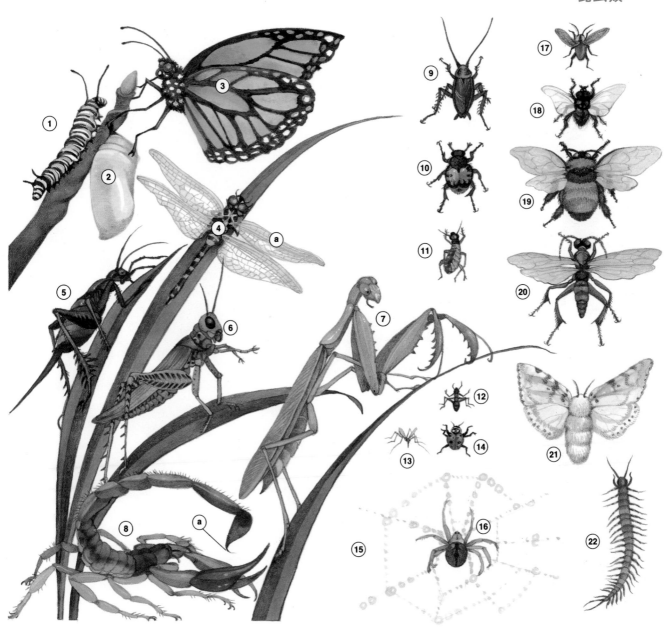

芋虫／青虫／毛虫	**1.** caterpillar	蠍	**8.** scorpion	くも[蜘蛛]の巣	**15.** web
繭	**2.** cocoon	毒針	**a.** sting	くも[蜘蛛]	**16.** spider
蝶	**3.** butterfly	ごきぶり[蜚蠊]	**9.** cockroach	蛍	**17.** firefly
とんぼ[蜻蛉／蜻蜓]	**4.** dragonfly	甲虫	**10.** beetle	蠅	**18.** fly
羽根	**a.** wing	白蟻	**11.** termite	蜜蜂	**19.** bee
こおろぎ[蟋蟀]	**5.** cricket	蟻	**12.** ant	雀蜂	**20.** wasp
ばった[飛蝗／蝗虫]	**6.** grasshopper	蚊	**13.** mosquito	蛾	**21.** moth
かまきり[蟷螂／螳螂]	**7.** mantis	天道虫[瓢虫]	**14.** ladybug	むかで[百足／蜈蚣]	**22.** centipede

鳥類

鳩／大鳩	**1.** pigeon
翼／翅	**a.** wing
蜂鳥	**2.** hummingbird
烏／鴉	**3.** crow
（鋭い）喙／嘴	**a.** beak
海鴎	**4.** sea gull
鷲鷹	**5.** eagle
梟／（みみ）ずく［木菟］	**6.** owl
鷹	**7.** hawk
羽／羽毛	**a.** feather
青懸巣	**8.** blue jay
駒鶫／渡り鶫	**9.** robin
雀	**10.** sparrow
紅冠鳥	**11.** cardinal
駝鳥	**12.** ostrich
卵	**13.** egg
カナリア／カナリヤ［金糸雀］	**14.** canary
小型いんこ［鸚哥］	**15.** parakeet
鸚鵡	**16.** parrot
きつつき［啄木鳥］	**17.** woodpecker
孔雀	**18.** peacock
雉（子）／山鳥	**19.** pheasant
七面鳥	**20.** turkey
雄鶏	**21.** rooster
雛	**22.** chick
鶏	**23.** chicken
ペリカン	**24.** pelican
（平たい）喙／嘴	**a.** bill
鴨／あひる［家鴨］	**25.** duck
雁／鴈／鵞鳥	**26.** goose
ペンギン	**27.** penguin
白鳥	**28.** swan
紅鶴／フラミンゴ	**29.** flamingo
鸛	**30.** stork
（鳥の）巣	**31.** nest
道走り	**32.** roadrunner

魚類および爬行動物
<small>はこう</small>

魚類

竜の落し子[海馬]
鱒<small>ます</small>
梶木[旗魚]（鮪）<small>かじき まぐろ</small>
尾／尻尾<small>しっぽ</small>
鰭／背鰭<small>ひれ せびれ</small>
鰓<small>えら</small>
鰻<small>うなぎ</small>
鮫／鱶<small>さめ ふか</small>

A. Fish

1. sea horse
2. trout
3. swordfish
　a. tail
　b. fin
　c. gill
4. eel
5. shark

（赤）鱝／鱏<small>えい えい</small>
　鰈<small>かれい</small>

両生類／両棲類<small>せい</small>
および爬行動物<small>はこう</small>

アメリカ鰐<small>わに</small>
（ガーター）蛇
がらがら蛇／響尾蛇<small>きょうびだ</small>
コブラ／眼鏡蛇

6. stingray
7. flounder

B. Amphibians and
　　Reptiles

8. alligator
9. (garter) snake
10. rattlesnake
11. cobra

亀／海亀／（小型の）陸亀<small>かめ がめ がめ</small>
イグアナ
山椒魚／半割／半裂<small>しょう</small>
とかげ[石竜子]／蜥蜴<small>げっちょう</small>
お玉杓子[蝌蚪]<small>じゃくし</small>
蛙<small>かえる</small>
（陸上・淡水の）亀<small>かめ</small>
甲羅

12. turtle
13. iguana
14. salamander
15. lizard
16. tadpole
17. frog
18. tortoise
　a. shell

哺乳動物 I

有袋類、貧歯類、飛行哺乳動物	Pouched, Toothless, or Flying Mammals
コアラ／袋熊	1. koala
アルマジロ	2. armadillo
カンガルー	3. kangaroo
尾／尻尾	a. tail
後脚／後足	b. hind legs
袋	c. pouch
前脚／前足	d. forelegs
こうもり［蝙蝠］	4. bat
ありくい［食蟻獣］	5. anteater

齧歯動物	Rodents
縞りす［栗鼠］	6. chipmunk
野鼠／溝鼠	7. rat
地りす［栗鼠］／	8. gopher
畑りす［栗鼠］	
二十日鼠／家鼠	9. mouse
りす［栗鼠］	10. squirrel
山荒らし	11. porcupine
針	a. quill
ビーバー／海狸	12. beaver
兎	13. rabbit

有蹄動物	Hoofed Mammals
河馬	14. hippopotamus
ラマ	15. llama
犀	16. rhinoceros
角	a. horn
象	17. elephant
象の鼻	a. trunk
牙／象牙	b. tusk
縞馬	18. zebra

バイソン/アメリカ野牛	**19.** bison	羊	**25.** sheep	乳牛/雌牛/牝牛	**32.** cow
ポニー/小型の馬	**20.** pony	鹿	**26.** deer	(二瘤)駱駝	**33.** camel
馬	**21.** horse	子鹿	**27.** fawn	瘤	**a.** hump
鬣 / 鬐	**a.** mane	やぎ[山羊]	**28.** goat	雄牛/牡牛	**34.** bull
子馬	**22.** foal	ジラフ/きりん	**29.** giraffe	ムース/アメリカ箆鹿	**35.** moose
驢馬	**23.** donkey	豚	**30.** hog	枝角	**a.** antler
子羊	**24.** lamb	子牛	**31.** calf	蹄	**b.** hoof

哺乳動物 II

ひょう
豹   **1.** leopard
とら
虎   **2.** tiger
かぎづめ
鉤爪   **a.** claw
ライオン／獅子 **3.** lion
猫   **4.** cat

子猫   **5.** kitten
きつね
狐   **6.** fox
あらいぐま
洗熊   **7.** raccoon
スカンク **8.** skunk

水生／水棲哺乳動物   **Aquatic Mammals**
鯨   **9.** whale
うそ
(川) 獺／らっこ [海獺／猟虎] **10.** otter

セイウチ [海象]   **11.** walrus
あざらし [海豹] ／あしか [海驢] ／   **12.** seal
おっとせい [膃肭獣] ／とど [胡獰]
ひれ
鰭足   **a.** flipper
いるか [海豚]   **13.** dolphin

<ruby>哺<rt>ほ</rt></ruby>乳動物　Ⅱ

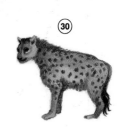

霊長類	**Primates**	熊<rt>くま</rt>	**Bears**	犬	**Dogs**
（小型の）猿	**14.** monkey	パンダ／ジャイアントパンダ／	**20.** panda	スパニエル犬	**24.** spaniel
ギボン／手長猿	**15.** gibbon	大パンダ／白黒熊<rt>ぐま</rt>		テリヤ	**25.** terrier
チンパンジー／黒猩猩<rt>しょうじょう</rt>	**16.** chimpanzee	黒熊<rt>ぐま</rt>	**21.** black bear	レトレーバー	**26.** retriever
ゴリラ／大猩猩<rt>しょうじょう</rt>	**17.** gorilla	北極熊<rt>ぐま</rt>／白熊<rt>ぐま</rt>	**22.** polar bear	子犬	**27.** puppy
オランウータン／猩猩<rt>しょうじょう</rt>	**18.** orangutan	グリズリー／灰色熊<rt>ぐま</rt>	**23.** grizzly bear	シェパード／	**28.** shepherd
狒狒<rt>ひひ</rt>	**19.** baboon			セパード／牧羊犬	
				狼<rt>おおかみ</rt>	**29.** wolf
				足	**a.** paw
				ハイエナ／鬣<rt>たてがみ</rt>犬	**30.** hyena

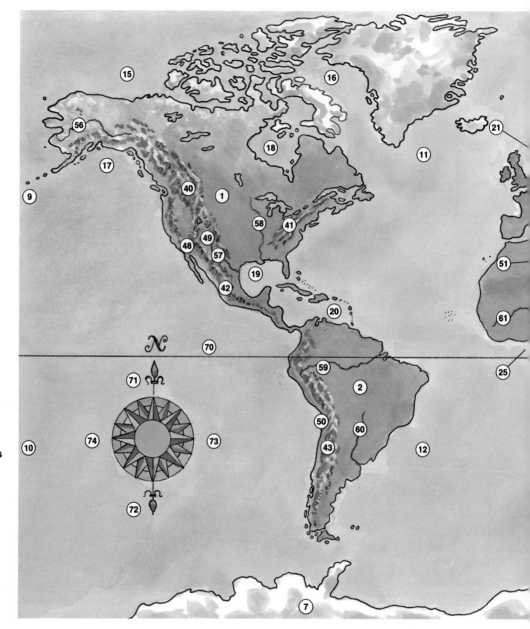

大陸   Continents

北アメリカ大陸/ 北米	**1.** North America
南アメリカ大陸/ 南米	**2.** South America
ヨーロッパ大陸/ 欧州	**3.** Europe
アフリカ大陸	**4.** Africa
アジア大陸	**5.** Asia
オーストラリア大陸/ 豪州	**6.** Australia
南極大陸	**7.** Antarctica

大洋   Oceans

北氷洋/北極海	**8.** Arctic
北太平洋	**9.** North Pacific
南太平洋	**10.** South Pacific
北大西洋	**11.** North Atlantic
南大西洋	**12.** South Atlantic
インド洋	**13.** Indian
南氷洋/南極海	**14.** Antarctic

海、湾、入り江   Seas, Gulfs, and Bays

ボーフォート海	**15.** Beaufort Sea
バフィン湾	**16.** Baffin Bay
アラスカ湾	**17.** Gulf of Alaska
ハドソン湾	**18.** Hudson Bay
メキシコ湾	**19.** Gulf of Mexico
カリブ海	**20.** Caribbean Sea
北海	**21.** North Sea
バルト海/ バルチック海	**22.** Baltic Sea
バレンツ海	**23.** Barents Sea
地中海	**24.** Mediterranean Sea
ギニア湾	**25.** Gulf of Guinea
黒海	**26.** Black Sea
カスピ海	**27.** Caspian Sea
ペルシャ湾	**28.** Persian Gulf
紅海	**29.** Red Sea
アラビア海	**30.** Arabian Sea
カラ海	**31.** Kara Sea
ベンガル湾	**32.** Bay of Bengal
ラプテフ海	**33.** Laptev Sea
ベーリング海	**34.** Bering Sea
オホーツク海	**35.** Sea of Okhotsk
日本海/東海	**36.** Sea of Japan
黄海	**37.** Yellow Sea
東シナ海	**38.** East China Sea
南シナ海	**39.** South China Sea

	河川		**Rivers**
	ユーコン川	**56.**	Yukon
	リオグランデ川	**57.**	Rio Grande
	ミシシッピー川	**58.**	Mississippi
	アマゾン川	**59.**	Amazon
	パラナ川	**60.**	Paraná
	ニジェール川	**61.**	Niger
	コンゴ川	**62.**	Congo
	ナイル川	**63.**	Nile
	オビ川	**64.**	Ob
	エニセイ川	**65.**	Yenisey
	レナ川	**66.**	Lena
	ガンジス川	**67.**	Ganges
	黄河	**68.**	Huang
	揚子江/長江	**69.**	Yangtze

山脈	**Mountain Ranges**		砂漠/沙漠	**Deserts**
ロッキー山脈	**40.** Rocky Mountains		モハーベ砂漠	**48.** Mojave
アパラチア山脈	**41.** Appalachian Mountains		五色砂漠	**49.** Painted
シエラマドレ山脈	**42.** Sierra Madre		アタカマ砂漠	**50.** Atacama
アンデス山脈	**43.** Andes		サハラ砂漠	**51.** Sahara
アルプス山脈	**44.** Alps		ルブアルハーリー砂漠	**52.** Rub' al Khali
カフカス山脈	**45.** Caucasus		タクラマカン砂漠	**53.** Takla Makan
ウラル山脈	**46.** Urals		ゴビ砂漠	**54.** Gobi
ヒマラヤ山脈	**47.** Himalayas		グレートサンジー砂漠	**55.** Great Sandy

赤道	**70.** equator
北	**71.** north
南	**72.** south
東	**73.** east
西	**74.** west

アメリカ合衆国

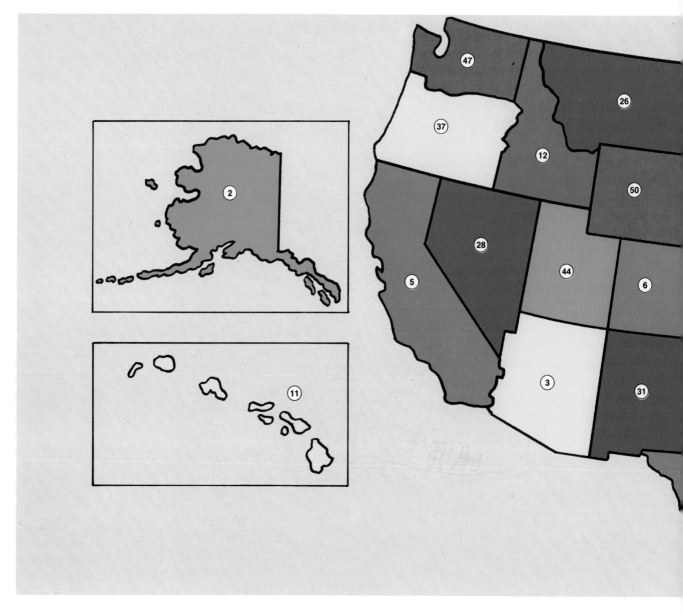

アラバマ州	**1.** Alabama	フロリダ州	**9.** Florida	ケンタッキー州	**17.** Kentucky	
アラスカ州	**2.** Alaska	ジョージア州	**10.** Georgia	ルイジアナ州	**18.** Louisiana	
アリゾナ州	**3.** Arizona	ハワイ州	**11.** Hawaii	メーン州	**19.** Maine	
アーカンソー州	**4.** Arkansas	アイダホ州	**12.** Idaho	メリーランド州	**20.** Maryland	
カリフォルニア州	**5.** California	イリノイ州	**13.** Illinois	マサチューセッツ州	**21.** Massachusetts	
コロラド州	**6.** Colorado	インジアナ州	**14.** Indiana	ミシガン州	**22.** Michigan	
コネチカット州	**7.** Connecticut	アイオワ州	**15.** Iowa	ミネソタ州	**23.** Minnesota	
デラウエア州	**8.** Delaware	カンザス州	**16.** Kansas	ミシシッピー州	**24.** Mississippi	

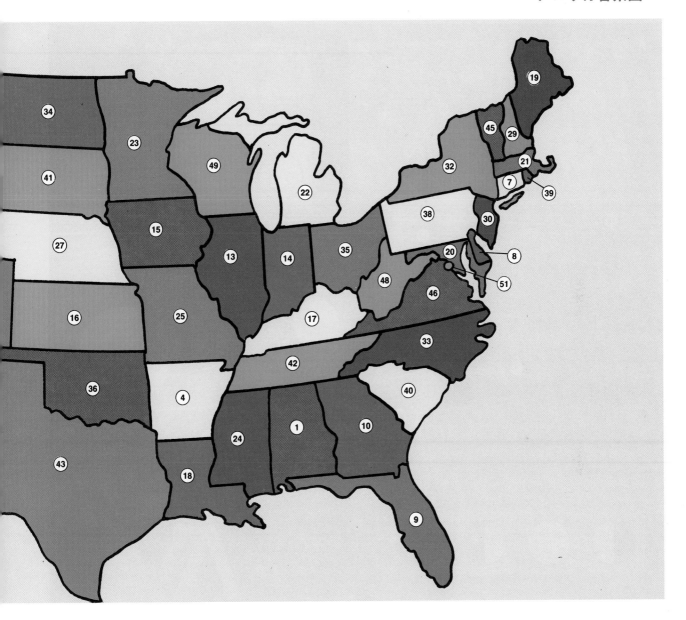

ミズーリ州	**25.** Missouri	ノースダコタ州	**34.** North Dakota	テキサス州	**43.** Texas
モンタナ州	**26.** Montana	オハイオ州	**35.** Ohio	ユタ州	**44.** Utah
ネブラスカ州	**27.** Nebraska	オクラホマ州	**36.** Oklahoma	バーモント州	**45.** Vermont
ネバダ州	**28.** Nevada	オレゴン州	**37.** Oregon	バージニア州	**46.** Virginia
ニューハンプシャー州	**29.** New Hampshire	ペンシルベニア州	**38.** Pennsylvania	ワシントン州	**47.** Washington
ニュージャージー州	**30.** New Jersey	ロードアイランド州	**39.** Rhode Island	ウエストバージニア州	**48.** West Virginia
ニューメキシコ州	**31.** New Mexico	サウスカロライナ州	**40.** South Carolina	ウイスコンシン州	**49.** Wisconsin
ニューヨーク州	**32.** New York	サウスダコタ州	**41.** South Dakota	ワイオミング州	**50.** Wyoming
ノースカロライナ州	**33.** North Carolina	テネシー州	**42.** Tennessee	コロンビア特別区	**51.** District of Columbia

大宇宙

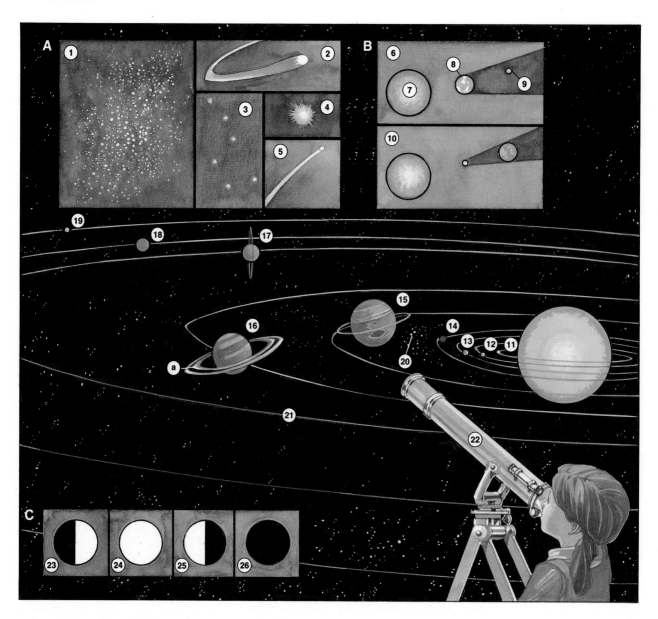

宇宙空間	**A. Outer Space**	惑星/遊星	**The Planets**
星雲/銀河(系)	**1.** galaxy	水星	**11.** Mercury
彗星/箒星	**2.** comet	金星	**12.** Venus
(北斗七星の)星座	**3.** (Big Dipper) constellation	地球	**13.** Earth
恒星	**4.** star	火星	**14.** Mars
流星(体)/流れ星	**5.** meteor	木星	**15.** Jupiter
		土星	**16.** Saturn
		環	**a.** ring
太陽系	**B. The Solar System**	天王星	**17.** Uranus
月食/月蝕	**6.** lunar eclipse	海王星	**18.** Neptune
太陽	**7.** Sun	冥王星	**19.** Pluto
地球	**8.** Earth		
月	**9.** Moon	小惑星/小遊星	**20.** asteroid
日食/日蝕	**10.** solar eclipse	(公転/周転)軌道	**21.** orbit
		(天体)望遠鏡	**22.** telescope
		月の形相	**C. Phases of the Moon**
		上弦(の月)	**23.** first quarter
		満月	**24.** full moon
		下弦(の月)	**25.** last quarter
		新月	**26.** new moon

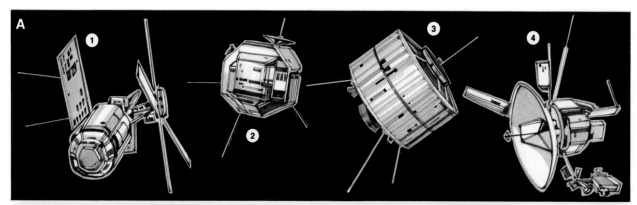

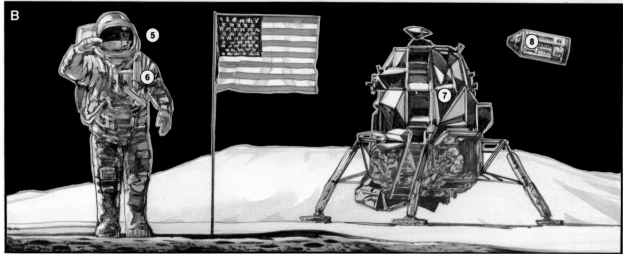

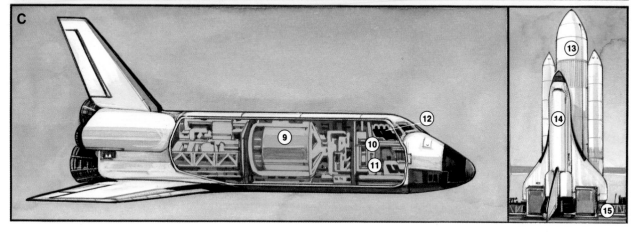

宇宙船	**A. Spacecraft**	月面着陸	**B. Landing on**	スペースシャトル	**C. The Space Shuttle**
宇宙ステーション	**1.** space station		**the Moon**	荷物室	**9.** cargo bay
通信衛星	**2.** communication satellite			操縦室	**10.** flight deck
気象衛星	**3.** weather satellite	宇宙飛行士	**5.** astronaut	居住区	**11.** living quarters
宇宙探査機	**4.** space probe	宇宙服	**6.** space suit	乗員/乗組員	**12.** crew
		月着陸船	**7.** lunar module	ロケット/推進装置	**13.** rocket
		司令船	**8.** command module	スペースシャトル	**14.** space shuttle
				発射台/打ち上げ台	**15.** launchpad

旗/国旗	**1.** flag	チョーク/白墨	**10.** chalk	鉛筆削り	**20.** pencil sharpener
(掛け)時計	**2.** clock	黒板消し/黒板拭き	**11.** eraser	消しゴム/字消し	**21.** pencil eraser
スピーカー/拡声器	**3.** loudspeaker	廊下	**12.** hall	ボールペン	**22.** ballpoint pen
教員/先生	**4.** teacher	(ルーズリーフ)用紙	**13.** (loose-leaf) paper	物差/物指/定規/定木	**23.** ruler
黒板	**5.** chalkboard	リングバインダー	**14.** ring binder	鉛筆	**24.** pencil
ロッカー	**6.** locker	螺旋ノート	**15.** spiral notebook	画鋲/押しピン	**25.** thumbtack
掲示板	**7.** bulletin board	机	**16.** desk	教科書	**26.** (text) book
コンピューター/	**8.** computer	接着剤/糊	**17.** glue	オーバーヘッドプロジェクター/	**27.** overhead projector
電算機(の)端末		筆/刷毛	**18.** brush	頭上投影器	
チョーク受け/白墨受け	**9.** chalk tray	生徒	**19.** student		

学校での動作

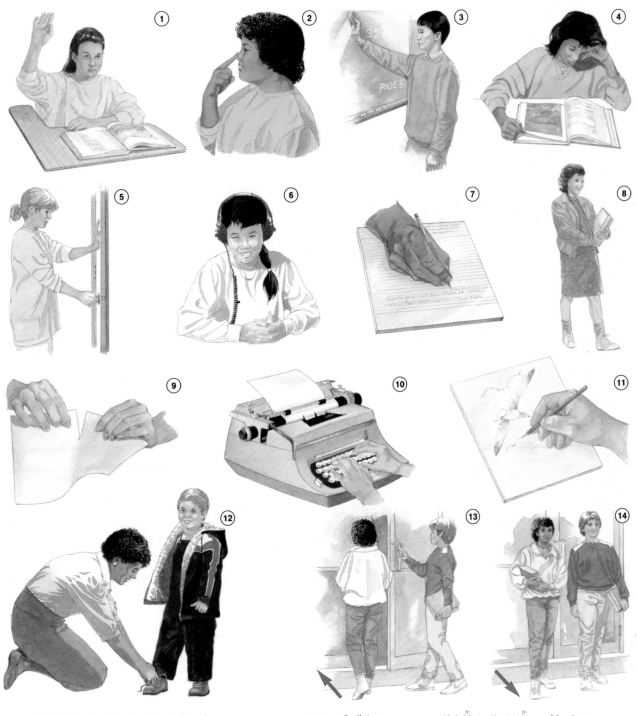

（手を）挙げる	**1.** raise (one's hand)	聴く	**6.** listen
触る／触れる	**2.** touch	書く	**7.** write
消す	**3.** erase	歩く	**8.** walk
読む	**4.** read	破る／裂く	**9.** tear
閉じる／閉める	**5.** close	タイプする	**10.** type

絵を描く／線画を描く	**11.** draw
結ぶ／縛る	**12.** tie
出る／退出する	**13.** leave
入る／入室する	**14.** enter

プリズム／分光器	**1.** prism	タイマー／	**13.** timer	作業台	**24.** bench
フラスコ／水差し	**2.** flask	ストップウォッチ		目盛りつきシリンダー／	**25.** graduated
ペトリ皿／培養皿	**3.** petri dish	ピペット	**14.** pipette	計量器	cylinder
衡／秤／天秤	**4.** scale	拡大鏡／虫眼鏡／ルーペ	**15.** magnifying glass	スポイト	**26.** medicine
錘／分銅	**5.** weights	濾過紙／濾し紙	**16.** filter paper		dropper
金網	**6.** wire mesh	じょうご／漏斗	**17.** funnel	磁石	**27.** magnet
	screen	ゴムホース／ゴム管	**18.** rubber tubing	鉗子	**28.** forceps
留め金／締め具／	**7.** clamp	リングスタンド／	**19.** ring stand	試験管挟み	**29.** tongs
クランプ		リング立て		顕微鏡	**30.** microscope
試験管立て	**8.** rack	ブンゼンバーナー／	**20.** Bunsen burner	スライドガラス／検鏡板	**31.** slide
試験管	**9.** test tube	ブンゼン灯		ピンセット	**32.** tweezers
栓	**10.** stopper	炎／焔	**21.** flame	解剖用具	**33.** dissection kit
グラフ用紙	**11.** graph paper	温度計	**22.** thermometer	腰掛け	**34.** stool
保護眼鏡	**12.** safety glasses	ビーカー	**23.** beaker		

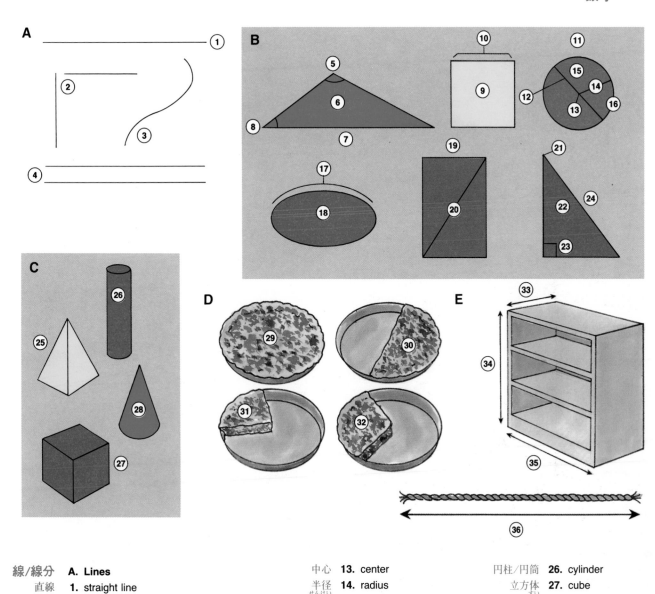

線/線分	**A. Lines**
直線	**1.** straight line
直交線	**2.** perpendicular lines
曲線	**3.** curve
平行線	**4.** parallel lines

幾可図形	**B. Geometrical Figures**
鈍角	**5.** obtuse angle
三角形	**6.** triangle
底辺	**7.** base
鋭角	**8.** acute angle
正方形	**9.** square
辺	**10.** side
円	**11.** circle
直径	**12.** diameter

中心	**13.** center
半径	**14.** radius
扇形	**15.** section
(円)弧	**16.** arc
円周	**17.** circumference
楕円/長円(形)	**18.** oval
直角形/長方形/矩形	**19.** rectangle
対角線	**20.** diagonal
頂点	**21.** apex
直角三角形	**22.** right triangle
直角	**23.** right angle
斜辺	**24.** hypotenuse

立体図形	**C. Solid Figures**
角錐	**25.** pyramid

円柱/円筒	**26.** cylinder
立方体	**27.** cube
円錐	**28.** cone

分数	**D. Fractions**
全体	**29.** whole
二分の一/半分	**30.** a half (1/2)
四分の一	**31.** a quarter (1/4)
三分の一	**32.** a third (1/3)

寸法	**E. Measurement**
奥行き	**33.** depth
高さ	**34.** height
幅	**35.** width
長さ	**36.** length

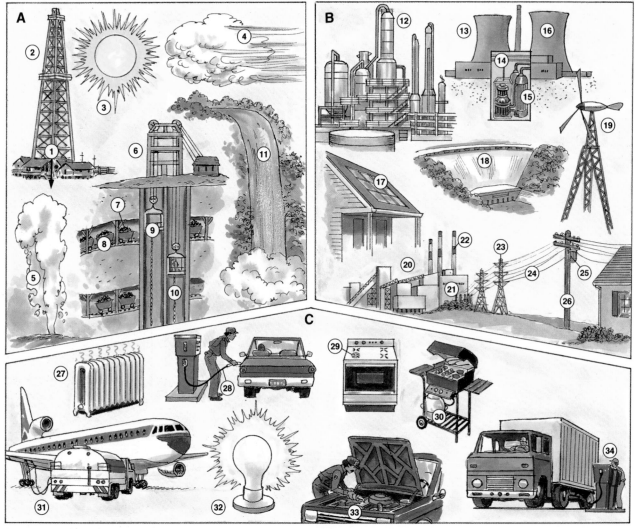

動力源	**A. Sources of Power**	発電	**B. Generation of Power**	高圧線／送電線	**24.** power lines
油井	**1.** oil well	精油所	**12.** refinery	変圧器／トランス	**25.** transformer
油井 櫓	**2.** derrick	原子炉	**13.** nuclear reactor	電柱／電信柱	**26.** utility pole
太陽	**3.** sun	炉心	**14.** core		
風力	**4.** wind	ウラニウム棒／	**15.** uranium rods	**用途と製品**	**C. Uses and Products**
間欠泉／間歇泉	**5.** geyser	ウラン棒		（温）熱／暖房	**27.** heat
炭鉱	**6.** coal mine	冷却塔	**16.** cooling tower	ガソリン／揮発油	**28.** gas(oline)
石炭	**7.** coal	太陽熱収集器／	**17.** solar collector	天然ガス	**29.** natural gas
トロッコ	**8.** shuttle car	蒐 集器／		プロパンガス	**30.** propane gas
エレベーター／	**9.** elevator	温水器		ジェット燃料	**31.** jet fuel
昇降機		ダム	**18.** dam	電気	**32.** electricity
縦坑／竪坑	**10.** shaft	風車	**19.** windmill	エンジンオイル	**33.** motor oil
滝／瀑布	**11.** waterfall	発電所	**20.** power station	ディーゼルオイル／重油／軽油	**34.** diesel fuel
		発電機	**21.** electrical generator		
		煙突	**22.** smokestack		
		高圧線鉄塔／	**23.** transmission towers		
		送電塔			

酪農場	**A. Dairy Farm**		羊	10. sheep			<ruby>畝<rt>うね</rt></ruby><ruby>畝<rt>うね</rt></ruby>	18. row
果樹園	1. orchard		乳牛	11. dairy cow			かかし[案山子]	19. scarecrow
果樹	2. fruit tree							
農場内住居	3. farmhouse		**小麦農場**	**B. Wheat Farm**			**牧畜場**	**C. Ranch**
サイロ／貯蔵・<ruby>醸酵<rt>はっこう</rt></ruby>塔	4. silo		家畜	12. livestock			牛(の群れ)	20. (herd of) cattle
<ruby>乾<rt>ほ</rt></ruby>し草・家畜・農器具置場／	5. barn		<ruby>乾<rt>ほ</rt></ruby>し草(の<ruby>梱<rt>こり</rt></ruby>)	13. (bale of) hay			牧童／牧畜業者(男子)	21. cowboy
農場内物置			<ruby>三叉<rt>みつまた</rt></ruby>	14. pitchfork			牧童／牧畜業者(女子)	22. cowgirl
放牧場	6. pasture		トラクター／<ruby>牽引<rt>けん</rt></ruby>車	15. tractor			馬	23. horses
農場経営者／農業就労者	7. farmer		(小麦)畑／畠	16. (wheat) field			囲い	24. corral
納屋回り	8. barnyard		コンバイン／	17. combine			<ruby>飼葉桶<rt>おけ</rt></ruby>／水飲み場	25. trough
垣根／<ruby>柵<rt>さく</rt></ruby>	9. fence		複式収穫機					

建設現場	A. Construction Site	セメント	10. cement	道路工事	B. Road Work
垂木／椽	1. rafters	基礎／土台	11. foundation	円錐標識	19. cone
柿（板）／木端	2. shingle	煉瓦	12. bricks	旗	20. flag
水準器／水平器	3. level	鶴嘴	13. pickax	バリケード／柵	21. barricade
安全帽／ヘルメット	4. hard hat	建設作業員	14. construction worker	掘削機／掘鑿機／	22. jackhammer
建設業者	5. builder	シャベル	15. shovel	削岩ドリル	
青写真／青焼き	6. blueprints	板材／厚板	16. board	（一輪）手押し車	23. wheelbarrow
足場（組み）	7. scaffolding	電線工事作業員	17. linesman	中央分離壁	24. center divider
梯子	8. ladder	高所作業用クレーン	18. cherry picker	セメント車／	25. cement mixer
（梯子の）段	9. rung			コンクリートミキサー	
				ショベルカー	26. backhoe
				ブルドーザー	27. bulldozer

（電話）交換手	**1.** switchboard operator	秘書	**11.** secretary	書類綴じ	**22.** file folder
イヤフォーン型送受話器	**2.** headset	未決箱／書類入れ	**12.** in-box	ファイル係	**23.** file clerk
（電話）交換機	**3.** switchboard	（事務）机	**13.** desk	コピー機／複写機	**24.** photocopier
プリンター／印字機	**4.** printer	ローロデックス／	**14.** rolodex	メモ用紙／連絡票	**25.** message pad
個室	**5.** cubicle	回転式検索簿		（8.5×14インチの）	**26.** (legal) pad
タイピスト	**6.** typist	電話（器）	**15.** telephone	法律用箋	
ワープロ／	**7.** word processor	コンピューター／	**16.** computer	ホッチキス／針金綴じ器	**27.** stapler
ワードプロセッサー		電算機（の端末）		（ゼム）クリップ／	**28.** paper clips
プリントアウト／	**8.** printout	タイプ用椅子	**17.** typing chair	ゼムピン	
ハードコピー		部長／課長	**18.** manager	針金剥し	**29.** staple remover
カレンダー／	**9.** calendar	（卓上）計算器	**19.** calculator	鉛筆削り	**30.** pencil sharpener
掛け暦／七曜表		書棚／本箱	**20.** bookcase	封筒	**31.** envelope
タイプライター	**10.** typewriter	ファイルキャビネット	**21.** file cabinet		

職業I：アメリカの典型的本通り

薬剤士	**1.** pharmacist	洋服屋/仕立屋	**6.** tailor	花屋 **11.** florist
自動車修理工	**2.** mechanic	八百屋/青物屋/青果店	**7.** greengrocer	宝石商 **12.** jeweller
散髪屋/床屋/理髪師	**3.** barber	パン職人/パン屋	**8.** baker	肉屋 **13.** butcher
旅行業務取扱者	**4.** travel agent	眼科医/光学技師	**9.** optician	
修理屋/修理工	**5.** repairperson	理髪師/美容師	**10.** hairdresser	

営繕維持	**A. Repair and Maintenance**
鉛管屋/配管工	**1.** plumber
大工	**2.** carpenter
庭師	**3.** gardener
錠前師	**4.** locksmith
不動産仲介人	**5.** real estate agent
電気工	**6.** electrician
ペンキ屋/塗装工	**7.** painter

家事	**B. Household Services**
家政婦	**8.** housekeeper
用務員/掃除夫	**9.** janitor
配達員	**10.** delivery boy
門衛/玄関番	**11.** doorman

工場作業	**C. Factory Work**
工員	**12.** shop worker
現場主任/監督	**13.** foreman

マスコミと芸能	**A. Media and Arts**	建築家	**8.** architect	警備員	**14.** security guard
天気予報官	**1.** weather forecaster	ディスクジョッキー	**9.** disc jockey (DJ)	窓口係員	**15.** teller
ニュースキャスター	**2.** newscaster	カメラマン/撮影班	**10.** cameraperson		
画家/美術担当者	**3.** artist	レポーター/取材記者	**11.** reporter	業務関係者	**C. Business Workers**
写真家/撮影係	**4.** photographer	販売員/店員	**12.** salesperson	プログラマー	**16.** computer programmer
モデル	**5.** model			受付係	**17.** receptionist
ファッションデザイナー	**6.** fashion designer	銀行	**B. Banking**	経理担当者	**18.** accountant
作家/脚本家	**7.** writer	役職者	**13.** officer	連絡係/メッセンジャー	**19.** messenger

動物園	**1.** zoo	(あひる[家鴨]の)池	**8.** (duck) pond	遊び場	**15.** playground
野外音楽堂	**2.** band shell	ジョギングコース	**9.** jogging path	ぶらんこ/鞦韆	**16.** swings
物売り	**3.** vendor	ベンチ/長椅子	**10.** bench	ジャングルジム	**17.** jungle gym
手押し車	**4.** hand truck	屑入れ/芥箱	**11.** trash can	シーソー	**18.** seesaw
回転木馬	**5.** merry-go-round	滑り台/辷り台	**12.** slide	水飲み場	**19.** water fountain
乗馬している人	**6.** horseback rider	砂場	**13.** sandbox		
乗馬(専用)道	**7.** bridle path	噴水/噴き上げ	**14.** sprinkler		

野外活動

台地	**1.** plateau	（魚）釣り	**Fishing**	ピクニック場	**Picnic Area**	
ハイカー	**2.** hikers	小川	**6.** stream	グリル／網焼き炉	**12.** grill	
渓谷／谿谷	**3.** canyon	釣り竿	**7.** fishing rod	ピクニック籠	**13.** picnic basket	
小山	**4.** hill	釣り糸	**8.** fishing line	魔法瓶／保温瓶	**14.** thermos	
森林警備隊員	**5.** park ranger	釣り用網	**9.** fishing net	ピクニックテーブル	**15.** picnic table	
		ウエーダー／防水長靴	**10.** waders			
		岩／石／岩石	**11.** rocks			

川下り	**Rafting**	登山	**Mountain Climbing**	キャンプ/野営/露営	**Camping**
ゴムボート	16. raft	山	19. mountain	テント/天幕	24. tent
急流	17. rapids	頂上/山頂	20. peak	キャンプ用焜炉	25. camp stove
滝/瀑布	18. waterfall	崖/厓/断崖/絶壁	21. cliff	シュラーフザック/寝袋	26. sleeping bag
		装帯/ハーネス/ベルト	22. harness	野外生活用具	27. gear
		綱/ロープ	23. rope	枠つきリュックサック	28. frame backpack
				ランプ/洋灯	29. lantern
				杭/杙	30. stake
				キャンプファイヤー	31. campfire
				森	32. woods

板敷き遊歩道	**1.** boardwalk	見張り台	**8.** lifeguard chair	ビーチタオル	**15.** beach towel
飲食物販売店/売店	**2.** refreshment stand	浮き袋/救命具	**9.** life preserver	バケツ[馬穴]	**16.** pail
モーテル	**3.** motel	救命ボート/救命艇	**10.** lifeboat	スコップ	**17.** shovel
自転車に乗っている人	**4.** biker	ビーチボール	**11.** beach ball	水着/海水着/水泳着	**18.** bathing suit
笛	**5.** whistle	砂丘	**12.** sand dunes	日光浴をしている人	**19.** sunbather
救助員	**6.** lifeguard	フリスビー	**13.** Frisbee™	デッキチェアー	**20.** beach chair
双眼鏡	**7.** binoculars	サングラス/日除け眼鏡	**14.** sunglasses	ビーチパラソル	**21.** beach umbrella

たこ・いか・いかのぼり 凧 [紙鳶]	**22.** kite	海水	**30.** water	びれ 足鰭/フリッパー	**36.** flippers
駆け足/駈足をしている人	**23.** runners	砂	**31.** sand	酸素ボンベ	**37.** scuba tank
波	**24.** wave	砂の城/砂楼	**32.** sandcastle	ウエットスーツ	**38.** wet suit
サーフボード/波乗り板	**25.** surfboard	海水パンツ/	**33.** bathing trunks	日焼け止め化粧水	**39.** suntan lotion
空気マット	**26.** air mattress	水泳パンツ		貝/貝殻	**40.** shell
ビート板/ばた足練習ボード	**27.** kickboard	シュノーケル	**34.** snorkel	冷蔵箱/	**41.** cooler
泳いでいる人/遊泳者	**28.** swimmer	水中眼鏡/ゴーグル	**35.** mask	アイスボックス	
チューブの浮き袋	**29.** tube				

チームスポーツ

野球	**Baseball**	ソフトボール	**Softball**	バスケットボール/	**Basketball**
審判/主審/	1. umpire	ソフトボールの球	10. softball	籠球	
アンパイアー/		野球帽	11. cap	バックボード/背板	19. backboard
アンパイヤー		グラブ/グローブ	12. glove	バスケットネット	20. basket
捕手/キャッチャー	2. catcher			バスケットボールの球	21. basketball
キャッチャーマスク	3. catcher's mask	アメリカンフットボール	**Football**		
キャッチャーミット	4. catcher's mitt	フットボールの球	13. football	バレーボール/	**Volleyball**
バット	5. bat	ヘルメット	14. helmet	排球	
ヘルメット	6. batting helmet			バレーボールの球	22. volleyball
打者/バッター	7. batter	ラクロス	**Lacrosse**	ネット	23. net
		顔面保護マスク	15. face guard		
リトルリーグ	**Little League**	ラクロスのスティック	16. lacrosse stick	サッカー/蹴球	**Soccer**
	Baseball			ゴールキーパー	24. goalie
リトルリーグの選手	8. Little Leaguer	アイスホッケー	**Ice Hockey**	ゴール	25. goal
ユニフォーム	9. uniform	パック/ゴム製円盤	17. puck	サッカーボール	26. soccer ball
		ホッケーのスティック	18. hockey stick		

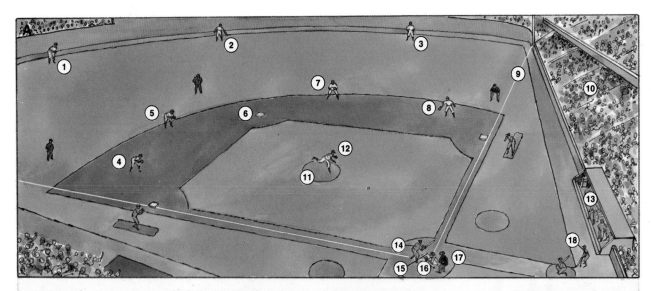

野球のダイヤモンド	**A. Baseball Diamond**	打者／バッター	**14.** batter	エンドゾーン	**23.** end zone
左翼手／レフト	**1.** left fielder	本塁／ホームプレート	**15.** home plate	スプリットエンド	**24.** split end
中堅手／センター	**2.** center fielder	捕手／キャッチャー	**16.** catcher	レフトタックル	**25.** left tackle
右翼手／ライト	**3.** right fielder	審判／主審／アンパイアー／	**17.** umpire	レフトガード	**26.** left guard
三塁手／サード	**4.** third baseman	アンパイヤー		センター	**27.** center
遊撃手／ショート	**5.** shortstop	バットボーイ	**18.** batboy	ライトガード	**28.** right guard
塁／ベース	**6.** base	備品管理係／球拾い		ライトタックル	**29.** right tackle
二塁手／セカンド	**7.** second baseman			タイトエンド	**30.** tight end
一塁手／ファースト	**8.** first baseman	**アメリカンフット**	**B. Football Field**	フランカー	**31.** flanker
ファウルライン	**9.** foul line	**ボール競技場**		クォーターバック	**32.** quarterback
スタンド／観客席	**10.** stands	スコアボード	**19.** scoreboard	ハーフバック	**33.** halfback
ピッチャーマウンド	**11.** pitcher's mound	チアリーダー／応援団	**20.** cheerleaders	フルバック	**34.** fullback
投手／ピッチャー	**12.** pitcher	コーチ／監督	**21.** coach	ゴールポスト	**35.** goalpost
ダッグアウト／	**13.** dugout	審判	**22.** referee		
選手控え席					

個人スポーツ

テニス/庭球	**Tennis**
テニスボール	**1.** tennis ball
ラケット	**2.** racket

ボーリング	**Bowling**
ガター	**3.** gutter
レーン	**4.** lane
ピン	**5.** pin
ボーリングのボール	**6.** bowling ball

ゴルフ	**Golf**
ゴルフボール	**7.** golf ball
ホール	**8.** hole
パター	**9.** putter
ゴルフをしている人/	**10.** golfer
ゴルファー	

ハンドボール/送球	**Handball**
グラブ	**11.** glove
ハンドボールの球	**12.** handball
コート	**13.** court

ボクシング/拳闘	**Boxing**
ヘッドプロテクター	**14.** head protector
グラブ	**15.** glove
レフェリー/レフリー	**16.** referee
リング	**17.** ring

ピンポン/卓球	**Ping-Pong**
ラケット	**18.** paddle
ピンポンボール	**19.** ping-pong ball

競馬	**Horse Racing**
鞍	**20.** saddle
騎手/ジョッキー	**21.** jockey
手綱	**22.** reins

体操	**Gymnastics**
体操選手	**23.** gymnast
平均台	**24.** balance beam

アイススケート	**Ice Skating**
スケートリンク	**25.** rink
スケート靴	**26.** skate
スケートの刃	**27.** blade

ラケットボール/壁内テニス	**Racquetball**
保護ゴーグル	**28.** safety goggles
ラケット	**29.** racquet
ラケットボールの球	**30.** racquetball

陸上競技	**Track and Field**
走者	**31.** runner
競技用トラック	**32.** track

クロスカントリースキー	**Cross-Country Skiing**
スキー	**33.** skis
ストック	**34.** pole
スキーをしている人/	**35.** skier
スキーヤー	

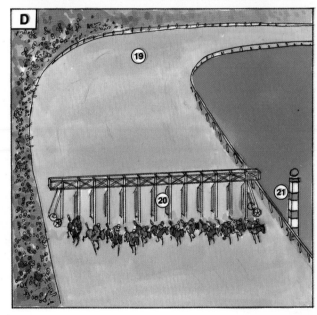

テニスコート	**A. Tennis Court**
サービスコート	**1.** service court
ネット	**2.** net
サービスライン	**3.** service line
ベースライン	**4.** baseline

ゴルフコース	**B. Golf Course**
クラブ	**5.** clubs
ラフ	**6.** rough
ゴルフバッグ	**7.** golf bag
ゴルフカート	**8.** golf cart
フラッグ	**9.** flag

グリーン	**10.** green
バンカー	**11.** sand trap
フェアウエー	**12.** fairway
ティー	**13.** tee

スキー斜面/ スキー場	**C. Ski Slope**
ストック	**14.** pole
スキー靴	**15.** ski boot
ビンディング/締め具	**16.** binding
スキー板	**17.** ski
スキーリフト	**18.** ski lift

競馬場	**D. Race Track**
ストレッチ/直線コース	**19.** stretch
（スターティング）ゲート	**20.** starting gate
フィニッシュ/決勝線	**21.** finish line

スポーツに関する動作

打つ／返す	**1.** hit	捕る／捕球する	**4.** catch	転ぶ／転倒する／落ちる／落下する	**7.** fall
サーブする	**2.** serve	パスする	**5.** pass	ジャンプする／跳躍する／飛び跳ねる	**8.** jump
蹴る／キックする	**3.** kick	走塁する／走る	**6.** run		

滑べる	**9.** skate	波乗りをする	**12.** surf	運転する／操縦する	**15.** drive
投球する／投げる	**10.** throw	乗馬する／乗る	**13.** ride	シュートする／射る／放つ	**16.** shoot
ドリブルする／バウンドする	**11.** bounce	飛び込む／潜る	**14.** dive		

楽器

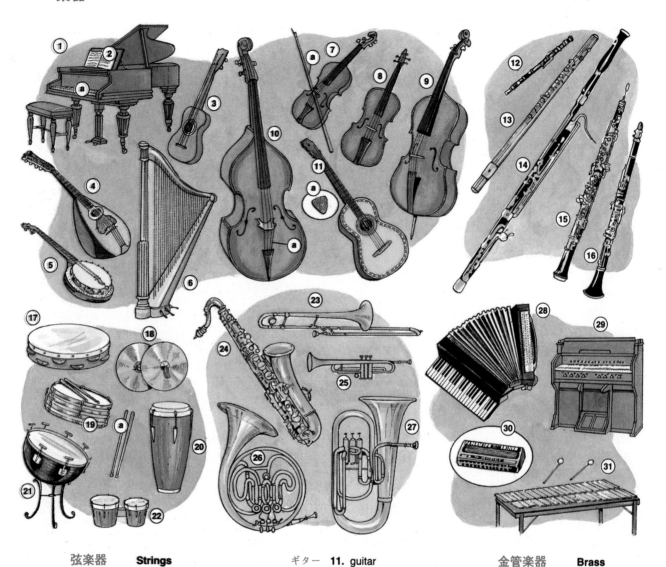

弦楽器	**Strings**		ギター	**11.** guitar		金管楽器	**Brass**
ピアノ	**1.** piano		ピック	**a.** pick		トロンボーン	**23.** trombone
鍵盤	**a.** keyboard					サキソホン／	**24.** saxophone
楽譜	**2.** sheet music		木管楽器	**Woodwinds**		サキソフォン／サックス	
ウクレレ	**3.** ukulele		ピッコロ	**12.** piccolo		トランペット	**25.** trumpet
マンドリン	**4.** mandolin		フルート／フリュート	**13.** flute		フレンチホルン	**26.** French horn
バンジョー	**5.** banjo		バスーン／ファゴット	**14.** bassoon		チューバ	**27.** tuba
ハープ	**6.** harp		オーボエ／オーボー	**15.** oboe			
バイオリン／	**7.** violin		クラリネット／	**16.** clarinet		その他の楽器	**Other Instruments**
ヴァイオリン／			クラリオネット			アコーデオン／	**28.** accordion
提琴						アコーディオン／	
弓	**a.** bow		打楽器	**Percussion**		手風琴	
ビオラ／ヴィオラ	**8.** viola		タンバリン／タンブリン	**17.** tambourine		オルガン／風琴	**29.** organ
チェロ／セロ	**9.** cello		シンバル	**18.** cymbals		ハーモニカ／	**30.** harmonica
コントラバス／	**10.** bass		ドラム／小太鼓	**19.** drum		ハモニカ／口風琴	
（ダブル）ベース			撥	**a.** drumsticks		シロホン／シロフォン／	**31.** xylophone
弦	**a.** string		コンガ	**20.** conga		木琴／鉄琴	
			ケトルドラム	**21.** kettledrum			
			ボンゴ	**22.** bongos			

バレー/ バレエ	**A. The Ballet**	
カーテン/ 緞帳/幕	**1.** curtain	
背景	**2.** scenery	
踊り手/ダンサー	**3.** dancer	
スポットライト	**4.** spotlight	
舞台	**5.** stage	
管弦楽団	**6.** orchestra	
指揮台/指魔台	**7.** podium	
指揮者/指魔者	**8.** conductor	
指揮棒/指魔棒	**9.** baton	
楽団員	**10.** musician	

ボックス席	**11.** box seat
一階正面席/平土間席	**12.** orchestra seating
二階正面桟敷	**13.** mezzanine
桟敷	**14.** balcony
観客/聴衆	**15.** audience
案内係	**16.** usher
プログラム	**17.** programs

ミュージカル コメディー/ 音楽喜劇	**B. Musical** 　**Comedy**
合唱団/合唱隊	**18.** chorus
男優	**19.** actor
女優	**20.** actress

ロックバンド	**C. Rock Group**
シンセサイザー	**21.** synthesizer
キーボード奏者	**22.** keyboard player
ベースギター奏者	**23.** bass guitarist
歌手	**24.** singer
リードギター奏者	**25.** lead guitarist
エレキギター/ エレキ/電気ギター	**26.** electric guitar
ドラム奏者	**27.** drummer

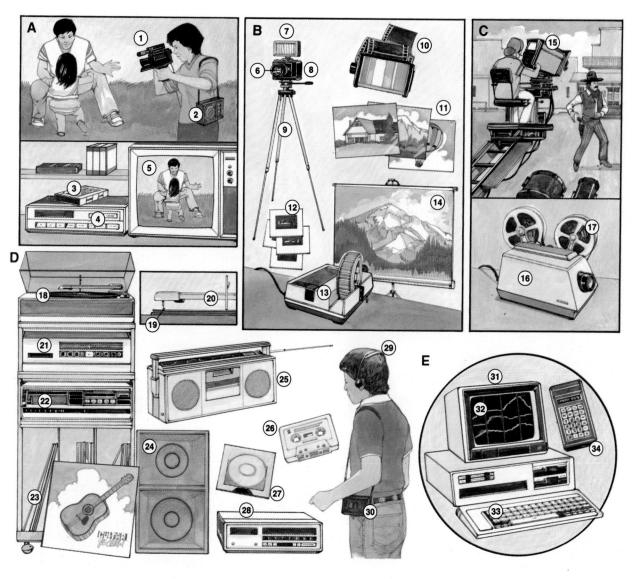

映像録画	A. Video	スライド映写機	13. slide projector	スピーカー	24. speaker
ビデオカメラ	1. video camera	スクリーン／銀幕	14. screen	ステレオカセットプレーヤー	25. stereo cassette player
ミニカム／小型ビデオ	2. Minicam™				
ビデオカセット	3. videocassette (tape)	映画	C. Film	カセット	26. cassette
ビデオ／録画・再生装置	4. VCR (videocassette recorder)	映画カメラ／映画撮影機	15. movie camera	コンパクトディスク／CD	27. compact disc (CD)
				CD プレーヤー	28. compact disc player
テレビ（受像器）／テレビジョン技術	5. television	映写機	16. projector	ヘッドホーン／ヘッドフォーン	29. headphones
		フィルム（一巻）	17. (reel of) film	ウォークマン	30. Sony Walkman
写真術	B. Photography	音響製品	D. Audio		
レンズ	6. lens	ターンテーブル	18. turntable	コンピューター／電算機	E. Computers
フラッシュ／閃光電球	7. flash	埋めこみ式／差し込み式レコード針	19. cartridge needle	パソコン	31. personal computer (PC)
カメラ／写真機	8. camera	アーム	20. arm	ディスプレー	32. monitor
三脚	9. tripod	受信機／チューナー	21. receiver	キーボード	33. keyboard
フィルム（一本）	10. (roll of) film	カセットデッキ	22. cassette deck	（卓上）計算器	34. calculator
プリント／紙焼き	11. prirts	レコード／音盤	23. records		
スライド	12. slides				

裁縫/	**A. Sewing**	縁縫い	**11.** hem	その他の針仕事	**B. Other Needlecrafts**
縫い物/お針		バイアステープ/	**12.** hem binding	編み物	**22.** knitting
ミシン	**1.** sewing machine	バイヤステープ		毛糸	**23.** wool
糸(一巻き)	**2.** (spool of) thread	ホック/スナップ	**13.** snap	桛/束	**24.** skein
針山/針刺し/	**3.** pincushion	鉤ホック	**14.** hook and eye	編み棒	**25.** knitting needle
針立て/針坊主		メジャー/巻き尺	**15.** tape measure	針編みレース	**26.** needlepoint
布地	**4.** material	ファスナー/チャック	**16.** zipper	刺繡	**27.** embroidery
ピンキング鋏	**5.** pinking shears	鋏(一丁)	**17.** (pair of) scissors	クロセ編み/	**28.** crochet
型紙	**6.** pattern piece	縫い針	**18.** needle	レース編み	
型紙セット	**7.** pattern	縫い目/針目	**19.** stitch	クロセ針/鉤針	**29.** crochet hook
ボタン孔	**8.** buttonhole	待ち針	**20.** pin	織物	**30.** weaving
ボタン	**9.** button	指貫き/指挿し	**21.** thimble	織り糸	**31.** yarn
縫い目	**10.** seam			キルティング/	**32.** quilting
				刺し子(縫い)	

場所を表わす前置詞

（窓）のところに／で	**1.** at (the window)	（引き出し［抽斗]）の中に／で	**7.** in (the drawer)
（黒猫）より上に／で	**2.** above (the black cat)	（机）の（真）下に／で	**8.** under (the desk)
（白猫）より下に／で	**3.** below (the white cat)	（椅子）の（真）後ろに／で、の陰に／で	**9.** behind (the chair)
（クッションとクッションと）の間に／で	**4.** between (the pillows)	（テーブル）の天辺に／で	**10.** on top of (the table)
（敷物）の上に乗って	**5.** on (the rug)	（テレビ）の脇に／で	**11.** next to (the TV)
（暖炉）の（真ん）前に／で	**6.** in front of (the fireplace)		

（炉台）を通り抜けて／突き抜けて	**1.** through (the lighthouse)	（ホール）の方に／に向かって	**4.** toward (the hole)	（池）の中から外へ	**7.** out of (the water)
（炉台）の周りを／周を／に／で	**2.** around (the lighthouse)	（ホール）から遠ざかって／と逆の方向に	**5.** away from (the hole)	（橋）を越えて／渡って	**8.** over (the bridge)
（小山）を下りて／下って	**3.** down (the hill)	（池）を横切って／越えて	**6.** across (the water)	（コース）へ	**9.** to (the course)
				（コース）から	**10.** from (the course)
				（小山）を上って	**11.** up (the hill)
				（ホール）の中へ	**12.** into (the hole)

付録

曜日の名称	**Days of the Week**
日曜日	Sunday
月曜日	Monday
火曜日	Tuesday
水曜日	Wednesday
木曜日	Thursday
金曜日	Friday
土曜日	Saturday

月の名称	**Months of the Year**
一月	January
二月	February
三月	March
四月	April
五月	May
六月	June
七月	July
八月	August
九月	September
十月	October
十一月	November
十二月	December

数の言い方		**Numbers**
ゼロ／零	0	zero
一	1	one
二	2	two
三	3	three
四	4	four
五	5	five
六	6	six
七	7	seven
八	8	eight
九	9	nine
十	10	ten
十一	11	eleven
十二	12	twelve
十三	13	thirteen
十四	14	fourteen
十五	15	fifteen
十六	16	sixteen
十七	17	seventeen
十八	18	eighteen
十九	19	nineteen
二十	20	twenty
二十一	21	twenty-one
三十	30	thirty
四十	40	forty
五十	50	fifty
六十	60	sixty
七十	70	seventy
八十	80	eighty
九十	90	ninety
百	100	a/one hundred
五百	500	five hundred
六百二十一	621	six hundred (and) twenty-one
千	1,000	a/one thousand
百万	1,000,000	a/one million

色の名称 **Colors**

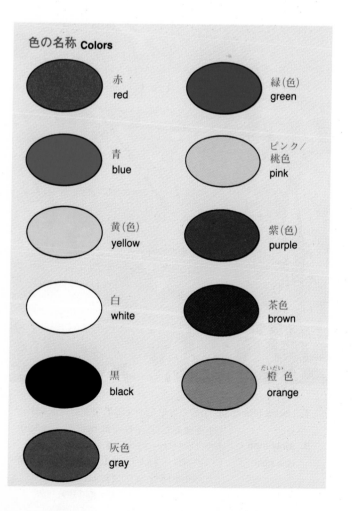

赤 red		緑（色） green	
青 blue		ピンク／桃色 pink	
黄（色） yellow		紫（色） purple	
白 white		茶色 brown	
黒 black		だいだい 橙色 orange	
灰色 gray			

英語と日本語の索引では、各項目に続く最初の数字(太字)がその項目の現れるページ数を、後の数字(細字)がページ内でのその項目の番号を示します。例えば above [ə bŭvʹ] **102 2** とあれば、above という語が102ページの2番目の項目であることを示します。

英語索引の各項目には発音記号が付けてあります。出版社の意向により国際音標文字(IPA)を使わず、綴り字に近い記号体系を使用していますので、その対照関係を以下に示します。

子音

本書		IPA	例語	本書		IPA	本書		IPA	例語	本書		IPA
[b]	=	/b/	back	[băk]	=	/bæk/	[ng]	=	/ŋ/	ring	[rĭng]	=	/rɪŋ/
[ch]	=	/tʃ/	cheek	[chēk]	=	/tʃik/	[p]	=	/p/	pack	[păk]	=	/pæk/
[d]	=	/d/	date	[dāt]	=	/det/	[r]	=	/r/	rake	[rāk]	=	/rek/
[dh]	=	/ð/	the	[dhə]	=	/ðə/	[s]	=	/s/	sand	[sănd]	=	/sænd/
[f]	=	/f/	face	[fās]	=	/fes/	[sh]	=	/ʃ/	shell	[shĕl]	=	/ʃɛl/
[g]	=	/g/	gas	[găs]	=	/gæs/	[t]	=	/t/	tape	[tāp]	=	/tep/
[h]	=	/h/	half	[hăf]	=	/hæf/	[th]	=	/θ/	three	[thrē]	=	/θri/
[j]	=	/dʒ/	jack	[jăk]	=	/dʒæk/	[v]	=	/v/	vine	[vĭn]	=	/vaɪn/
[k]	=	/k/	kite	[kīt]	=	/kaɪt/	[w]	=	/w/	waste	[wāst]	=	/weᴵst/
[l]	=	/l/	leaf	[lēf]	=	/lif/	[y]	=	/y/	yam	[yăm]	=	/yæm/
[m]	=	/m/	man	[măn]	=	/mæn/	[z]	=	/z/	zoo	[zōō]	=	/zu/
[n]	=	/n/	neck	[nĕk]	=	/nɛk/	[zh]	=	/ʒ/	measure	[mezhʹər]	=	/ˈmeʒər/

母音

本書		IPA	例語	本書		IPA	本書		IPA	例語	本書		IPA
[ā]	=	/eᴵ/	bake	[bāk]	=	/bek/	[ŏ]	=	/a(ː)/	box	[bŏks]	=	/baks/
[ă]	=	/æ/	back	[băk]	=	/bæk/	[ü]	=	/ɔ(ː)/	claw	[klö]	=	/klɔ/
[ä]	=	/a(ɚ)/	bar	[bär]	=	/bar/	[ö]	=	/ɔ(ɚ)/	for	[för]	=	/fɔr/
[ē]	=	/i/	beat	[bēt]	=	/bit/	[ōō]	=	/uː/	cool	[kōōl]	=	/kul/
[ĕ]	=	/ɛ/	bed	[bĕd]	=	/bɛd/	[ŏŏ]	=	/ʊ/	book	[bŏŏk]	=	/bʊk/
[ë]	=	/ɛ(ɚ)/	bear	[bër]	=	/bɛr/	[ow]	=	/aʊ/	cow	[kow]	=	/kaʊ/
[ī]	=	/aᴵ/	lime	[līm]	=	/laɪm/	[oy]	=	/ɔᴵ/	boy	[boy]	=	/bɔɪ/
[ĭ]	=	/ɪ/	lip	[lĭp]	=	/lɪp/	[ŭ]	=	/ᴵə/	cut	[kŭt]	=	/kʌt/
[ï]	=	/ɪ(ɚ)/	beer	[bïr]	=	/bɪr/	[ü]	=	/(ɚː)/	curb	[kürb]	=	/kərb/
[ō]	=	/oʊ/	post	[pōst]	=	/post/	[ə]	=	/ə/	above	[ə bŭvʹ]	=	/əˈbʌv/

変音符合 [̈] は、後続する [r] の影響で母音の音色が変わり、その母音と [r] との間に「渡り音」が生じることを示します: [är, ër, ïr, ör, ür] → /aər, ɛər, ɪər, ɔər ər /。その際 /ər/ 部は融合して「母音がかった r」(/ɚ/) となり、各々二重母音 (または長母音) の /aɚ, ɛɚ, ɪɚ, ɔɚ, ɚː/ となります。[ōōr] にも渡り音が生じ (/ʊɚ/). 実際の発音は /ʊɚ/ となります。[ö] は [r] に先行しないこと (/ɔ(ː)/) もありますが、その場合は [ŏ] (/a(ː)/) に合流するのが普通です。[ə] は強勢を受けることがなく、その音価は [ŭ] (/ᴵə /) を弱めたものと同じです。[ər] は融合して /ɚ/ となります。

二重母音や長母音に (同じ音節内で) [l] が続くときにも渡り音が生じます: [āl, ēl, īl, ōl, ōōl, owl, oyl] → /eᴵəl, iːəl, aᴵəl, oʊəl, uːəl, /。また [ärl, ürl] → /aɚəl, əːəl/ となります。

[́] は直前の音節が第一強勢を受けることを、[̀] は直前の音節が第二強勢を受けることを示します。但し、単音節語には強勢符合を省略してあります。

音節の切れ目はスペースを空けて示してあります。

above [ə bŭv/] **102** 2

abdomen [ăb/də mən] **4** 14

accelerator [ăk sĕl/ə rā/tər] **50** 27

accordion [ə kör/dē ən] **98** 28

accountant [ə kown/tənt] **86** 18

acorn [ā/körn] **61** 33b

acorn squash [ā/körn skwŏsh/] **7** 28

across [ə krös/] **103** 6

actor [ăk/tər] **99** 19

actress [ăk/trəs] **99** 20

acute angle [ə kyoot/ăng/gəl] **79** 8

address [ă/drĕs] **46** 11

adjectives [ăj/ĭk tĭvz] **24, 25**

aerial tramway [ĕr/ē əl trăm/wā] **55** 31

Africa [ă/frĭ kə] **70** 4

after-shave lotion [ăf/tər shāv lō/shən]
    23 21

ailments [āl/mənts] **40**

air conditioner [ĕr/kən dĭ/shə nər]
    32 11

air filter [ĕr/fĭl/tər] **51** 52

Air Force [ĕr/förs/] **48** 19

air mattress [ĕr/mă/trəs] **91** 26

air pump [ĕr/ pŭmp/] **53** 13

air travel [ĕr/ tră/vəl] **56**

aircraft [ĕr/krăft/] **57**

aircraft carrier [ĕr/krăft kăr/yər] **48** 4

aircraft types [ĕr/krăft tīps/] **57**

(airmail) envelope
    [ĕr/māl ĕn/və lōp] **46** 16

airman [ĕr/mən] **48** 20

airport check-in [ĕr/pört chĕk/ĭn] **56**

aisle [ī/əl] **14** 10, **56** 23

Alabama [ăl/ə bă/mə] **72** 1

alarm clock [ə lärm/ klŏk] **32** 8

Alaska [ə lăs/kə] **72** 2

alcohol [ăl/kə höl/] **39** 22

alligator [ăl/ə gā/tər] **65** 8

almond(s) [ö/mənd(z)] **9** 31

Alps [ălps] **70** 44

Amazon River [ă/mə zŏn rĭv/ər]
    71 59

ambulance [ăm/byə ləns] **42** 6

amphibians [ăm fĭ/bē ənz] **65**

ammunition [ăm/yə nĭsh/ən] **48**

anchor [ăng/kər] **58** 24

Andes [ăn/dēz] **71** 43

ankle [ăng/kəl] **5** 49

animals [ăn/ə məlz] **62-69**

ant [ănt] **63** 12

Antarctic Ocean [ănt ärk/tĭk ō/ shən]
    70 14

Antarctica [ănt ärk/tĭ kə] **70** 7

anteater [ănt/ē/tər] **66** 5

antenna [ăn tĕn/ə] **51** 46, **62** 1b

antler [ănt/lər] **67** 35a

apartment house
    [ə pärt/mənt hows/] **45** 23

apex [ā/pĕks] **79** 21

Appalachian Mountains
    [ăp/ə lā/chē ən mown/ tənz] **71** 41

apple [ă/pəl] **8** 2

apricot [ăp/rə kŏt/] **9** 25

apron [ā/prən] **16** 6

aquatic mammals
    [ə kwŏ/tĭk·mă/məlz] **68**

Arabian Sea [ə rā/bē ən sē/] **70** 30

arc [ärk] **79** 16

architect [är/kə tĕkt/] **86** 8

Arctic [ärk/tĭk] **70** 8

Arizona [ăr/ə zō/nə] **72** 3

Arkansas [är/kən sö/] **72** 4

arm [ärm] **4** 6, **100** 20

armadillo [är/ mə dĭl/ō] **66** 2

armed forces [ärmd/ för/səz] **48**

armpit [ärm/pĭt/] **4** 10

armrest [ärm/rĕst/] **50** 3

Army [är/mē] **48** 15

around [ə rownd/] **103** 2

artery [är/tə rē] **5** 69

artichoke [är/tə chōk/] **6** 11

artist [är/təst] **86** 3

arts [ärts] **86**

ashtray [ăsh/trā/] **16** 29

Asia [ā/zhə] **70** 5

asparagus [ə spăr/ə gəs] **6** 18

asteroid [ăs/tə royd/] **74** 20

astronaut [ăs/trə nŏt/] **75** 5

at [ăt] **102** 1

Atacama Desert
    [ăt/ə kŏ/mə dĕz/ərt] **71** 50

athletic supporter
    [ăth lĕ/tĭk sə pör/tər] **22** 4

atlas [ăt/ləs] **47** 20

attachments [ə tăch/mənts] **35** 17

attendant [ə tĕn/dənt] **39** 8, **53** 12

audience [ö/dē əns] **99** 15

audio [ö/dē ō/] **100**

aunt [ănt] **3** 6

Australia [ö strāl/yə] **70** 6

author [ö/thər] **47** 8

automatic transmission
    [ö/ tə măt/ĭk trănz mĭ/shən] **50**

avocado [ăv/ə kŏ/dō] **9** 33

away from [ə wā/ frŭm] **103** 5

axe [ăks] **42** 14

baboon [bă boon/] **69** 19

baby [bā/bē] **2** 5

baby carriage [bā/bē kăr/ĭj] **45** 27

baby lotion [bā/bē lō/shən] **33** 6

baby powder [bā/bē pow/dər] **33** 7

baby wipes [bā/bē wīps/] **33** 8

baby's room [bā/bēz room/] **33**

back [băk] **4** 11, **23** 19

backache [băk/āk/] **40** 8

backboard [băk/börd/] **92** 19

backhoe [băk/hō/] **82** 26

backpack [băk/păk/] **19** 4

backseat [băk/sēt/] **50** 32

backyard [băk/yärd/] **27**

back-up light [băk/əp līt/] **50** 30

bacon [bā/kən] **10** 11, **18,** 33

badge [băj] **43** 5

Baffin Bay [băf/ən bā/] **70** 16

bag [băg] **12** 8, **15** 25, **21** 35

baggage [băg/ĭj] **56** 8

bake [bāk] **31** 14

baked beans [bākt/ bēnz/] **18** 3

baked goods [bākt goodz/] **14** 11

baked potato [bākt/ pə tā/tō] **18** 20

baker [bā/kər] **84** 8

bakery [bā/kə rē] **44** 6

balance beam [băl/əns bēm/] **94** 24

balcony [băl/kə nē] **99** 14

(bale of) hay [bāl/ əv hā/] **81** 13

ball [böl] **5** 52

ballet [bă lā/] **99**

ballfields [böl/fēldz/] **93**

ballpoint pen [böl/poynt pĕn/] **76** 22

Baltic Sea [böl/tĭk sē/] **70** 22

bananas [bə nă/nəz] **9** 20

Band-Aid [bănd/ ād/] **39** 4

band shell [bănd/ shĕl/] **87** 2

bandage [băn/dĭj] **39** 24

banister [băn′ə stər] **28** 11

banjo [băn′jō′] **98** 5

banking [băng′kĭng] **86**

bar [bär] **13** 18, **16** 24

bar stool [bär′stool′] **16** 25

barber [bär′bər] **84** 3

Barents Sea [băr′ənts sē′] **70** 23

barge [bärj] **58** 12

bark [bärk] **61** 35c

barn [bärn] **81** 5

barnyard [bärn′yärd′] **81** 8

barrel [băr′əl] **48** 23

barricade [băr′ə kād′] **82** 21

bartender [bär′těn′dər] **16** 21

base [bās] **79** 7, **93** 6

baseball [bās′böl′] **92**

baseball diamond [bās′böl dī′mənd] **93**

baseline [bās′līn′] **95** 4

basin [bā′sən] **39** 16

basket [băs′kət] **92** 20

basketball [băs′kət böl′] **92**, **92** 21

bass [bās] **98** 10

bass guitarist [bās′gə tär′əst] **99** 23

bassoon [bă soon′] **98** 14

bat [băt] **66** 4, **92** 5

batboy [băt′boy′] **93** 18

bath mat [băth′măt′] **34** 12

bath towel [băth′ tow′əl] **34** 24

bathing suit [bā′dhĭng soot′] **90** 18

bathing trunks [bā′ dhĭng trŭngks′] **91** 33

bathrobe [băth′rōb] **22** 20

bathroom [băth′room′] **34**

bathtub [băth′tŭb′] **34** 11

baton [bə tŏn′] **99** 9

batter [băt′ər] **92** 7, **93** 14

battery [băt′ə rē] **51** 54

batting helmet [băt′ĭng hĕl′mət] **92** 6

battleship [băt′əl shĭp′] **48** 5

Bay of Bengal [bā′ əv běn göl′] **70** 32

bayonet [bā′ə nět′] **48** 24

bays [bāz] **70**

beach [bēch] **90**

beach ball [bēch′ böl′] **90** 11

beach chair [bēch′ chër′] **90** 20

beach towel [bēch′ tow′ əl] **90** 15

beach umbrella [bēch′əm brěl′ə] **90** 21

beads [bēdz] **23** 7

beak [bēk] **64** 3a

beaker [bē′kər] **78** 23

beard [bïrd] **4** 39

bears [bërz] **69**

beat [bēt] **31** 8

Beaufort Sea [bō′ fərt sē′] **70** 15

beaver [bē′vər] **66** 12

bed [běd] **32** 21

bed rest [běd′ rěst′] **41** 1

bedroom [běd′room′] **32**

bedspread [běd′sprěd′] **32** 23

bee [bē] **63** 19

beef [bēf] **10** 1

beef stew [bēf′ stoo′] **18** 14

beer [bïr] **16** 23

beet(s) [bēts] **7** 33

beetle [bē′təl] **63** 10

behind [bə hīnd′] **102** 9

below [bə lō′] **102** 3

belt [bělt] **20** 16

bench [běnch] **43** 16, **44** 14, **78** 24, **87** 10

beret [bə rā′] **19** 22

Bering Sea [bër′ĭng sē′] **70** 34

berries [bër′ēz] **8**

between [bə twēn′] **102** 4

beverages [běv′rə jəz] **14** 14

bib [bĭb] **33** 20

bicycle [bī′sĭ kəl] **52** 15

big [bĭg] **24** 8

(Big Dipper) constellation [bĭg′ dĭ′pər kŏn stə lā′shən] **74** 3

big toe [bĭg′ tō′] **5** 53

bike stand [bīk′ stănd′] **52** 14

biker [bī′kər] **90** 4

bikes [bīks] **52**

(bikini) panties [bə kē′ nē păn′ tēz] **22** 11

bill [bĭl] **64** 24a

bin [bĭn] **15** 16

binding [bīn′ dĭng] **95** 16

binoculars [bə nŏk′ yə lərs] **90** 7

birch [bürch] **61** 32

birds [bürdz] **64**

biscuit [bĭs′ kət] **18** 27

bison [bī′sən] **67** 19

bit [bĭt] **37** 43a

black bear [blăk′ bër′] **69** 21

black bean(s) [blăk′ běn(z)′] **6** 14

black eye [blăk′ ī′] **40** 5

Black Sea [blăk′ sē′] **70** 26

blackberries [blăk′ bër′ēz] **8** 12

bladder [blă′ dər] **5** 72

blade [blād] **94** 27

blanket [blăng′ket] **32** 20

blazer [blā′ zer] **20** 2

bleach [blēch] **35** 26

blender [blěn′ dər] **30** 12

blimp [blĭmp] **57** 5

blinds [blīndz] **32** 12

block [blŏk] **33** 32

blouse [blows] **21** 34

blue jay [bloo′ ja′] **64** 8

(blue) jeans [bloo′ jēnz′] **19** 6

blueberries [bloo′ bër′ēz] **8** 14

blueprints [bloo′ prĭnts′] **82** 6

blush [blŭsh] **23** 32

board [börd] **82** 16

boarding [bör′dĭng] **56**

boarding pass [bör′dĭng păs′] **56** 18

boardwalk [börd′wök′] **90** 1

body [bŏ′dē] **4**

boil [boyl] **31** 16

bollard [bŏl′ ərd] **58** 26

bolt [bōlt] **37** 38

bomb [bŏm] **48** 3

bomber [bŏm′ ər] **48** 2

bongos [bŏng′ gōz] **98** 22

book [book] **13** 17

(book of) matches [book′ əv mă′ chəz] **16** 28

bookcase [book′ kās] **28** 22, **83** 20

bookstore [book′ stör] **45** 18

boom [boom] **59** 7

booth [booth] **16** 9

boots [boots] **19** 21, **21** 32

bottle [bŏt′ əl] **12** 3, **33** 17

bottle opener [bŏt′ əl ō′ pə nər] **30** 6

bounce [bowns] **97** 11

bow [bō] **98** 7a

bow [bow] **58** 5

bowl [bōl] **13** 23

bowling [bōl′ĭng] **94**

bowling ball [bōl/ĭng böl/] **94** 6

box [bŏks] **13** 12

box seat [bŏks/ sēt/] **99** 11

box spring [bŏks/ sprĭng/] **32** 18

boxer shorts [bŏk/ sər shörts/] **22** 2

boxing [bŏk/ sĭng] **94**

boy's frame [boyz/ frām/] **52** 11

bra(ssiere) [brŏ]/[brə zïr/] **22** 13

brace [brās] **36** 9

bracelet [brās/lət] **23** 9

brain [brān] **5** 57

brake [brāk] **50** 26, **52** 17

brake light [brāk/lĭt/] **50** 29

branch [brănch] **61** 35a

brass [brăs] **98**

bread [brĕd] **14** 12

bread and butter plate
[brĕd/ ənd bŭt/ ər plāt/] **29** 11

break [brāk] **31** 7

breast [brĕst] **11** 21

bricks [brĭks] **82** 12

bridle path [brīd/ əl păth/] **87** 7

briefcase [brēf/kās/] **21** 37

briefs [brēfs] **22** 12

broccoli [brŏk/ ə lē] **6** 2

broil [broyl] **31** 13

broiler [broy/lər] **30** 33

broken bone [brō/kən bōn/] **40** 15

broom [brōōm] **35** 7

brother [brŭdh/ər] **3** 9

brother-in-law [brŭdh/ ər ən lö/] **3** 11

bruise [brōōz] **40** 17

brush [brŭsh] **76** 18

brussels sprouts [brŭs/ əl sprowts/] **6** 4

bucket [bŭk/ət] **35** 15

bucket seat [bŭk/ ət sēt/] **50** 16

buckle [bŭk/əl] **20** 17

bud [bŭd] **60** 18a

buffet [bə fā/] **29** 29

builder [bĭl/dər] **82** 5

building number [bĭl/ dĭng nŭm/ bər]
45 24

bulb [bŭlb] **60** 8a

bull [bŏŏl] **67** 34

bulldozer [bŏŏl/ dō/ zər] **82** 27

bullet [bŏŏl/ĭt] **48** 26

bulletin board [bŏŏl/ ĭ tən börd/] **76** 7

bumper [bŭm/pər] **33** 5

bun [bŭn] **18** 7

bunch [bŭnch] **8** 1

Bunsen burner [bŭn/ sən bür/ nər]
78 20

buoy [bōō/ē]/[boy] **58** 16

bureau [byŏŏr/ō] **32** 9

burn [bürn] **17** 14, **40** 18

burner [bür/nər] **30** 29

bus [bŭs] **53** 20, **54**

bus driver [bŭs/drī/vər] **54** 3

bus stop [bŭs/stŏp/] **44** 13

busboy [bŭs/boy/] **16** 3

bushes [bŏŏsh/ əz] **61** 41

business workers [biz/nəs wür/kərz] **86**

butcher [bŏŏ/chər] **84** 13

butter [bŭt/ər] **18** 18

buttercup [bŭt/ ər kŭp/] **60** 17

butterfly [bŭt/ ər flī/] **63** 3

buttocks [bŭt/əks] **4** 15

button [bŭt/ən] **20** 3, **101** 9

buttonhole [bŭt/ ən hōl/] **101** 8

C-clamp [sē/klămp/] **36** 2

cab driver [kăb/drī/ vər] **55** 26

cabbage [kăb/ĭj] **6** 3

cabin [kăb/ĭn] **56** 19

cabin cruiser [kăb/ĭn krōō/ zər] **59** 16

cabinet [kăb/ ə nət] **30** 22

cable [kā/bəl] **52** 23

cable car [kā/ bəl kär/] **55** 32

cactus [kăk/təs] **61** 40

calculator [kăl/kyə lā/ tər] **83** 19,
100 34

calendar [căl/ ən dər] **83** 9

calf [kăf] **4** 20, **67** 31

California [kăl/ ə för/ nyə] **72** 5

call card [köl/kärd/] **47** 6

call number [köl/ nŭm/ bər] **47** 6

call slip [köl/slĭp/] **47** 12

camel [kăm/əl] **67** 33

camera [kăm/ər ə] **100** 8

cameraperson [kăm/ ər ə pür/ sən] **86** 10

camisole [kăm/ ə sōl/] **22** 9

camp stove [kămp/stōv/] **89** 25

camper [kăm/pər] **53** 16

campfire [kămp/fīr/] **89** 31

camping [kăm/pĭng] **89**

can [kăn] **12** 10

can opener [kăn/ ō/ pə nər] **30** 4

canary [kə nër/ ē] **64** 14

candle [kăn/dəl] **29** 27

candlestick [kăn/dəl stĭk/] **29** 28

canister [kăn/ ə stər] **30** 15

canned goods [kănd/ gŏŏdz/] **14** 13

cannon [kăn/ ən] **48** 11

canoe [kə nōō/] **59** 2

cantaloupe [kăn/ tə lōp/] **9** 36

canyon [kăn/ yən] **88** 3

cap [kăp] **19** 2, **21** 43, **92** 11

capsule [kăp/ səl] **41** 5

car [kär] **54** 9

card catalog [kärd/ kăt/ ə lög] **47** 4

cardigan [kär/dĭ gən] **21** 26

cardinal [kärd/nəl] **64** 11

cargo [kär/gō] **58** 10

cargo area [kär/gō ër/ ē ə] **57** 12

cargo bay [kär/gō bā/] **75** 9

cargo door [kär/gō dör/] **57** 13

Caribbean Sea [kăr/ ə bē/ ən sē/]
70 20

carpenter [kär/pən tər] **85** 2

carpenter's rule [kär/ pən tərz rōōl/]
36 1

carrot(s) [kăr/ ət(s)] **7** 32

carry [kăr/ē] **26** 16

carry-on bag [kăr/ē ŏn băg/] **56** 2

cars [kärz] **50-51**

carton [kär/tən] **12** 1

cartridge needle [kär/trĭj nē/ dəl]
100 19

carve [kärv] **31** 6

cash register [kăsh/rĕ/ jə stər] **15** 21

cashew(s) [kăsh/ ōō(z)] **9** 27

cashier [kă shïr/] **15** 22

Caspian Sea [kăs/pē ən sē/] **70** 27

casserole dish [kăs/ ə rōl dĭsh/] **30** 14

cassette [kə sĕt/] **100** 26

cassette deck [kə sĕt/ dĕk/] **100** 22

cast [kăst] **39** 5

cat [kăt] **68** 4

catch [kăch] **96** 4

catcher [kăch/ ər] **92** 2, **93** 16

catcher's mask [kăch/ərz măsk/] **92** 3

catcher's mitt [kăch/ərz mĭt/] **92** 4

caterpillar [kăt/ ər pĭl/ər] **63** 1

cattle [kăt/ əl] **81** 20

Caucasus [kö/kə səs] **71** 45

cauliflower [kŏl′ ə flow′ ər] **6** 1

ceiling [sē′lĭng] **28** 2

ceiling fan [sē′ lĭng făn′] **28** 1

celery [sĕl′ ə rē] **6** 10

cello [chĕl′o] **98** 9

cement [sə mĕnt′] **82** 10

cement mixer [sə mĕnt′ mĭk′ sər] **82** 25

cement truck [sə mĕnt′ trŭk′] **49** 13

center [sĕn′ tər] **79** 13, **93** 27

center divider [sĕn′ tər də vī′ dər] **53** 18, **82** 24

center fielder [sĕn′ tər fēl′ dər] **93** 2

center lane [sĕn′ tər lān′] **53** 6

centerboard [sĕn′ tər börd′] **59** 6

centipede [sĕn′ tə pēd′] **63** 22

chain [chān] **23** 5, **52** 18

chair [chër] **29** 17

chalk [chök] **76** 10

chalk tray [chök′ trā′] **76** 9

chalkboard [chök′ börd′] **76** 5

chandelier [shăn′ də lïr′] **29** 3

change (the sheets) [chānj′ dhə shēts′] **38** 13

changing table [chān′ jĭng tā′ bəl] **33** 9

charcoal briquettes [chär′ kōl brĭ kĕts′] **27** 23

chart [chärt] **39** 10

check [chĕk] **15** 27, **16** 14

checked [chĕkt] **24** 18

checkout counter [chĕk′ owt kown′ tər] **15** 26

checkout desk [chĕk′ owt dĕsk′] **47** 2

cheerleaders [chïr′ lē′ dərz] **93** 20

cheek [chēk] **4** 35

cherries [chër′ ēz] **9** 19

cherry picker [chër′ ē pĭk′ ər] **82** 18

chest [chĕst] **4** 12

chest of drawers [chĕst′ əv drörz′] **32** 30

chestnut(s) [chĕs′ nŭt(s)] **9** 32

chick [chĭk] **64** 22

chicken [chĭk′ ən] **11** 24, **64** 23

child's seat [chīldz′ sēt′] **50** 33

children [chĭl′ drən] **2** 7

chills [chĭlz] **40** 4

chimney [chĭm′ nē] **27** 9

chimpanzee [chĭm păn′ zē] **69** 16

chin [chĭn] **4** 3

china [chī′ nə] **29** 1

china closet [chī′ nə klŏz′ ət] **29** 2

chipmunk [chĭp′ mŭnk] **66** 6

chop [chŏp] **26** 11, **31** 11

chops [chŏps] **10** 9, **10** 15

chorus [kör′ əs] **99** 18

(chrysanthe)mum [krə săn′ thə məm]/[mŭm] **60** 4

cigarette [sĭg′ ə rĕt′] **16** 31

circle [sür′ kəl] **79** 11

circuit breaker [sür′ kət brā′ kər] **35** 5

circular saw [sür′ kyə lər sö′] **36** 20

circumference [sür kŭm′ fə rəns] **79** 17

citrus fruits [sĭ′ trəs froots′] **8**

city [sĭt′ ē] **44-45**

clam(s) [klăm(z)] **11** 32

clamp [klămp] **78** 7

clarinet [klăr′ə nĕt′] **98** 16

clasp [klăsp] **23** 17

classroom [klăs′ room′] **76**

claw [klö] **62** 13a, **68** 2a

clean [klēn] **24** 6, **26** 2

cleanser [klĕn′ zər] **35** 9

clear [klïr] **17** 6

cliff [klĭf] **89** 21

clip-on earring [klĭp′ ŏn ïr′ ĭng] **23** 15

clock [klŏk] **76** 2

close (v) [klōz] **77** 5

closed [klōzd] **24** 16

closet [klŏz′ ət] **32** 3

cloth diaper [klöth′ dī′ pər] **33** 13

clothes [klōz] **19-24**

clothesline [klōz′ līn′] **35** 19

clothespins [klōz′ pĭnz′] **35** 20

cloudy [klow′ dē] **25** 2

clove [klōv] **7** 25a

cloverleaf [klō′ vər lēf′] **53** 4

clubs [klŭbz] **95** 5

clutch [klŭch] **50** 25

coach [kōch] **93** 21

coal [kōl] **80** 7

coal mine [kōl′ mīn′] **80** 6

coaster [kō′ stər] **16** 27

coat [kōt] **19** 24, **42** 13

cob [kŏb] **6** 12a

cobra [kō′ brə] **65** 11

cockpit [kŏk′ pĭt′] **56** 13

cockroach [kŏk′ rōch′] **63** 9

cocktail lounge [kŏk′ tāl lownj′] **16**

cocktail waitress [kŏk′ tāl wā′ trəs] **16** 32

cocoon [kə koon′] **63** 2

coconut [kō′ kə nŭt′] **8** 3

coffee [kö′ fē] **18** 35

coffee maker [kö′ fē mā′ kər] **30** 31

coffeepot [kö′ fē pŏt′] **29** 18

coffee table [kö′ fē tā′ bəl] **28** 26

coins [koynz] **13** 26

colander [kŏl′ ən dər] **30** 7

cold [kōld] **25** 10, **40** 11

cold water faucet [kōld′ wŏ tər fö′ sət] **34** 18

collar [kŏl′ ər] **20** 20

colonial-style house [kə lō′ nē əl stīl hows′] **27**

Colorado [kŏl′ə rŏd′ ō] **72** 6

column [kŏl′ əm] **50** 13

comb [kōm] **32** 6

combine (n) [kŏm′ bīn] **81** 17

comet [kŏm′ ət] **74** 2

comforter [kŭm′ fər tər] **32** 22

command module [kə mănd′ mŏj′ ool] **75** 8

communication satellite [kə myoo′ nə kā shən săt′ ə līt] **75** 2

commuter [kə myoo′ tər] **55** 17

commuter train [kə myoo′ tər trān′] **55** 14

compact disc (CD) [kŏm′ păkt dĭsk′]/[sē′ dē′] **100** 27

compact disc player [kŏm′ păkt dĭsk′ plā′ ər] **100** 28

computer [kəm pyoo′ tər] **76** 8, **83** 16, **100**

computer programmer [kəm pyoo′ tər prō′ grăm ər] **86** 16

conductor [kən dŭk′ tər] **54** 7, **99** 8

cone [kōn] **61** 34b, **79** 28, **82** 19

conga [kŏng′ gə] **98** 20

Congo River [kŏng′ gō rĭv′ ər] **71** 62

Connecticut [kə nĕ′ tĭ kət] **72** 7

constellation [kŏn′ stə lā′ shən] **74** 3

construction [kən strŭk′ shən] **82**

(construction) boots [kən strŭk′ shən boots′] **21** 32

construction site [kən strŭk′ shən sīt′] **82**

construction worker
   [kən strŭk′ shən wür′ kər] **82** 14

container [kən tā′nər] **12** 2, **58** 7

(container)ship [kən tā′ nər shĭp′] **58** 9

containers [kən tā′ nərz] **12**

continents [kŏn′ tə nənts] **70**

control tower [kən trōl′ tow′ər] **57** 20

conveyor belt [kən vā′ər bĕlt] **15** 23,
  56 12

cook (n) [kŏok] **17** 4

cook (v) [kŏok] **17** 4

cookie [kŏok′ ē] **18** 22

cool [kŏol] **25** 9

cooler [kŏo′ lər] **91** 41

cooling tower [kŏo′lĭng tow′ər] **80** 16

copilot [kō′pī lət] **56** 16

cord [körd] **32** 26a, **54** 1

(corduroy) pants [kör′ də roy pănts′]
  21 27

core [kör] **8** 2b, **80** 14

cork [körk] **16** 18

corkscrew [körk′ skrŏo′] **16** 17

corn [körn] **6** 12, **60** 24

corner [kör′ nər] **44** 3

corral [kə răl′] **81** 24

cosmetics [kŏz mĕt′ ĭks] **23**

cotton balls [kŏt′ ən bölz′] **39** 23

cotton swab [kŏt′ ən swŏb′] **33** 10

counter [kown′ tər] **30** 27

court [kört] **43**, **94** 13

court officer [kört′ ö′ fə sər] **43** 19

court reporter [kört′ rə pör′ tər] **43** 14

cousin [kŭz′ən] **3** 7

cow [kow] **67** 32

cowboy [kow′ boy′] **81** 21

cowgirl [kow′ gürl′] **81** 22

crab(s) [kră b(z)] **11** 36, **62** 9

cradle [krā′ dəl] **33** 26

cranberries [krăn′ bër′ ēz] **8** 13

crane [krān] **58** 6

creamer [krē′ mər] **29** 24

crew [krŏo] **75** 12

(crewneck) sweater
  [krŏo′ nĕk swĕt′ ər] **19** 7

crib [krĭb] **33** 4

criket [krĭk′ ət] **63** 5

crime [krīm] **43**

crochet [krō shā′] **101** 28

crochet hook [krō′ shā′ hŏok′] **101** 29

crocus [krō′ kəs] **60** 9

cross-country skiing
  [krös′ kŭn trē skē′ ĭng] **94**

crosswalk [krös′ wök′] **44** 4

crow [krō] **64** 3

crutch [krŭch] **39** 7

cube [kyŏob] **79** 27

cubicle [kyŏo′ bə kəl] **83** 5

cucumber(s) [kyŏo′ kŭm bər(z)] **7** 20

cuff links [kŭf′ lĭnks′] **23** 12

cup [kŭp] **13** 19, **29** 20

curb [kürb] **45** 26

curtain [kür′ tən] **32** 10, **99** 1

curtain rings [kür′ tən rĭngz′] **34** 2

curtain rod [kür′ tən rŏd′] **34** 1

curve [kürv] **79** 3

cushion [kŏosh′ ən] **28** 24

customer [kŭs′ tə mər] **15** 17

cut (v) [kŭt] **31** 9

cut (n) [kŭt] **40** 16

cutting board [kŭt′ ĭng börd′] **30** 26

cylinder [sĭl′ ĭn dər] **79** 26

cymbals [sĭm′ bəlz] **98** 18

daffodil [dăf′ ə dĭl] **60** 8

dairy cow [dër′ ē kow′] **81** 11

dairy farm [dër′ ē färm′] **81**

dairy products [dër′ ē prŏd′ ŭkts] **14** 4

daisy [dā′ zē] **60** 5

dam [dăm] **80** 18

dance [dăns] **99**

dancer [dăn′ sər] **99** 3

dark [därk] **24** 10

dashboard [dăsh′ börd′] **50** 19

date [dāt] **9** 23

daughter [dö′ tər] **3** 15

deck [dĕk] **27** 5, **58** 22

deer [dïr] **67** 26

defendant [də fĕn′ dənt] **43** 23

defense attorney [də fĕns′ ə tür′ nē]
  43 22

Delaware [dĕl′ ə wăr′] **72** 8

deli counter [dĕl′ ē kown′ tər] **14** 1

delivery boy [də lĭv′ ə rē boy′] **85** 10

delivery person [də lĭv′ ə rē pür′ sən]
  49 10

dental care [dĕn′ təl kër′] **39**

dentist [dĕn′ tĭst] **39** 17

department store [də pärt′ mənt stör′]
  44 5

depth [dĕpth] **79** 33

derrick [dĕr′ ĭk] **80** 2

deserts [dĕz′ ərts] **71**

desk [dĕsk] **28** 14, **76** 16, **83** 13

detective [də tĕk′ tĭv] **43** 2

diagonal [dī ăg′ ə nəl] **79** 20

diameter [dī ăm′ ə tər] **79** 12

dictionary [dĭk′ shə nër′ ē] **47** 24

diesel fuel [dē′ zəl fyŏo′ əl] **80** 34

dig [dĭg] **26** 3

dime [dīm] **13** 29

dinghy [dĭng′ ē] **59** 18

dining room [dī′ nĭng rŏom′] **29**

dipstick [dĭp′ stĭk′] **51** 58

dirt bike [dürt′ bīk′] **52** 8

disc jockey (DJ) [dĭsk′ jŏk′ ē]/[dē′ jā]
  86 9

dirty [dür′ tē] **24** 5

dish drainer [dĭsh′ drā′ nər] **30** 2

dish towel [dĭsh′ tow′ əl] **30** 18

dishwasher [dĭsh′ wŏsh′ ər] **30** 1

dishwashing liquid
  [dĭsh′ wŏsh ĭng lĭ′ kwĭd] **30** 10

disposable diaper
  [dīs pō′ zə bəl dī′ pər] **33** 12

dissection kit [dĭ sĕk′ shən kĭt′] **78** 33

dive [dīv] **97** 14

dock [dŏk] **58** 28

doctor [dŏk′ tər] **39** 11

dogs [dögz] **69**

dogwood [dög′ wŏod′] **61** 28

doll [dŏl] **33** 28

doll house [dŏl′ hows′] **33** 25

dollar bills [dŏl′ər bĭlz′] **13** 25

dolly [dŏl′ ē] **56** 6

dolphin [dŏl′ fĭn] **68** 13

donkey [dŏng′ kē] **67** 23

door handle [dör′ hăn′ dəl] **50** 4

door lock [dör′ lŏk′] **50** 1

doorman [dör′ mən] **85** 11

down [down] **103** 3

down vest [down′ vĕst′] **19** 12

dragonfly [drăg′ ən flī′] **63** 4

drain [drān] **34** 9

drainpipe [drān′ pīp′] **27** 18

drapes [drāps] **28** 23

draw [drö] **77** 11

drawer [drör] **47** 5

dress [drĕs] **20** 22

dried fruits [drīd/ frōōts/] **9**

drill [drĭl] **39** 15

drink [drĭngk] **17** 2

drive [drīv] **97** 15

driveway [drīv/ wā/] **27** 1

drugstore [drŭg/ stör/] **45** 22

drum [drŭm] **98** 19

drummer [drŭm/ ər] **99** 27

drumsticks [drŭm/ stĭks/] **98** 19a

dry [drī] **25** 14, **38** 9

dryer [drī/ ər] **35** 24

duck [dŭk] **11** 25, **64** 25

(duck) pond [dŭk/ pŏnd/] **87** 8

dugout [dŭg/ owt/] **93** 13

dump truck [dŭmp/ trŭk/] **49** 14

dust [dŭst] **38** 15

dustpan [dŭst/ păn/] **35** 8

eagle [ē/ gəl] **64** 5

ear [ïr] **4** 34

(ear of) corn [ïr/ əv körn/] **6** 12

earmuffs [ïr/ mŭfs/] **19** 10

earrings [ïr/ ĭngz] **23** 1

Earth [ürth] **74** 8, **13**

east [ēst] **71** 73

East China Sea [ēst/ chī/ nə sē/] **70** 38

eat [ēt] **17** 1

eel [ēl] **65** 4

egg [ĕg] **18** 32, **64** 13

egg roll [ĕg/ rōl/] **18** 25

eggplant [ĕg/ plănt/] **7** 21

elbow [ĕl/ bō] **4** 8

electric drill [ĭ lĕk/ trĭk drĭl/] **37** 43

electric guitar [ĭ lĕk/ trĭk gĭ tär/] **99** 26

electric generator [ĭ lĕk/ trĭk gĕn/ ə rā tər] **80** 21

electrical tape [ĭ lĕk/ trĭ kəl tāp/] **37** 34

electrician [ĭ lĕk trĭ/ shən] **85** 6

electricity [ĭ lĕk trĭs/ ĭ tē] **80** 32

electronics [ĭ lĕk trŏn/ ĭks] **100**

elephant [ĕl/ ə fənt] **66** 17

elevator [ĕl/ ə vā/ tər] **45** 17, **80** 9

elm [ĕlm] **61** 36

embroidery [ĕm broi/ də rē] **101** 27

emergency brake [ĭ mür/ jən sē brāk/] **50** 15

emery board [ĕm/ ə rē börd/] **23** 24

encyclopedia [ĕn sī/ klə pē/ dē ə] **47** 25

end table [ĕnd/ tā/ bəl] **28** 29

end zone [ĕnd/ zōn/] **93** 23

energy [ĕn/ ər jē] **80**

engagement ring [ĕn gāj/ mənt rĭng/] **23** 3

engine [ĕn/ jən] **51, 52** 32

engineer [ĕn/ jə nïr/] **55** 15

enter [ĕn/ tər] **77** 14

entrance ramp [ĕn/ trəns rămp/] **53** 21

envelope [ĕn/ və lōp/] **46** 16, **83** 31

equator [ĭ kwā/ tər] **71** 70

erase [ĭ rās/] **77** 3

eraser [ĭ rā/ sər] **76** 11

escarole [ĕs/ kə rōl/] **6** 7

esophagus [ĭ sŏf/ ə gəs] **5** 61

eucalyptus [yōō/ kə lĭp/ təs] **61** 27

Europe [yōōr/ əp] **70** 3

examining table [ĭg zăm/ ə nĭng tā/ bəl] **39** 6

exhaust pipe [ĭg zöst/ pīp/] **52** 33

exit ramp [ĕg/ zĭt rămp/] **53** 2

exit sign [ĕg/ zĭt sīn/] **53** 24

Express Mail (package) [ĭk sprĕs/ māl păk/ ĭj] **46** 23

extension cord [ĭk stĕn/ shən körd/] **36** 5

eye [ī] **5**

eye drops [ī/ drŏps/] **41** 10

eye shadow [ī/ shă/ dō] **23** 30

eyebrow [ī/ brow/] **5** 44

eyebrow pencil [ī/ brow pĕn/ səl] **23** 26

eyelashes [ī/ lăsh/ əz] **5** 46

eyelid [ī/ lĭd/] **5** 45

eyeliner [ī/ lī/ nər] **23** 33

fabric softener [făb/ rĭk sö/ fə nər] **35** 27

face [fās] **4** 1

face guard [fās/ gärd/] **92** 15

factory work [făk/ tə rē würk/] **85**

fairway [fĕr/ wā/] **95** 12

fall [föl] **96** 7

Fall [föl] **26**

family [făm/ ə lē] **3**

family restaurant [făm/ ə lē rĕs/ tər ənt] **16**

fan belt [făn/ bĕlt/] **51** 53

fare [fĕr] **55** 21

fare box [fĕr/ bŏks/] **54** 5

farmhouse [färm/ hows/] **81** 3

farmer [fär/ mər] **81** 7

farming [fär/ mĭng] **81**

fashion designer [făsh/ ən də zī/ nər] **86** 6

father [fŏdh/ ər] **3** 5

faucet [fö/ sĭt] **34** 17, 18

fawn [fön] **67** 27

feather [fĕdh/ ər] **64** 7a

feather duster [fĕdh/ ər dŭs/ tər] **35** 2

fence [fĕns] **81** 9

fender [fĕn/ dər] **52** 10

ferry [fĕr/ ē] **58** 17

fever [fē/ vər] **40** 2

field [fēld] **81** 16

fields and courses [fēldz/ ənd kör/ səz] **95**

fig [fĭg] **9** 21

fighter plane [fī/ tər plān/] **48** 1

file cabinet [fīl/ kăb/ ə nət] **83** 21

file clerk [fīl/ klürk/] **83** 23

file folder [fīl/ fōl/ dər] **83** 22

filet [fĭ lā/] **11** 28

fill [fĭl] **26** 9

film [fĭlm] **100** 10, **100** 17

filter paper [fĭl/ tər pā/ pər] **78** 16

fin [fĭn] **65** 3b

finger [fĭng/ gər] **4** 25

fingernail [fĭng/ gər nāl/] **4** 23

fingerprints [fĭng/ gər prĭnts/] **43** 24

finish line [fĭn/ ĭsh līn/] **95** 21

fire [fīr] **28** 9, **42** 5

fire engine [fīr/ ĕn/ jən] **42** 2

fire escape [fīr/ ə skāp/] **42** 4

fire extinguisher [fīr/ ĭk stĭng/ gwĭ shər] **42** 11

fire fighter [fīr/ fī/ tər] **42** 10

fire hydrant [fīr/ hī/ drənt] **42** 9

fire truck [fīr/ trŭk/] **42** 3

firefighting [fīr/ fī/ tĭng] **42**

firefly [fīr/ flī/] **63** 17

fireplace [fīr′ plās′] **28** 8

first baseman [fürst′ bās′ mən] **93** 8

first quarter [fürst′ kwör′ tər] **74** 23

fish [fĭsh] **11** 26, **65**

fisherman [fĭsh′ ər mən] **58** 2

fishing [fĭsh′ ĭng] **88**

fishing boat [fĭsh′ ĭng bōt′] **58** 1

fishing line [fĭsh′ ĭng līn′] **88** 8

fishing net [fĭsh′ ĭng nĕt′] **88** 9

fishing rod [fĭsh′ ĭng rŏd′] **88** 7

flag [flăg] **76** 1, **82** 20, **95** 9

flame [flām] **29** 26, **78** 21

flamingo [flə mĭng′ gō] **64** 29

flanker [flăng′ kər] **93** 31

flannel shirt [flăn′ əl shürt′] **19** 3

flare [flër] **51** 41

flash [flăsh] **100** 7

flashlight [flăsh′ līt′] **35** 3

flask [flăsk] **78** 2

(flat) sheet [flăt′ shēt′] **32** 19

flatbed [flăt′ bĕd′] **49** 18

flight attendant [flīt′ ə tĕn′ dənt] **56** 20

flight deck [flīt′ dĕk′] **75** 10

flight engineer [flīt′ ĕn jə nïr′] **56** 17

flipper [flĭp′ ər] **68** 12a

flippers [flĭp′ ərz] **91** 36

floor [flör] **32** 29

Florida [flör′ ə də] **72** 9

florist [flör′ ĭst] **84** 11

flounder [flown′ dər] **65** 7

flowers [flow′ ərz] **60**

flute [floōt] **99** 13

fly [flī] **63** 18

flying mammal [flī′ ĭng mă′ məlz] **66**

foal [fōl] **67** 22

foggy [fög′ ē] **25** 12

fold [fōld] **38** 1

food [foōd] **6-18**

foot [foōt] **5**

football [foōt′ böl′] **92, 92** 13

football field [foōt′ böl fēld′] **93**

forceps [för′ səps] **78** 28

forearm [för′ ärm] **4** 9

forehead [för′ hĕd′] **4** 32

forelegs [för′ lĕgz′] **66** 3d

foreman [för′ mən] **85** 13

fork [förk] **29** 12

forklift [förk′ lĭft′] **58** 4

foul line [fowl′ līn′] **93** 9

foundation [fown dā′ shən] **82** 11

four-door hatchback [för′ dör hăch′ băk] **51**

fox [fŏks] **68** 6

fractions [frăk′ shənz] **79**

frame [frām] **28** 4

frame backpack [frām′ băk′ păk] **89** 28

freezer [frē′ zər] **14** 3, **30** 20

freezing [frē′ zĭng] **25** 11

french fries [frĕnch′ frīz′] **18** 28

French horn [frĕnch′ hörn′] **98** 26

fried chicken [frīd′ chĭk′ ən] **18** 29

Frisbee™ [frĭz′ bē] **90** 13

frog [frŏg] **65** 17

from [frŭm] **103** 10

front bumper [frŭnt′ bŭm′ pər] **51** 51

frozen foods [frō′zən foōdz′] **14** 2

fruit and vegetable market [froōt′ ənd vĕj′ tə bəl mär′ kət] **44** 28

fruit tree [froōt′ trē′] **81** 2

fruits [froōts] **8**

fry [frī] **31** 15

frying pan [frī′ ĭng păn′] **30** 5

fuel truck [fyoō′ əl trŭk′] **49** 3

full moon [foōl′ moōn′] **74** 24

full slip [foōl′ slĭp′] **22** 10

fullback [foōl′ băk′] **93** 34

funnel [fŭn′ əl] **78** 17

fuselage [fyoō′ sə lŏj′] **57** 14

galaxy [găl′ək sē] **74** 1

Ganges River [găn′ jēz rĭv′ ər] **71** 67

gangway [găng′ wā′] **58** 20

garage [gə rŏj′] **27** 2

garbage can [gär′ bĭj kăn′] **35** 31

garbage truck [gär′ bĭj trŭk′] **49** 6

garden hose [gär′ dən hōs′] **27** 14

gardenia [gär dēn′ yə] **60** 14

gardener [gärd′ nər] **85** 3

garlic [gär′ lĭk] **7** 25

garment bag [gär′ mənt băg′] **56** 1

garter belt [gär′ tər bĕlt′] **22** 14

(garter) snake [gär′ tər snāk′] **65** 9

gas gauge [găs′ gāj′] **50** 9

gas pump [găs′ pŭmp′] **53** 14

gas tank [găs′ tănk′] **50** 34

gas(oline) [găs′ ə lēn′] **80** 28

(gauze) bandage [göz′ băn′ dĭj] **39** 24

gauze pads [göz′ pădz′] **39** 25

gavel [găv′ əl] **43** 12

gear [gïr] **89** 27

gear changer [gïr′ chān′ jər] **52** 22

gearshift [gïr′ shĭft′] **50** 17

geometrical figures [jē′ ə mĕ′ trĭ kəl fĭg′ yərz] **79**

Georgia [jör′ jə] **72** 10

geyser [gī′ zər] **80** 5

gibbon [gĭb′ ən] **69** 15

gill [gĭl] **65** 3c

giraffe [jə răf′] **67** 29

girdle [gür′ dəl] **22** 15

girl [gürl] **2** 9

girl's frame [gürlz′ frām′] **52** 3

give [gĭv] **17** 9

glass [glăs] **12** 20

glasses [glăs′ əz] **21** 44

glider [glī′ dər] **57** 4

globe [glōb] **47** 19

glove [glŭv] **92** 12, **94** 11, **94** 15

glove compartment [glŭv′ kəm pärt′ mənt] **50** 20

gloves [glŭvz] **19** 1

glue [gloō] **36** 33, **76** 17

goal [gōl] **92** 25

goalie [gōl′ ē] **92** 24

goalpost [gōl′ pōst′] **93** 35

goat [gōt] **67** 28

Gobi Desert [gō′ bē dĕz′ ərt] **71** 54

golf [gŏlf] **94**

golf bag [gŏlf′ băg′] **95** 7

golf ball [gŏlf′ böl′] **94** 7

golf cart [gŏlf′ kärt′] **95** 8

golf course [gŏlf′ körs′] **95**

golfer [gŏl′ fər] **94** 10

goose [goōs] **64** 26

gooseberries [goōs′ bër′ ēz] **8** 11

gopher [gō′ fər] **66** 8

gorilla [gə rĭl′ ə] **69** 17

graduated cylinder [grăj′ oō ā tĭd sĭl′ ən dər] **78** 25

grains [grānz] **60**

granddaughter [grănd′ dö′ tər] **2** 11

grandfather [grănd′ fŏ′ dhər] **3** 2

grandmother [grănd′ mŭ′ dhər] **3** 1

grandparents [grănd pär′ ənts] **2** 10

grandson [grănd′ sŭn′] **2** 12

grapefruit [grăp′ fro͞ot′] **8** 7

grapes [grāps] **8** 1

graph paper [grăf′ pā′ pər] **78** 11

grass [grăs] **27** 15

grasses [grăs′ əz] **60**

grasshopper [grăs′ hŏp′ ər] **63** 6

grate [grāt] **31** 2

Great Sandy Desert
 [grāt′ săn′ dē dĕz′ ərt] **71** 55

green [grēn] **95** 10

greengrocer [grēn′ grō′ sər] **84** 7

grill [grĭl] **27** 22, **88** 12

grizzly bear [grĭz′ lē bër′] **69** 23

groceries [grō′ sə rēz] **15** 24

ground beef [grownd′ bēf′] **10** 2

grounding plug [grown′ dĭng plŭg′]
 36 7

guitar [gĭ tär′] **98** 11

Gulf of Alaska [gŭlf′ əv ə lăs′ kə]
 70 17

Gulf of Guinea [gŭlf′ əv gĭn′ ē] **70** 25

Gulf of Mexico [gŭlf′ əv mĕk sə kō]
 70 19

gulfs [gŭlfs] **70**

gun [gŭn] **43** 7

gun turret [gŭn′ tür′ ət] **48** 12

gutter [gŭt′ ər] **27** 10, **94** 3

gymnast [jĭm′ nəst] **94** 23

gymnastics [jĭm năs′ tĭks] **94**

hacksaw [hăk′ sö′] **36** 18

hair [hër] **4** 30

hair dryer [hër′ drī′ ər] **34** 26

hairbrush [hër′ brŭsh′] **32** 7

hairdresser [hër′ drĕs′ ər] **84** 10

half (1/2) [hăf] **79** 30

half slip [hăf′ slĭp′] **22** 8

halfback [hăf′ băk′] **93** 33

hall [höl] **76** 12

ham [hăm] **10** 12

hamburger [hăm′ bür′ gər] **18** 9

hammer [hăm′ ər] **36** 13

hammock [hăm′ ək] **27** 11

hamper [hăm′ pər] **34** 28

hand [hănd] **4**

hand brake [hănd′ brāk′] **52** 24

hand grenade [hănd′ grə nād′] **48** 29

hand towel [hănd′ tow′ əl] **34** 23

hand truck [hănd′ trŭk′] **87** 4

handball [hănd′ böl′] **94**, **94** 12

handcuffs [hănd′ kŭfs′] **43** 4

handicrafts [hăn′ dē krăfts′] **101**

handlebars [hăn′ dəl bärz′] **52** 2

hang [hăng] **38** 6

hang glider [hăng′ glī′ dər] **57** 6

hangar [hăng′ ər] **57** 17

hanger [hăng′ ər] **32** 2

hard hat [härd′ hăt′] **21** 28, **82** 4

harmonica [här mŏn′ ə kə] **98** 30

harness [här′ nəs] **89** 22

harp [härp] **98** 6

hat [hăt] **19** 18

hatchback [hăch′ băk′] **51** 43

hatchet [hăch′ ət] **36** 17

Hawaii [hə wŏ′ ē] **72** 11

hawk [hök] **64** 7

hay [hā] **81** 13

hazelnut(s) [hā′ zəl nŭt(s)′] **9** 30

head [hĕd] **4**, **36** 42a

(head of) cauliflower
 [hĕd′ əv kŏl ə flow′ ər] **6** 1

head protector [hĕd prə tĕk′ tər] **94** 14

headache [hĕd′ āk′] **40** 6

headboard [hĕd′ börd′] **32** 14

headlights [hĕd′ līts′] **51** 48

headphones [hĕd′ fōnz′] **100** 29

headrest [hĕd′ rĕst′] **50** 35

headset [hĕd′ sĕt′] **83** 2

heart [härt] **5** 64

heat [hēt] **80** 27

heating pad [hē′ tĭng păd′] **41** 3

hedge clippers [hĕj′ klĭp′ ərz] **27** 29

heel [hēl] **5** 50, **20** 5

heels [hēlz] **20** 25

height [hīt] **79** 34

helicopter [hĕl′ ə kŏp′ tər] **57** 2

helmet [hĕl′ mət] **42** 12, **52** 7, **92** 14

hem [hĕm] **101** 11

hem binding [hĕm′ bīn′ dĭng] **101** 12

herb(s) [ürb(z)] **6** 9

(herd of) cattle [hürd′ əv kăt′ əl] **81** 20

high [hī] **24** 11

high blood pressure [hī′ blŭd prĕsh′ ər]
 40 10

high chair [hī′ chër′] **16** 8

high heels [hī′ hēlz′] **20** 25

highway travel [hī′ wā trăv′ əl] **53**

hikers [hī′ kərz] **88** 2

hiking boots [hī′ kĭng bo͞ots′] **19** 9

hill [hĭl] **88** 4

Himalayas [hĭm′ ə lā′ əz] **70** 47

hind legs [hīnd′ lĕgz′] **66** 3b

hip [hĭp] **4** 16

hippopotamus [hĭp′ ə pŏt′ ə məs]
 66 14

hit [hĭt] **96** 1

hitchhiker [hĭch′ hī′ kər] **53** 9

hockey stick [hŏk′ ē stĭk′] **92** 18

hog [hög] **66** 30

hold [hōld] **17** 12, **58** 8

hole [hōl] **94** 8

holly [hŏl′ ē] **61** 37

holster [hōl′ stər] **43** 8

home plate [hōm′ plāt′] **93** 15

honeydew melon
 [hŭn′ ē do͞o mĕl′ ən] **9** 35

hood [ho͝od] **51** 47

hoof [ho͝of] **66** 35b

hoofed mammals [ho͝oft′ măm′ əlz] **66**

hook [ho͝ok] **32** 1, **36** 16

hook and eye [ho͝ok′ ənd ī′] **101** 14

horn [hörn] **50** 12, **52** 5, **66** 16a

horse [hörs] **66** 21

horse racing [hörs′ rā′ sĭng] **94**

horse-drawn carriage
 [hörs′ drön kăr′ ĭj] **54** 33

horseback rider [hörs′ băk rī′ dər]
 87 6

horses [hörs′ əz] **81** 23

hose [hōz] **42** 8, **50** 57

hot [hŏt] **25** 7

hot air balloon [hŏt′ ër bə lo͞on′] **57** 1

hot dog [hŏt′ dög′] **18** 2

hot water faucet [hŏt′ wŏt ər fö′ sət]
 34 17

house plants [hows′ plănts′] **60** 39

household items [hows′ hōld ī′ təmz]
 15 15

household services
 [hows′ hōld sür′ və səz] **85**

housekeeper [hows′ kē′ pər] **85** 8

houses [how′ zəz] **27**

housework [hows′ würk′] **38**

Huang River [hwöng′ riv′ ər] **71** 68

hubcap [hŭb′ kăp′] **50** 36

Hudson Bay [hŭd′ sən bā′] **70** 18
human body [hyōō′ mən bŏd′ ē] **4**
hummingbird [hŭm′ ĭng bürd′] **64** 2
hump [hŭmp] **67** 33a
husband [hŭz′ bənd] **2** 3, **3** 12
hyacinth [hī′ə sĭnth] **60** 10
hyena [hī ē′ nə] **68** 30
hypotenuse [hī pŏt′ə nōōs′] **79** 24
ice cream cone [īs′ krēm cōn′] **18** 36
ice hockey [īs′ hŏk′ ē] **92**
ice pack [īs′ păk′] **41** 4
ice skates [īs′ skāts′] **19** 15
ice skating [īs′ skā′ tĭng] **94**
ice tray [īs′ trā′] **30** 21
icy [ī′ sē] **25** 16
Idaho [ī′ də hō′] **72** 12
ignition [ĭg nĭsh′ ən] **50** 14
iguana [ĭ gwŏ′ nə] **65** 13
Illinois [ĭl′ ə noy′] **72** 13
in [ĭn] **102** 7
in front of [ĭn frŭnt′ əv] **102** 6
in-box [ĭn′ bŏks] **83** 12
(index) finger [ĭn′ dĕks fing′ gər] **4** 25
Indian Ocean [ĭn′ dē ən ō′ shən′] **70** 13
Indiana [ĭn′ dē ăn′ ə] **72** 14
individual sports
   [ĭn′ də vĭj′ ōō əl spörts′] **94**
infection [ĭn fĕk′ shən] **40** 14
inflatable raft [ĭn flā′ tə bəl răft′] **59** 20
information desk
   [ĭn′ fər mā′ shən dĕsk′] **47** 22
injection [ĭn jĕk′ shən] **41** 8
injuries [ĭn′ jə rēz] **40**
insect bite [ĭn′ sĕkt bīt′] **40** 3
insects [ĭn′ sĕkts] **63**
instep [ĭn′ stĕp′] **5** 51
instruments [ĭn′ strə mənts]
   39 13, **56** 14, **98**
internal organs [ĭn tür′ nəl ör′ gənz] **5**
intersection [ĭn′ tər sĕk′ shən] **44** 11
interstate highway
   [ĭn′ tər stāt hī′ wā] **53** 1
intestines [ĭn tĕs′ tənz] **5** 67
into [ĭn′ tōō] **103** 12
Iowa [ī′ə wə] **72** 15
iris [ī′ rəs] **5** 47, **60** 11
iron (n) [ī′ ərn] **35** 12
iron (v) [ī′ ərn] **38** 11

ironing board [ī′ər nĭng börd′] **35** 13
jack [jăk] **32** 26b, **50** 38
jacket [jăk′ ət] **19** 17, **21** 33
jackhammer [jăk′ hăm′ər] **82** 22
jail [jāl] **43** 1
janitor [jăn′ə tər] **85** 9
jar [jär] **12** 9
jaw [jö] **4** 38
jeans [jēnz] **19** 6
jeep [jēp] **48** 9
jelly [jĕl′ ē] **18** 31
jellyfish [jĕl′ ē fĭsh′] **62** 12
jet engine [jĕt′ ĕn′ jən] **57** 11
jet fuel [jĕt′ fyōō′ əl] **80** 31
(jet) plane [jĕt′ plān′] **57** 18
jeweller [jōō′ ə lər] **84** 12
jewelry [jōō′ əl rē] **23**
jewelry box [jōō′ əl rē bŏks′] **32** 4
jigsaw [jĭg′ sö] **36** 3
jockey [jŏk′ ē] **94** 21
jogging path [jŏg′ ĭng păth′] **87** 9
judge [jŭj] **43** 10
jukebox [jōōk′ bŏks′] **16** 12
jump [jŭmp] **96** 8
jungle gym [jŭng′ əl jĭm′] **87** 17
Jupiter [jōō′ pə tər] **74** 15
jury [jōor′ ē] **43** 21
jury box [joor′ ē bŏks′] **43** 20
kangaroo [kăng′ gə rōō′] **66** 3
Kansas [kăn′ zəs] **72** 16
Kara Sea [kär′ ə sē′] **70** 31
kayak [kī′ ăk] **59** 17
Kentucky [kĕn tŭk′ ē] **72** 17
ketchup [kĕch′ əp] **16** 4
kettledrum [kĕt′ əl drŭm′] **98** 21
keyboard [kē′ börd] **98** 1a, **100** 33
keyboard player [kē′ börd plā′ ər] **99** 22
kickstand [kĭk′ stănd′] **52** 9
kidney [kĭd′ nē] **5** 70
kidney bean(s) [kĭd′ nē bēn(z)′] **6** 13
kitchen [kĭch′ ən] **30**
kite [kīt] **91** 22
kitten [kĭt′ ən] **68** 5
knee [nē] **4** 19
knee socks [nē′ sŏks′] **22** 16
knife [nīf] **29** 15
knitting [nĭt′ ĭng] **101** 22
knitting needle [nĭt′ ĭng nē′ dəl] **101** 25

knuckle [nŭk′ əl] **4** 22
koala [kō ŏl′ ə] **66** 1
label [lā′ bəl] **46** 21
lacrosse [lə krös′] **92**
lacrosse stick [lə krös′ stĭk′] **92** 16
ladder [lăd′ ər] **42** 1, **82** 8
ladybug [lā′ dē bŭg′] **63** 14
lamb [lăm] **10** 13, **67** 24
lamp [lămp] **28** 28
lampshade [lămp′ shād′] **28** 27
landing gear [lăn′ dĭng gĭr′] **57** 15
lane [lān] **94** 4
lantern [lăn′ tərn] **88** 29
lapel [lə pĕl′] **20** 1
Laptev Sea [lăp′ tĕv sē′] **70** 33
last quarter [lăst′ kwör′ tər] **74** 25
launchpad [lönch′ păd′] **75** 15
laundry [lön′ drē] **35** 28
laundry basket [lön′ drē băs′ kət] **35** 29
laundry detergent [lön′ drē də tür′ jənt]
   35 25
lawn mower [lön′ mō′ ər] **27** 12
lead guitarist [lēd′ gĭ tär′ ĭst] **99** 25
leaf [lēf] **60** 36a
leave [lēv] **77** 13
left fielder [lĕft′ fēl′ dər] **93** 1
left guard [lĕft′ gärd′] **93** 26
left lane [lĕft′ lān′] **53** 5
left tackle [lĕft′ tăk′ əl] **93** 25
leg [lĕg] **4** 17, **10** 14, **11** 20
(legal) pad [lē′ gəl păd′] **83** 26
lemon [lĕm′ ən] **8** 9
Lena River [lē′ nə rĭv′ ər] **71** 66
length [lĕngth] **79** 36
lens [lĕnz] **100** 6
leopard [lĕp′ ərd] **68** 1
letter [lĕt′ ər] **46** 7
letter carrier [lĕt′ər kăr′ yər] **46** 3
lettuce [lĕt′ əs] **6** 6
level [lĕv′ əl] **82** 3
librarian [lī brĕr′ ē ən] **47** 23
library card [lī′ brĕr ē kärd′] **47** 3
library clerk [lī′ brĕr ē klürk′] **47** 1
license plate [lī′ səns plāt′] **50** 28
lid [lĭd] **30** 9
life jacket [līf′ jăk′ ət] **59** 1
life preserver [līf′ prə zür′ vər] **90** 9
lifeboat [līf′ bōt′] **58** 19, **90** 10

lifeguard [līf′ gärd′] **90** 6

lifeguard chair [līf′ gärd chër′] **90** 8

light (v) [līt] **17** 13

light (adj) [līt] **24** 9

light switch [līt′ swĭch′] **32** 25

lightbulb [līt′ bŭlb′] **35** 22

lighter [lī′ tər] **16** 30

lighthouse [līt′ hows′] **58** 14

lily [lĭl′ ē] **60** 3

lima bean(s) [lī′ mə bēn(z)′] **6** 16

lime [līm] **8** 10

line [līn] **58** 25

lines [līnz] **79**

linesman [līnz′ mən] **82** 17

lion [lī′ ən] **68** 3

lip [lĭp] **4** 43

lipstick [lĭp′ stĭk′] **23** 29

liquor (bottle) [lĭk′ ər bŏt′ əl] **16** 22

listen [lĭs′ ən] **77** 6

little finger [lĭt′ əl fĭng′ gər] **4** 28

little league baseball [lĭt′ əl lēg bās′ böl]
   92

Little Leaguer [lĭt′ əl lēg′ ər] **92** 8

little toe [lĭt′ əl tō′] **5** 55

liver [lĭv′ ər] **5** 65

livestock [līv′ stŏk′] **81** 12

living quarters [lĭv′ ĭng kwör′ tərz]
   75 11

living room [lĭv′ ĭng rōōm′] **28**

lizard [lĭz′ ərd] **65** 15

llama [lŏm′ ə] **66** 15

loaf [lōf] **12** 7

loafer [lō′ fər] **21** 42

lobby [lŏb′ ē] **44** 2

lobster [lŏb′ stər] **10** 30, **62** 13

lock [lŏk] **52** 13

locker [lŏk′ ər] **76** 6

locksmith [lŏk′ smĭth′] **85** 4

log [lög] **28** 10

long [löng] **24** 2

long johns [löng′ jŏnz′] **22** 7

long sleeve [löng′ slēv′] **20** 15

loose [lōōs] **24** 4

(loose-leaf) paper [lōōs′ lēf pā′ pər]
   76 13

loudspeaker [lowd′ spē′ kər] **76** 3

Louisiana [lōō ē′ zē ăn′ ə] **72** 18

lounge chair [lownj′ chër′] **27** 24

low [lō] **24** 12

lunar eclipse [lōō′ nər ĭ klĭps′] **74** 6

lunar module [lōō′ nər mŏj′ ōōl] **75** 7

lunch box [lŭnch′ bŏks′] **20** 31

lunch truck [lŭnch′ trŭk′] **49** 8

lung [lŭng] **5** 63

machine gun [mə shēn′ gŭn′] **48** 25

magazine [măg′ ə zēn′] **47** 16

magnet [măg′ nət] **78** 27

magnifying glass [măg′ nə fĭ ĭng glăs′]
   78 15

magnolia [măg nōl′ yə] **61** 29

mail [māl] **46** 2

mail slot [māl′ slŏt′] **46** 13

mail truck [māl′ trŭk′] **46** 5

mailbag [māl′ băg′] **46** 4

mailbox [māl′ bŏks′] **46** 1

Maine [mān] **72** 19

maintenance [mān′ tə nəns] **95**

make (the bed) [māk′ dhə bĕd′] **38** 8

makeup [māk′ ŭp′] **23**

mallet [măl′ ĭt] **36** 11

mammals [măm′ əlz] **66-69**

man [măn] **2** 2

manager [măn′ ĭ jər] **83** 18

mandolin [măn′ də lĭn′] **98** 4

mane [mān] **66** 21a

mango [măng′ gō] **8** 5

manhole [măn′ hōl′] **45** 32

mantel [măn′ təl] **28** 7

mantis [măn′ tĭs] **63** 7

manual transmission
   [măn′ yōō əl trănz mĭsh′ ən] **50**

map [măp] **70**

maple [mā′ pəl] **61** 38

marigold [măr′ ə gōld′] **60** 6

marine [mə rēn′] **48** 18

Marines [mə rēnz′] **48** 17

Mars [märz] **74** 14

Maryland [mër′ ə lənd] **72** 20

mascara [mă skăr′ ə] **23** 28

mashed potatoes [măsht′ pə tā tōz]
   18 17

mask [măsk] **91** 35

Massachusetts [măs′ ə chōō′ sĭts]
   72 21

mast [măst] **59** 8

mat [măt] **50** 22

matches [măch′ əz] **16** 28

material [mə tïr′ ē əl] **101** 4

math [măth] **79**

mattress [mă′ trəs] **32** 17

measurement [mĕzh′ ər mənt] **79**

meat [mēt] **10**

meatballs [mēt′ bölz′] **18** 11

mechanic [mə kăn′ ĭk] **84** 2

media [mē′ dē ə] **86**

medical care [mĕd′ ə kəl kër′] **39**

medicine [mĕd′ ə sən] **41**

medicine chest [mĕd′ ə sən chĕst′]
   34 14

medicine dropper [mĕd′ ə sən drŏp′ ər]
   78 26

Mediterranean Sea
   [mĕd′ ĭ tə rā′ nē ən sē′] **70** 24

melon [mĕl′ ən] **9** 35

menu [mĕn′ yōō] **16** 7

Mercury [mür′ kyə rē] **74** 11

merry-go-round [mër′ ē gō rownd′]
   87 5

message pad [mĕs′ ĭj păd′] **83** 25

messenger [mĕs′ ən jər] **86** 19

metal detector [mĕt′ əl də tĕk′ tər]
   56 10

meteor [mē′ tē ər] **74** 5

meter [mē′ tər] **55** 23

mezzanine [mĕz′ ə nēn′] **99** 13

Michigan [mĭsh′ ə gən] **72** 22

microfilm [mī′ krə fĭlm′] **47** 13

microfilm reader [mī′ krə fĭlm rē′ dər]
   47 14

microscope [mī′ krə skōp′] **78** 30

microwave oven [mī′ krə wāv ŭv′ ən]
   30 23

middle finger [mĭd′ əl fĭng′ gər] **4** 26

milk [mĭlk] **14** 5

Minicam™ [mĭn′ ē kăm′] **100** 2

Minnesota [mĭn′ ə sō′ tə] **72** 23

mirror [mïr′ ər] **32** 5

Mississippi [mĭs′ ə sĭp′ ē] **72** 24

Mississippi River [mĭs′ ə sĭp′ ē rĭv′ ər]
   71 58

Missouri [mĭ zōōr′ ē] **73** 25

mitt [mĭt] **27** 20

mittens [mĭt′ ənz] **19** 11

mixed vegetables [mĭkst′ věj′ tə bəlz]
    18 16

mixing bowl [mĭk′ sĭng bōl′] **30** 24

mobile [mō′ bēl] **33** 2

model [mŏd′ əl] **86** 5

Mojave Desert [mō hŏv′ ē děz′ ərt]
    71 48

money [mŭn′ ē] **12**

money order [mŭn′ ē ör′ dər] **46** 18

monitor [mŏn′ ə tər] **100** 32

monkey [mŭng′ ke] **69** 14

monkey wrench [mŭng′ kē rěnch′]
    36 12

monorail [mŏn′ ə rāl′] **55** 29

Montana [mŏn tăn′ ə] **73** 26

Moon [mōōn] **74** 9

mooring [mŏŏr′ ĭng] **59** 19

moose [mōōs] **67** 35

mop [mŏp] **35** 6

(mop) refill [mŏp′ rē′ fĭl] **35** 11

mortar [mör′ tər] **48** 28

mosquito [mə skē′ tō] **63** 13

motel [mō těl′] **90** 3

moth [mŏth] **63** 21

mother [mŭdh′ ər] **3** 4

motor oil [mōt′ ər oyl′] **80** 33

motor scooter [mōt′ ər skōō′ tər] **52** 29

motorboat [mōt′ ər bōt′] **59** 13

motorcycle [mōt′ ər sī′ kəl] **52** 30,
    53 19

mountain [mown′ tən] **89** 19

mountain climbing [mown′ tən klīm′ ĭng]
    89

mountain ranges [mown′ tən rān′ jəz] **71**

mouse [mows] **66** 9

mousetrap [mows′ trăp′] **35** 32

mouth [mowth] **4** 2

mover [mōō′ vər] **49** 12

movie camera [mōō′ vē kăm′ ə rə]
    100 15

moving van [mōō′ vĭng văn′] **49** 11

mow [mō] **26** 6

mum [mŭm] **60** 4

muscle [mŭs′ əl] **5** 62

mushroom(s) [mŭsh′ rōōm(z)] **7** 30

music [myōō′ zĭk] **99**

musical comedy
    [myōō′ zə kəl kŏm′ ə dē] **99**

musical instruments
    [myōō′ zə kəl ĭn′ strə mənts] **98**

musician [myōō zĭsh′ ən] **99** 10

mussel(s) [mŭs′ əl(z)] **11** 34, **62** 3

mustache [mŭs′ tăsh] **4** 40

mustard [mŭs′ tərd] **18** 1

nail [nāl] **37** 41

nail clippers [nāl klĭp′ ərz] **23** 31

nail polish [nāl′ pŏl′ ĭsh] **23** 25

nailbrush [nāl′ brŭsh′] **34** 20

napkin [năp′ kĭn] **29** 14

natural gas [năch′ ər əl găs′] **80** 29

Navy [nā′ vē] **48** 13

Nebraska [nə brăs′ kə] **73** 27

neck [něk] **4** 4

necklace [něk′ lĭs] **23** 6

nectarine [něk′ tə rēn′] **8** 17

needle [nē′ dəl] **39** 26, **60** 34a, **101** 18

needlecrafts [nē′ dəl krăfts′] **101**

needlepoint [nē′ dəl poynt′] **101** 26

neighborhood parks
    [nā′ bər hŏŏd pärks′] **87**

nephew [něf′ yōō] **3** 13

Neptune [něp′ tōōn] **74** 18

nest [něst] **64** 31

net [nět] **92** 23

Nevada [nə văd′ ə] **73** 28

new [nōō] **24** 13

New Hampshire [nōō′ hămp′ shər]
    72 29

New Jersey [nōō′ jür′ ze] **73** 30

New Mexico [nōō′ měk′ sə kō] **73** 31

new moon [nōō′ mōōn′] **74** 26

New York [nōō′ yörk′] **73** 32

newscaster [nōōz′ kăs′ tər] **86** 2

newspaper [nōōz′ pā′ pər] **21** 48

newsstand [nōōz′ stănd′] **45** 30

next to [někst′ tōō] **102** 11

nickel [nĭk′ əl] **13** 28

niece [nēs] **3** 14

Niger River [nī′ jər rĭv′ ər] **71** 61

night table [nīt′ tā′ bəl] **32** 27

nightgown [nīt′ gown′] **22** 21

nightstick [nīt′ stĭk′] **43** 9

Nile River [nīl′ rĭv′ ər] **71** 63

nipple [nĭp′ əl] **33** 18

north [nörth] **71** 71

North America [nörth′ ə měr′ ə kə]
    70 1

North Atlantic [nörth′ ăt lăn′ tĭk] **70** 11

North Carolina [nörth′ kăr ə lī′ nə]
    73 33

North Dakota [nörth′ də kō′ tə] **73** 34

North Pacific [nörth′ pə sĭf′ ĭk] **70** 9

North Sea [nörth′ sē′] **70** 21

nose [nōz] **4** 36, **57** 8

nostril [nŏs′ trĭl] **4** 37

nozzle [nŏz′ əl] **42** 17

nuclear reactor [nōō′ klē ər rē ăk′ tər]
    80 13

nurse [nürs] **39** 19

nut [nŭt] **37** 39

nuts [nŭts] **9**

oak [ōk] **61** 33

oar [ör] **59** 22

oarlock [ör′ lŏk′] **59** 21

oats [ōts] **60** 23

Ob River [ŏb′ rĭv′ ər] **71** 64

oboe [ō′ bō] **98** 15

obtuse angle [ŏb tōōs′ ăng′ gəl] **79** 5

occupations [ŏk′ yə pā′ shənz] **84-86**

ocean liner [ō′ shən lī′ nər] **58** 27

oceans [ō′ shənz] **70**

octopus [ŏk′ tə pəs] **62** 6

office [ö′ fĭs] **83**

office building [ö′ fĭs bĭl′ dĭng] **44** 1

officer [ö′ fĭ sər] **86** 13

Ohio [ō hī′ ō] **73** 35

oil [oyl] **38** 12

oil well [oyl′ wĕl′] **80** 1

ointment [oynt′ mənt] **41** 9

Oklahoma [ō′ klə hō′ mə] **73** 36

old [ōld] **24** 14

on [ŏn] **102** 5

on top of [ŏn tŏp′ əv] **102** 10

onion(s) [ŭn′ yən(z)] **7** 31

open [ō′ pən] **24** 15, **31** 3

optician [ŏp tĭsh′ ən] **84** 9

oral hygienist [ör′ əl hī jē′ nĭst] **39** 14

orange [ör′ ĭnj] **8** 8

orangutan [ə răng′ ə tăn′] **69** 18

orbit [ör′ bĭt] **74** 21

orchard [ör′ chərd] **81** 1

orchestra [ör′ kə strə] **99** 6

orchestra seating [ör′ kə strə sēt′ ĭng]
   99 12
orchid [ör′ kĭd] **60** 12
order [ör′ dər] **17** 5
Oregon [ör′ ə gən] **73** 37
organ [ör′ gən] **98** 29
ostrich [ŏs′ trĭch] **64** 12
otter [ŏt′ ər] **68** 10
out of [owt′ əv] **103** 7
outboard motor [owt′ börd mō′ tər]
   59 12
outer space [owt′ər spās′] **74**
outlet [owt′ lət] **36** 6
oval [ō′ vəl] **79** 18
oven [ŭv′ ən] **30** 32
over [ō′ vər] **103** 8
overalls [ō′ vər ölz′] **21** 30
overcoat [ō′ vər kōt′] **19** 20
overhead projector
   [ō′ vər hĕd prə jĕk′ tər] **76** 27
overpass [ō′ vər păs′] **53** 3
owl [owl] **64** 6
oyster(s) [oy′ stər(z)] **11** 33, **62** 2
pacifier [păs′ ə fī′ ər] **33** 22
pack [păk] **13** 16
package [păk′ ĭj] **12** 4, **46** 19
pad [păd] **83** 26
paddle [păd′ əl] **59** 3, **94** 18
pail [pāl] **90** 16
paint (v) [pānt] **26** 1
paint (n) [pānt] **37** 31
paintbrush [pānt′ brŭsh′] **37** 30
Painted Desert [pān′ təd dez′ ərt] **71** 49
painter [pān′ tər] **85** 7
painting [pān′ tĭng] **28** 5
(pair of) scissors [për′ əv sĭz′ ərz]
   101 17
pajamas [pə jŏm′ əz] **22** 19
palm [pŏm] **4** 29, **61** 26
pan [păn] **37** 28
pancakes [păn′ kāks′] **18** 5
pancreas [pang′ krē əs] **5** 71
panda [păn də] **69** 20
panel truck [păn′ əl trŭk′] **49** 9
pansy [păn′ zē] **60** 2
panties [păn′ tēz] **22** 11
pants [pănts] **21** 27
pantyhose [păn′ tē hōz′] **22** 5

papaya [pə pī′ yə] **8** 6
paper [pā′ pər] **76** 13
paper clips [pā′ pər klĭps′] **83** 28
paper towels [pā′ pər tow′əlz] **35** 23
parachute [păr′ ə shoot′] **48** 6
parakeet [păr′ ə kēt] **64** 15
parallel lines [păr′ə lĕl līnz′] **79** 4
paramedic [păr′ ə mĕd′ ĭk] **42** 7
Parana River [păr′ ə nŏ′ rĭv′ ər] **71** 60
parents [păr′ ənts] **2** 6
park [pärk] **87**
park ranger [pärk′ rān′ jər] **88** 5
parka [pär′ kə] **19** 8
parking lights [pär′ kĭng līts′] **51** 49
parking garage [pär′ kĭng gə rŏj′]
   45 19
parking meter [pär′ kĭng mē′ tər]
   45 20
parrot [păr′ ət] **64** 16
part [pärt] **4** 31
pass [păs] **96** 5
passenger [păs′ ĭn jər] **55** 25
passenger car [păs′ ĭn jər kär′] **53** 15
pasture [păs′ chər] **81** 6
patient [pā ′shənt] **39** 20
patio [păt′ ē ō′] **27** 17
pattern [păt′ ərn] **101** 7
pattern piece [păt′ ərn pēs′] **101** 6
paw [pö] **69** 29a
pay [pā] **17** 7
pea(s) [pē(z)] **6** 17
peach [pēch] **9** 37
peacock [pē′ kŏk′] **64** 18
peak [pēk] **89** 20
peanut(s) [pē′ nŭt(s)′] **9** 28
pear [për] **8** 18
pedal [pĕd′ əl] **39** 18, **52** 19
pedestrian [pə dĕs′ trē ən] **44** 12
peel (n) [pēl] **9** 20a
peel (v) [pēl] **31** 5
pegboard [pĕg′ börd′] **36** 15
pelican [pĕl′ ə kən] **64** 24
pencil [pĕn′ səl] **76** 24
pencil eraser [pĕn′ səl ə rā′ sər] **76** 21
pencil sharpener
   [pĕn′ səl shär′ pə nər] **76** 20, **83** 30
Pennsylvania [pĕn səl vān′ yə] **73** 38
penny [pĕn′ ē] **13** 27

penguin [pĕn′ gwĭn] **64** 27
people [pē′ pəl] **2**
pepper shaker [pĕp′ ər shā′ kər] **29** 9
pepper(s) [pĕp′ ər(z)] **7** 22
percussion [pər kŭsh′ ən] **98**
perfume [pür′ fyoom] **23** 27
periodicals section
   [pïr′ ē ŏd′ ə kəlz sĕk′ shən] **47** 15
periscope [pĕr′ə skōp′] **48** 8
perpendicular lines
   [pür′ pən dĭk′ yə lər līnz′] **79** 2
Persian Gulf [pür′ zhən gŭlf ′] **70** 28
personal computer (PC)
   [pür′ sə nəl kŭm pyoo′ tər]/
   [pē′ sē′] **100** 31
personnel [pür′ sə nĕl′] **48**
petal [pĕt′ əl] **60** 18b
petri dish [pĕt′ rē dĭsh′] **78** 3
petunia [pə toon′ yə] **60** 7
pharmacist [fär′ mə sĭst] **84** 1
phases of the moon
   [fā′ zəz əv dhə moon′] **74**
pheasant [fĕz′ ənt] **64** 19
Phillips screwdriver
   [fĭl′ ĭps skroo′ drī vər] **37** 25
phone [fōn] **32** 26
photocopier [fō′ tə kŏp′ ē ər] **83** 24
photocopy machine
   [fō tə kŏp ē mə shēn′] **47** 18
photographer [fə tŏg′ rə fər] **86** 4
photography [fə tŏg′ rə fē] **100**
piano [pē ăn′ ō] **98** 1
piccolo [pĭk′ ə lō′] **98** 12
pick (v) [pĭk] **26** 7
pick (n) [pĭk] **98** 11a
pickup truck [pĭk′ ŭp trŭk′] **49** 4
pickax [pĭk′ ăks′] **82** 13
pickle [pĭk′ əl] **18** 8
picnic area [pĭk′nĭk ër′ ē ə] **88**
picnic basket [pĭk′ nĭk băs′ kət] **88** 13
picnic table [pĭk′ nĭk tā′ bəl] **88** 15
piece [pēs] **12** 22
pier [pïr] **58** 3
pierced earring [pïrst′ ïr′ ĭng] **23** 16
pigeon [pĭj′ ən] **64** 1
pill [pĭl] **41** 7
pillow [pĭl′ ō] **32** 16
pillowcase [pĭl′ ō kās′] **32** 15

pilot [pī′lət] **56** 15

pin [pĭn] **23** 8, **94** 5, **101** 20

pincushion [pĭn′kŏŏsh′ən] **101** 3

pine [pīn] **60** 34

pineapple [pīn′ăp′əl] **8** 4

ping-pong [pĭng′pŏng′] **94**

ping-pong ball [pĭng′pŏng bŏl′] **94** 19

pinking shears [pĭng′kĭng shïrz′] **101** 5

pipe [pīp] **16** 26, **35** 18

pipette [pī pĕt′] **78** 14

pit [pĭt] **8** 37a

pitcher [pĭch′ər] **29** 4, **93** 12

pitcher's mound [pĭch′ərz mownd′] **93** 11

pitchfork [pĭch′förk′] **81** 14

pizza [pēt′sə] **18** 30

plaid [plăd] **24** 22

plane [plān] **57** 18

planets [plăn′əts] **74**

plant (v) [plănt] **26** 4

plants (n) [plănts] **60**

plate [plāt] **29** 13

plateau [plă tō′] **88** 1

platform [plăt′förm′] **54** 11

playground [plā′grownd′] **87** 15

playpen [plā′pĕn′] **33** 30

pleasure boating [plĕzh′ər bō′tĭng] **59**

pliers [plī′ərz] **36** 19

plug [plŭg] **37** 43d

plum [plŭm] **9** 34

plumber [plŭm′ər] **85** 1

plunger [plŭn′jər] **35** 14

Pluto [plōō′tō] **74** 19

pocket [pŏk′ət] **21** 41

pod [pŏd] **6** 17a

podium [pō′dē əm] **99** 7

poinsettia [poyn sĕt′ē ə] **60** 15

poison ivy [poy′zən ī′vē] **61** 45

poison oak [poy′zən ōk′] **61** 43

poison sumac [poy′zən sōō′măk] **61** 44

poisonous plants [poy′zə nəs plănts′] **61**

polar bear [pōl′ər bër′] **69** 22

pole [pōl] **94** 34, **95** 14

police officer [pə lēs′ öf′ə sər] **43** 6

police station [pə lēs′ stā′ shən] **43**

polish [pŏl′ĭsh] **38** 3

polka dot [pō′kə dŏt′] **24** 19

pond [pŏnd] **87** 8

pony [pō′nē] **67** 20

poplar [pŏp′lər] **61** 30

porch [pörch] **27** 6

porcupine [pör′kyə pīn′] **66** 11

pork [pörk] **10** 6

pork chops [pörk′chŏps′] **18** 15

port [pört] **58**

porter [pör′tər] **56** 5

porthole [pört′hōl′] **58** 21

post [pōst] **23** 18

post office [pōst′öf′ĭs] **44** 9, **46**

postal worker [pōs′təl wür′kər] **46** 14

postcard [pōst′kärd′] **46** 17

postmark [pōst′märk′] **46** 9

pot [pŏt] **30** 13

pot holder [pŏt′hōl′dər] **30** 34

potato chips [pə tā′tō chĭps′] **18** 4

potato(es) [pə tā′tō(z)] **7** 23

potty [pŏt′ē] **33** 33

pouch [powch] **66** 3c

pouched mammals [powcht′măm′əlz] **66**

poultry [pōl′trē] **10**

pour [pör] **31** 4

power lines [pow′ər līnz′] **80** 24

power sander [pow′ər săn′dər] **37** 26

power saw [pow′ər sö′] **27** 25

power station [pow′ər stā′shən] **80** 20

prepositions [prep′ə zĭ′shənz] **102**, **103**

primates [prī′māts] **69**

print [prĭnt] **24** 21

printer [prĭn′tər] **83** 4

printout [prĭnt′owt′] **83** 8

prints [prĭnts] **100** 11

prism [prĭz′əm] **78** 1

private jet [prī′vət jĕt′] **57** 3

produce [prŏd′ōōs] **14** 9

programs [prō′grămz] **99** 17

projector [prə jĕk′tər] **100** 16

propane gas [prō′pān găs′] **80** 30

propeller plane [prə pĕl′ər plān′] **57** 7

prosecuting attorney [prŏ′sə kyōō tĭng ə tür′nē] **43** 17

prune [prōōn] **9** 22

public library [pŭb′lĭk lī′brër ē] **47**

public transportation [pŭb′lĭk trăns pər tā′shən] **54**

public telephone [pŭb′lĭk tĕl′ə fōn] **44** 7

puck [pŭk] **92** 17

pump [pŭmp] **13** 14, **52** 21

pumpkin [pŭmp′kĭn] **7** 26

punishment [pŭn′ĭsh mənt] **43**

pupil [pyōō′pəl] **5** 48

puppy [pŭp′ē] **69** 27

purse [pürs] **20** 23

push [pŏŏsh] **26** 12

putter [pŭt′ər] **94** 9

puzzle [pŭz′əl] **33** 31

pyramid [pïr′ə mĭd′] **79** 25

quantities [kwŏn′tə tēz] **12**

quarter [kwör′tər] **11** 18, **13** 30, **79** 31

quarterback [kwör′tər băk′] **93** 32

quill [kwĭl] **66** 11a

quilting [kwĭl′tĭng] **101** 32

rabbit [răb′ĭt] **66** 13

raccoon [ră kōōn′] **68** 7

race track [rās′trăk′] **95**

(racing) handlebars [rā′sĭng hăn′dəl bärz] **52** 2

rack [răk] **47** 17, **78** 8

racket [răk′ĭt] **94** 2

racquet [răk′ĭt] **94** 29

racquetball [răk′ĭt böl′] **94** 30

radiator [rā′dē āt′ər] **51** 56

radio [rā′dē ō′] **50** 18

radish(es) [răd′ĭsh (əz)] **7** 29

radius [rā′dē əs] **79** 14

raft [răft] **89** 16

rafters [răf′tərz] **82** 1

rafting [răf′tĭng] **89**

rags [răgz] **35** 4

rain boots [rān′bōōts′] **19** 25

raincoat [rān′kōt′] **21** 38

rainy [rān′ē] **25** 1

raise (one's hand) [rāz′ wŭnz hănd′] **77** 1

raisin(s) [rā′zən(z)] **9** 24

rake (v) [rāk] **26** 10

rake (n) [rāk] **27** 30

ranch [rănch] **81**

ranch house [rănch′ hows′] **27**

ranching [rănch′ ĭng] **81**

rapids [răp′ ĭdz] **89** 17

rash [răsh] **40** 1

raspberries [răz′ běr′ ēz] **8** 16

rat [răt] **66** 7

rattle [răt′ əl] **33** 21

rattlesnake [răt′ əl snāk′] **65** 10

razor [rā′ zər] **23** 20

razor blades [rā′ zər blādz′] **23** 23

read [rēd] **77** 4

real estate agent [rēl′ ə stāt ā′ jənt] **85** 5

rear bumper [rïr′ bŭm′ pər] **50** 42

rearview mirror [rïr′ vyōo mïr′ ər] **50** 7

receipt [rə sēt′] **15** 20, **55** 24

receiver [rə sē′ vər] **100** 21

receptionist [rə sĕp′ shə nəst] **86** 17

recliner [rə klī′ nər] **28** 16

records [rĕk′ ərdz] **100** 23

rectangle [rĕk′ tăng′ gəl] **79** 19

Red Sea [rĕd′ sē′] **70** 29

redwood [rĕd′ wŏŏd′] **61** 25

(reel of) film [rēl′ əv fĭlm′] **100** 17

referee [rĕf′ ə rē′] **93** 22, **94** 16

reference section [rĕf′ ə rəns sĕk′ shən] **47** 21

(reference) librarian [rĕf′ ə rəns lī brër′ e ən] **47** 23

refill [rē′ fĭl′] **35** 11

refinery [rə fī′ nə rē] **80** 12

reflector [rə flĕk′ tər] **52** 25

refreshment stand [rə frĕsh′ mənt stănd′] **90** 2

refrigerator [rə frĭj′ ə rā′ tər] **30** 19

reins [rānz] **94** 22

relationshops [rə lā′ shən shĭps′] **2**

remedies [rĕm′ ə dēz] **41**

remote control [rə mōt′ kən trōl′] **28** 17

repair [rə për′] **38** 10

repairperson [rə për′ pür′ sən] **84** 5

reporter [rə pör′ tər] **86** 11

reptiles [rĕp′ tīlz] **65**

rescue [rĕs′ kyōo] **42**

restaurant [rĕs′ tə rənt] **16**

retriever [rə trē′ vər] **69** 26

return address [rə türn′ ă drĕs′] **46** 8

rhinoceros [rī nŏs′ ə rəs] **66** 16

Rhode Island [rōd′ ī′ lənd] **73** 39

rice [rīs] **60** 21

ride [rīd] **97** 13

rider [rī′ dər] **54** 6

rifle [rī′ fəl] **48** 21

right angle [rīt′ ăng′ gəl] **79** 23

right fielder [rīt′ fēl′ dər] **93** 3

right guard [rīt′ gärd′] **93** 28

right lane [rīt′ lān′] **53** 7

right tackle [rīt′ tăk′ əl] **93** 29

right triangle [rīt′ trī′ ăng gəl] **79** 22

rind [rīnd] **8** 8b

ring(s) [rĭng(z)] **23** 2, **74** 16a, **94** 17

ring binder [rĭng′ bīn′ dər] **76** 14

ring finger [rĭng′ fĭng′ gər] **4** 27

ring stand [rĭng′ stănd′] **78** 19

rink [rĭngk] **94** 25

Rio Grande River [rē′ ō grănd′ rĭv′ ər] **71** 57

rivers [riv′ ərz] **71**

road sign [rōd′ sīn′] **53** 23

road work [rōd′ würk′] **82**

roadrunner [rōd′ rŭn′ ər] **64** 32

roast [rōst] **10** 3, **10** 8

roasting pan [rōs′ tĭng păn′] **30** 17

robes [rōbz] **43** 11

robin [rŏb′ in] **64** 9

rock group [rŏk′ grōop′] **99**

rocket [rŏk′ ət] **75** 13

rocks [rŏks] **88** 11

rocking chair [rŏk′ ĭng chër′] **33** 16

Rocky Mountains [rŏk′ ē mown′ tənz] **71** 40

rodents [rō′ dənts] **66**

roll [rōl] **12** 11, **18** 19

(roll of) film [rōl′ əv fĭlm′] **100** 10

roller [rōl′ ər] **37** 29

rolling pin [rōl′ ĭng pĭn′] **30** 25

rolodex [rōl′ ə dĕks′] **83** 14

rooster [rōo′ stər] **64** 21

roof [rōof] **27** 4

root [rōot] **60** 35d

rope [rōp] **89** 23

rose [rōz] **60** 18

rotor [rō′ tər] **57** 2a

rough [rŭf] **95** 6

router [row′ tər] **37** 37

row [rō] **47** 11, **81** 18

rowboat [rō′ bōt′] **59** 23

Rub′ al Khali Desert [rōob′ ăl kŏl′ ē dĕz′ ərt] **71** 52

rubber tubing [rŭb′ ər tōob′ ĭng] **78** 18

rudder [rŭd′ ər] **59** 5

rug [rŭg] **32** 28

ruler [rōo′ lər] **76** 23

run [rŭn] **96** 6

rung [rŭng] **82** 9

runner [rŭn′ ər] **91** 23, **94** 31

runway [rŭn′ wā′] **57** 19

saddle [săd′ əl] **94** 20

safety glasses [săf′ tē glăs′ əz] **78** 12

safety goggles [săf′ tē gŏg′ əlz] **94** 28

safety pin [săf′ tē pĭn′] **33** 11

Sahara Desert [sə hër′ ə dĕz′ ərt] **71** 51

sail [sāl] **59** 9

sailboard [sāl′ börd′] **59** 15

sailboat [sāl′ bōt′] **59** 4

sailor [sāl′ ər] **48** 14

salad bowl [săl′ əd bōl′] **29** 25

salad dressing [săl′ əd drĕs′ ĭng] **18** 12

salamander [săl′ ə măn′ dər] **65** 14

salesperson [sālz′ pür′ sən] **86** 12

salt shaker [sölt′ shā′ kər] **29** 10

sand (v) [sănd] **26** 14

sand (n) [sănd] **90** 31

sand dunes [sănd′ dōonz′] **90** 12

sand trap [sănd′ trăp′] **95** 11

sandal [săn′ dəl] **20** 19

sandbox [sănd′ bŏks′] **87** 13

sandcastle [sănd′ kăs′ əl] **91** 32

sandpaper [sănd′ pā′ pər] **37** 27

sandwich [sănd′ wĭch] **16** 16

sanitation worker [săn ə tā′ shən wür′ kər] **49** 7

Saturn [săt′ ərn] **74** 16

saucepan [sös′ păn′] **30** 8

saucer [sö′ sər] **29** 21

sausage [sö′ sĭj] **10** 7

saw [sö] **36** 8

saxophone [săk′ sə fōn′] **98** 24

scaffolding [skăf′ əl dĭng] **82** 7

scale [skāl] **14** 7, **34** 32, **78** 4

scallop(s) [skăl′ əp(s)] **11** 35, **62** 10

scarecrow [skër′ krō′] **81** 19

scarf [skärf] **19** 19

scenery [sē′ nə rē] **99** 2

school [skool] **76, 77**

science lab [sī′ əns lăb′] **78**

scissors [sĭz′ərz] **101** 17

scoreboard [skör′ börd′] **93** 19

scorpion [skör′ pē ən] **63** 8

scouring pad [skowr′ ĭng păd′] **30** 11

scrape [skrāp] **26** 15

scraper [skrāp′ ər] **36** 14

screen [skrēn] **27** 19, **100** 14

screw [skroo] **37** 42

screwdriver [skroo′ drī′ vər] **37** 24

scrub [skrŭb] **38** 2

scuba tank [skoo′ bə tăngk′] **91** 37

sea gull [sē′ gŭl′] **64** 4

sea horse [sē′ hörs′] **65** 1

Sea of Japan [sē′ əv jə păn′] **70** 36

Sea of Okhotsk [sē′ əv ō kötsk′]
    70 35

seafood [sē′ food′] **10**

seal [sēl] **68** 12

seam [sēm] **101** 10

seas [sēz] **70**

seat [sēt] **52** 16, **54** 2

seat belt [sēt′ bĕlt] **50** 23

second baseman [sĕk′ ənd bās′ mən]
    93 7

secretary [sĕk′ rə tër′ ē] **83** 11

section [sĕk′ shən] **8** 8a, **79** 15

security [sə kyoor′ ə tē] **56**

security guard [sə kyoor′ ə tē gärd′]
    56 9, **86** 14

sedan [sə dăn′] **51**

seed [sēd] **8** 8c

seesaw [sē′ sö′] **87** 18

serve [sürv] **17** 3, **96** 2

service area [sür′ vəs ër′ ē ə] **53** 11

sevice court [sür′ vəs kört′] **95** 1

service line [sür′ vəs līn′] **95** 3

set (the table) [sĕt′ dhə tā′ bəl] **17** 8

sewing [sō′ ĭng] **101**

sewing machine [sō′ ĭng mə shēn′]
    101 1

shade [shād] **33** 1

shaft [shăft] **80** 10

shampoo [shăm poo′] **34** 8

shank [shăngk] **36** 43b

shark [shärk] **65** 5

shaving cream [shā′ vĭng krēm′] **23** 22

sheep [shēp] **67** 25, **81** 10

sheet [shēt] **32** 19

sheet music [shēt′ myoo′ zĭk] **98** 2

shelf [shĕlf] **14** 6, **47** 26

shell [shĕl] **48** 27, **62** 1a, **65** 18a,
    90 40

shellfish [shĕl′ fĭsh′] **11**

shepherd [shĕp′ ərd] **69** 28

shingle [shĭng′ gəl] **82** 2

ship [shĭp] **58** 9

shirt [shürt] **21** 46

shock absorbers [shŏk′ əb zör′ bərz]
    52 31

shoe [shoo] **21** 49

shoelace [shoo′ lās′] **20** 7

shoot [shoot] **97** 16

shop worker [shŏp′ wür′ kər] **85** 12

shopping bag [shŏp′ ĭng băg′] **20** 18

shopping basket [shŏp′ ĭng băs′ kət]
    14 8

shopping cart [shŏp′ ĭng kärt′] **15** 19

short [shört] **24** 1

short sleeve [shört′ slēv′] **20** 21

shorts [shörts] **20** 14

shortstop [shört′ stŏp′] **93** 5

shoulder [shōl′ dər] **4** 5, **53** 22

(shoulder) bag [shōl′ dər băg′] **21** 35

shovel (n) [shŭv′ əl] **27** 31, **82** 15,
    90 17

shovel (v) [shŭv′ əl] **26** 13

shower cap [show′ ər kăp′] **34** 3

shower curtain [show′ ər kür′ tən] **34** 5

shower head [show′ ər hĕd′] **34** 4

shrimp [shrĭmp] **11** 31, **62** 8

shutter [shŭt′ ər] **27** 8

shuttle car [shŭt′ əl kär′] **80** 8

side [sīd] **79** 10

side mirror [sīd′ mïr′ ər] **50** 2

sideburn [sīd′ bürn′] **4** 33

sidewalk [sīd′ wök′] **45** 25

Sierra Madre [sē ër′ ə mö′ drē] **71** 42

silo [sī′ lō] **81** 4

silverware [sĭl′ vər wër′] **29** 22

simple animals [sĭm′ pəl ăn′ ə məlz] **62**

singer [sĭng′ ər] **99** 24

sink [sĭngk] **34** 19

sister [sĭs′ tər] **3** 10

sister-in-law [sĭs′ tər ən lö′] **3** 8

six-pack [sĭks′ păk′] **13** 13

skate (n) [skāt] **94** 26

skate (v) [skāt] **97** 9

skein [skān] **101** 24

ski [skē] **95** 17

ski boot [skē′ boot′] **95** 15

ski cap [skē′ kăp′] **19** 16

ski lift [skē′ lĭft′] **95** 18

ski slope [skē′ slōp′] **95**

skier [skē′ ər] **94** 35

skis [skēz] **94** 33

skin [skĭn] **9** 37b

skirt [skürt] **21** 36

skunk [skŭngk] **68** 8

slacks [slăks] **20** 4

sleeping bag [slē′ pĭng băg′] **89** 26

sleepwear [slēp′ wër′] **22**

slice (n) [slīs] **13** 21

slice (v) [slīs] **31** 10

slide [slīd] **78** 31, **87** 12

slide projector [slīd′ prə jĕk′ tər]
    100 13

slides [slīdz] **100** 12

sling [slĭng] **39** 3

splippers [slĭp′ ərz] **22** 18

slug [slŭg] **62** 4

small [smöl] **24** 7

smoke [smōk] **42** 15

smoke detector [smōk′ də tĕk′ tər]
    33 15

smokestack [smök′ stăk′] **58** 18,
    80 22

snacks [snăks] **14** 18

snail [snāl] **62** 1

snake [snāk] **65** 9

snap [snăp] **101** 13

sneakers [snē′ kərz] **20** 11

snorkel [snör′ kəl] **91** 34

snow plow [snō′ plow′] **49** 5

snowy [snō′ e] **25** 3

soap [sōp] **34** 15

soap dish [sōp′ dĭsh′] **34** 6

soccer [sŏk′ ər] **92**

soccer ball [sŏk′ ər böl′] **92** 26

socks [sŏks] **22** 17

sofa [sō**′** fə] **28** 25

soft drink [söft**′** drĭngk**′**] **16** 11

softball [söft**′** böl**′**] **92, 92** 10

solar collector [sō**′** lər kə lĕk**′** tər] **80** 17

solar eclipse [sō**′** lər ĭ klĭps**′**] **74** 10

solar system [sō**′** lər sĭs**′** təm] **74**

soldier [sōl**′** jər] **48** 16

sole [sōl] **20** 6

solid [sŏl**′** əd] **24** 20

solid figures [sŏl**′** əd fĭg**′** yərz] **79**

son [sŭn] **3** 16

Sony Walkman [sō**′** nē wök**′** mən] **100** 30

sore throat [sör**′** thrōt**′**] **40** 12

south [sowth] **71** 72

South America [sowth**′** ə mër**′** ə kə] **70** 2

South Atlantic [sowth**′** ăt lăn**′** tək] **70** 12

South Carolina [sowth**′** kăr ə lī**′** nə] **73** 40

South China Sea [sowth**′** chi**′** nə sē**′**] **70** 39

South Dakota [sowth**′** də kō**′** tə] **73** 41

South Pacific [sowth pə sĭf**′** ək] **70** 10

space probe [spās**′** prōb] **75** 4

space program [spās**′** prō**′** grăm] **75**

space shuttle [spās**′** shŭt**′** əl] **75** 14

space station [spās**′** stā**′**_shən] **75** 1

space suit [spās**′** sōot**′**] **75** 6

spacecraft [spās**′** krăft**′**] **75**

spaghetti [spə gĕt**′** ē] **18** 10

spaniel [spăn**′** yəl] **69** 24

spare ribs [spër**′** rĭbz**′**] **10** 10

spare tire [spër**′** tīr**′**] **51** 39

sparrow [spăr**′** ō] **64** 10

spatula [spăch**′**ə lə] **27** 21

speaker [spē**′** kər] **28** 21, **100** 24

speed limit sign [spēd**′** lĭm ət sīn**′**] **53** 8

speedometer [spə dŏm**′**ə tər] **50** 10

spider [spī**′** dər] **63** 16

spinach [spĭn**′** əch] **6** 8

spinal cord [spī**′** nəl körd**′**] **5** 58

spiral notebook [spī**′** rəl nōt**′** bŏok] **76** 15

split [splĭt] **11** 17

split end [splĭt**′** ĕnd**′**] **93** 24

spoke [spōk] **52** 26

sponge [spŭnj] **34** 7

(sponge) mop [spŭnj**′** mŏp**′**] **35** 6

(spool of) thread [spōol**′** əv thrĕd**′**] **101** 2

spoon [spōon] **29** 8

sports car [spörts**′** kär**′**] **53** 17

sports [spörts] **92-97**

spotlight [spŏt**′** līt**′**] **99** 4

sprain [sprān] **40** 13

spray can [sprā**′** kăn**′**] **13** 24

spray starch [sprā**′** stärch**′**] **35** 21

spread [sprĕd] **17** 11

Spring [sprĭng] **26**

sprinkler [sprĭng**′** klər] **27** 13, **87** 14

sprocket [sprŏk**′** ət] **52** 20

square [skwër] **79** 9

squid [skwĭd] **62** 5

squirrel [skwür**′** əl] **66** 10

stage [stāj] **99** 5

staircase [stër**′** kās] **28** 12

stake [stāk] **89** 30

stamp [stămp] **46** 10

stands [stăndz] **93** 10

staple remover [stāp**′** əl rə moo**′** vər] **83** 29

stapler [stāp**′** lər] **83** 27

star [stär] **74** 4

starfish [stär**′** fĭsh**′**] **62** 7

starting gate [stär**′** tĭng gāt**′**] **95** 20

station [stā**′** shən] **55** 18

station wagon [stā**′** shən wăg**′** ən] **50**

steak [stāk] **10** 5, **11** 29, **18** 21

steam [stēm] **31** 12

steamer [stēm**′** ər] **30** 3

steering wheel [stĭr**′** ĭng wēl**′**] **50** 8

stem [stĕm] **8** 2a, **60** 1a

step [stĕp] **28** 13

stepladder [stĕp**′** lăd**′** ər] **35** 1

stereo cassette player [stër**′** ē ō kə sĕt plā**′** ər] **100** 25

stereo system [stër**′** ē ō sĭs**′** təm] **28** 20

stern [stürn] **58** 11

stethoscope [stĕth**′** ə skōp**′**] **39** 9

stewing meat [stoo**′** ĭng mēt] **10** 4

stick [stĭk] **12** 5

stick shift [stĭk**′** shĭft**′**] **50** 24

sting [stĭng] **63** 8a

stingray [stĭng**′** rā**′**] **65** 6

stir [stür] **31** 1

stitch [stĭch] **101** 19

stitches [stĭch**′** əz] **39** 21

stockings [stŏk**′** ĭngz] **22** 6

stomach [stŭm**′** ək] **5** 66

stomachache [stŭm**′** ək āk**′**] **40** 7

stool [stōol] **78** 34

stopper [stŏp**′** ər] **34** 10, **78** 10

stork [störk] **64** 30

stove [stōv] **30** 30

straight line [strāt**′** līn**′**] **79** 1

(strand of) beads [strănd**′** əv bēdz**′**] **23** 7

strap [străp] **54** 8

straw [strö] **16** 10

strawberry [strö**′** bër**′** ē] **8** 15

strawberry shortcake [strö**′** bër ē shört**′** kāk] **18** 26

stream [strēm] **88** 6

street [strēt] **45** 31

street cleaner [strēt**′** klē**′** nər] **49** 1

street sign [strēt**′** sīn**′**] **44** 8

streetcar [strēt**′** kär**′**] **55** 30

streetlight [strēt**′** līt**′**] **45** 29

stretch [strĕch] **95** 19

stretch bandage [strĕch**′** băn**′** dĭj] **40** 13a

stretcher [strĕch**′** ər] **39** 12

stretchie [strĕch**′** ē] **33** 19

string [strĭng] **46** 20, **98** 10a

string bean(s) [strĭng**′** bēn(z)**′**] **6** 15

strings [strĭngz] **98**

striped [strīpt] **24** 17

stroller [strō**′** lər] **33** 14

student [stōo**′** dənt] **76** 19

stuffed animal [stŭft**′** ăn ə məl] **33** 27

subject [sŭb**′** jəkt] **47** 10

submarine [sŭb**′** mə rēn**′**] **48** 7

subway [sŭb**′** wā**′**] **54**

subway station [sŭb**′** wā stā**′** shən] **44** 16

sugar (packet) [shōog**′** ər păk**′** ət] **16** 13

sugar bowl [shōog**′** ər bōl**′**] **29** 23

sugarcane [shōog**′** ər kān**′**] **60** 20

suitcase [sōot**′** kās**′**] **56** 7

Summer [sŭm**′** ər] **26**

sun [sŭn] **74** 7, **80** 3
sunbather [sŭn′ bā′ dhər] **90** 19
sundae [sŭn′ dē] **18** 23
sunflower [sŭn′ flŏw′ ər] **60** 19
sunglasses [sŭn′ glăs′ əz] **90** 14
sunny [sŭn′ ē] **25** 4
(sunnyside-up) egg
    [sŭn′ ē sīd ŭp′ ĕg′] **18** 32
sunroof [sŭn′ rōōf′] **51** 44
suntan lotion [sŭn′ tăn lō′ shən] **91** 39
supermarket [sōō′ pər mär′ kət] **14**
surf [sürf] **97** 12
surfboard [sürf′ börd′] **91** 25
surgery [sŭr′ jə rē] **41** 2
suspect [sŭs′ pĕkt] **43** 3
swan [swŏn] **64** 28
sweatband [swĕt′ bănd′] **20** 12
sweater [swĕt′ ər] **19** 7, **19** 13, **19** 23
sweatpants [swĕt′ pănts′] **20** 10
sweatshirt [swĕt′ shürt′] **20** 8
sweep [swēp] **38** 7
swimmer [swĭm′ ər] **91** 28
swing [swĭng] **33** 24
swings [swĭngz] **87** 16
switch [swĭch] **37** 43c
switchboard [swĭch′ börd′] **83** 3
switchboard operator
    [swĭch′ börd ŏp′ ə rā tər] **83** 1
swordfish [sörd′ fĭsh′] **65** 3
synthesizer [sĭn′ thə sī′ zər] **99** 21
syringe [sə rĭnj′] **39** 27
syrup [sĭr′ əp] **18** 6
T-shirt [tē′ shürt′] **21** 29
table [tā′ bəl] **29** 7
tablecloth [tā′ bəl klöth′] **29** 16
tablet [tăb′ lət] **41** 6
taco [tŏ′ kō] **18** 24
tadpole [tăd′ pōl′] **65** 16
tail [tāl] **57** 10, **65** 3a, **66** 3a
taillight [tāl′ līt′] **50** 31
tailor [tā′ lər] **84** 6
take [tāk] **17** 10
takeoff [tāk′ ŏf′] **57**
Takla Makan Desert
    [tŏk′ lə mə kŏn′ dĕz′ ərt] **71** 53
tambourine [tăm′ bə rēn′] **98** 17
tank [tăngk] **48** 10
tank top [tăngk′ tŏp′] **20** 13

tanker [tăngk′ ər] **58** 15
tap [tăp] **16** 20
tape [tāp] **46** 22
tape measure [tāp′ mĕzh′ ər] **36** 21,
    101 15
taxi [tăk′ sē] **55**
taxi stand [tăk′ sē stănd′] **55** 28
taxicab [tăk′ sē kăb′] **55** 27
tea [tē] **16** 15
teacher [tē′ chər] **76** 4
teakettle [tē′ kĕt′ əl] **30** 28
team sports [tēm′ spörts′] **92**
teapot [tē′ pŏt′] **29** 19
tear [tër] **77** 9
teddy bear [tĕd′ ē bër′] **33** 3
tee [tē] **95** 13
telephone [tĕl′ ə fōn′] **83** 15
telescope [tĕl′ ə skōp′] **74** 22
television [tĕl′ ə vĭzh′ ən] **28** 18, **100** 5
teller [tĕl′ ər] **86** 15
temperature [tĕm′ pər ə chər] **25** 6
Tennessee [tĕn′ ə sē′] **73** 42
tennis [tĕn′ əs] **94**
tennis ball [tĕn′ əs böl′] **94** 1
tennis court [tĕn′ əs kört′] **95**
tent [tĕnt] **89** 24
tentacle [tĕn′ tə kəl] **62** 12a
terminal [türm′ ə nəl] **51** 55, **58** 29
terminal building [türm′ ə nəl bĭl′ dĭng]
    57 16
termite [tür′ mīt] **63** 11
terrier [tĕr′ ē ər] **69** 25
test tube [tĕst′ tōōb′] **78** 9
Texas [tĕk′ səs] **73** 43
textbook [tĕkst′ bŏŏk′] **76** 26
theater [thē′ ə tər] **99**
thermometer
    [thər möm′ ə tər] **25** 5, **78** 22
thermos [thür′ məs] **88** 14
thigh [thī] **4** 18, **11** 19
thimble [thĭm′ bəl] **101** 21
third (1/3) [thürd] **79** 32
third baseman [thürd′ bās′ mən] **93** 4
thorn [thörn] **60** 18c
thread [thrĕd] **37** 42b, **101** 2
three-piece suit [thrē′ pēs sōōt] **21** 40
throat [thrōt] **5** 59
through [thrōō] **103** 1

throw [thrō] **97** 10
thumb [thŭm] **4** 24
thumbtack [thŭm′ tăk′] **76** 25
ticket [tĭk′ ət] **55** 16, **56** 4
ticket window [tĭk′ ət wĭn′ dō] **55** 19
tie (n) [tī] **21** 47
tie (v) [tī] **77** 12
tie clip [tī′ klĭp′] **23** 14
tie pin [tī′ pĭn′] **23** 13
tiger [tī′ gər] **68** 2
tight [tīt] **24** 3
tighten [tī′ tən] **38** 4
tight end [tīt′ ĕnd′] **93** 30
tights [tīts] **19** 14
tile [tīl] **34** 27
timer [tī′ mər] **78** 13
timetable [tīm′ tă′ bəl] **55** 20
tip [tĭp] **55** 22
tire [tīr] **50** 37, **52** 28
tissues [tĭsh′ ōōz] **32** 13
title [tī′ təl] **47** 9
to [tōō] **103** 9
toast [tōst] **18** 34
toaster [tōs′ tər] **30** 16
toe [tō] **5** 54
toenail [tō′ nāl′] **5** 56
toilet [toy′ lət] **34** 29
toilet brush [toy′ lət brŭsh′] **34** 31
toilet paper [toy′ lət pā′ pər] **34** 30
toiletries [toy′ lə trēz] **23**
token booth [tō′ kən bōōth′] **54** 13
tollbooth [tōl′ bōōth′] **53** 27
tomato(es) [tə mā′ tō(z)] **6** 19
tongs [tŏngz] **78** 29
tongue [tŭng] **4** 41
tongue depressor [tŭng′ də prĕs′ ər]
    40 12a
toolbox [tōōl′ bŏks′] **36** 23
toolshed [tōōl′ shĕd′] **27** 28
tooth [tōōth] **4** 42
toothache [tōōth′ āk′] **40** 9
toothbrush [tōōth′ brŭsh′] **34** 21
toothless mammals [tōōth′ ləs măm′ əlz]
    66
toothpaste [tōōth′ pāst′] **34** 16
tortoise [tör′ təs] **65** 18
tossed salad [töst′ săl′ əd] **18** 13
touch [tŭch] **77** 2

touring handlebars
  [tŏŏr/ ĭng hăn/ dəl bärz] **52** 12
tow truck [tō/ trŭk] **49** 2
toward [törd] **103** 4
towel rack [tow/ əl răk/] **34** 25
towrope [tō/ rōp/] **59** 11
toy chest [toy/ chĕst/] **33** 29
track [trăk] **54** 10, **94** 32
track and field [trăk/ ənd fēld/] **94**
tractor [trăk/ tər] **81** 15
tractor trailer [trăk/ tər trā/ lər] **49** 15
traffic cop [trăf/ ək kŏp/] **44** 10
traffic light [trăf/ ək līt/] **45** 21
trailer [trā/ lər] **53** 10
train [trān] **55**
training wheels [trān/ ĭng wēlz/] **52** 1
transcript [trăn/ skrĭpt] **43** 15
transfer [trăns/ fər] **54** 4
transformer [trăns för/ mər] **80** 25
transmission towers
  [trănz mĭsh/ ən tow/ ərz] **80** 23
transportation [trăns/ pər tā/ shən] **54**
transporter [trăns/ pör tər] **49** 17
trash basket [trăsh/ băs/ kət] **44** 15
trash can [trăsh/ kăn/] **87** 11
travel agent [trăv/ əl ā/ jənt] **84** 4
traveler [trăv/ ə lər] **56** 3
tray [trā] **16** 33
tray table [trā/ tā/ bəl] **56** 22
treatments [trēt/ mənts] **41**
tree [trē] **61** 35
trees [trēz] **60**
triangle [trī/ ăng/ gəl] **79** 6
tricycle [trī/ sĭ kəl] **52** 6
trigger [trĭg/ ər] **48** 22
tripod [trī/ pod] **100** 9
trim [trĭm] **26** 8
trombone [trŏm bōn/] **98** 23
trough [trŏf] **81** 25
trout [trowt] **65** 2
trowel [trow/ əl] **27** 27
truck [trŭk] **49**, **53** 25
truck driver [trŭk/ drī/ vər] **49** 16
trumpet [trŭm/ pət] **98** 25
trunk [trŭngk] **51** 40, **61** 35b, **66** 17a
tub [tŭb] **12** 6
tuba [tōō/ bə] **98** 27
tube [tōōb] **13** 15, **91** 29

tugboat [tŭg/ bōt/] **58** 13
tulip [tōō/ ləp] **60** 1
turkey [tür/ kē] **10** 23, **64** 20
turnip [tür/ nəp] **6** 34
turn signal lever [türn/ sĭg nəl lĕ/ vər]
  50 11
turn signal lights [türn/ sĭg nəl līts/]
  51 50
turnstile [türn/ stīl/] **54** 12
turntable [türn/ tā/ bəl] **100** 18
turtle [tür/ təl] **65** 12
(turtleneck) sweater
  [tür/ təl nĕk swĕ/ tər] **19** 13
tusk [tŭsk] **66** 17b
TV antenna [tē/ vē ăn tĕn/ ə] **27** 3
tweezers [twē/ zərz] **78** 32
twig [twĭg] **61** 33a
(two-door) sedan [tōō/ dör sə dăn/] **51**
type [tīp] **77** 10
typewriter [tīp/ rī/ tər] **83** 10
typing chair [tī/ pĭng chër/] **83** 17
typist [tī/ pəst] **83** 6
U.S. mailbox [yōō/ ĕs māl/ bŏks] **46** 6
U.S. Postal System
  [yōō/ ĕs pōs/ təl sĭs təm] **46**
ukulele [yōō/ kə lā/ lē] **98** 3
umbrella [ŭm brĕl/ ə] **20** 24
umpire [ŭm/ pīr] **92** 1, **93** 17
uncle [ŭng/ kəl] **3** 3
under [ŭn/ dər] **102** 8
underpants [ŭn/ dər pănts/] **22** 3
undershirt [ŭn/ dər shürt/] **22** 1
underwear [ŭn/ dər wër/] **22**
uniform [yōō/ nə förm/] **21** 45, **92** 9
United States of America
  [yōō nī/ təd stāts/ əv əmër/ ə kə] **72**
universe [yōō/ nə vürs/] **74**
up [ŭp] **103** 11
upper arm [ŭp/ ər ärm/] **4** 7
Urals [yōōr/ əlz] **71** 46
uranium rods [yōō rā/ nē əm rŏdz/]
  80 15
Uranus [yōōr/ ə nəs] **74** 17
usher [ŭsh/ ər] **99** 16
Utah [yōō/ tö] **73** 44
utility pole [yōō tĭl/ ə tē pōl/] **80** 26
utility room [yōō tĭl/ ə tē rōōm] **35**

(V-neck) sweater [vē/ nĕk swĕt/ ər]
  19 23
vacuum [văk/ yōōm] **38** 14
vacuum cleaner [văk/ yōōm klē/ nər]
  35 16
valve [vălv] **52** 27
van [văn] **53** 26
vase [vās] **28** 6
VCR (videocassette recorder)
  [vē/ sē är/]/
  [vĭd/ ē ō kə sĕt/ rə kör/ dər] **100** 4
vegetables [vĕj/ tə bəlz] **6**
vehicles and equipment
  [vē/ ə kəlz ənd ə kwĭp/ mənt] **48**
vein [vān] **5** 68
vendor [vĕn/ dər] **87** 3
vent [vĕnt] **50** 21
Venus [vē/ nəs] **74** 12
verbs [vürbz] **17**, **26**, **31**, **38**, **77**, **96**
Vermont [vür mŏnt/] **73** 45
vest [vĕst] **21** 39
video [vĭd/ē ō] **100**
video camera [vīd/ ē ō kăm/ ə rə]
  100 1
videocassette (tape)
  [vĭd/ ē ō kə sĕt/ tāp/] **100** 3
vine [vīn] **61** 42
viola [vē ōl/ə] **98** 8
violet [vī/ ə lət] **60** 16
violin [vī ə lĭn/] **98** 7
Virginia [vər jĭn/ yə] **73** 46
vise [vīs] **37** 36
visor [vĭz/ ər] **50** 5
volleyball [vŏl/ ē böl/] **92**, **92** 22
waders [wā/ dərz] **88** 10
waist [wāst] **4** 13
waiter [wā tər] **16** 5
waitress [wā/ trəs] **16** 2
walk [wök] **77** 8
walker [wök/ ər] **33** 23
wall [wöl] **28** 3
wall unit [wöl/ yōō/ nət] **28** 19
wall-to-wall carpeting
  [wöl/ tə wöl kär/ pə tĭng] **28** 15
wallet [wöl/ ət] **20** 9
walnut(s) [wöl/ nət(s)] **8** 29
walrus [wöl/ rŭs] **68** 11
warm [wörm] **25** 8

wash [wŏsh] **38** 16

washcloth [wŏsh′klöth′] **34** 22

washer [wŏsh′ər] **37** 40

washing machine
  [wŏsh′ĭng mə shēn′] **35** 30

Washington [wŏsh′ ĭng tən] **73** 47

wasp [wŏsp] **63** 20

wastepaper basket
  [wāst′ pā pər băs′ kət] **34** 13

watch [wŏch] **23** 10

watchband [wŏch′bănd′] **23** 11

water (n) [wŏt′ ər] **42** 16, **91** 30

water (v) [wŏt′ ər] **26** 5

water fountain [wŏt′ ər fown′ tən]
  87 19

water glass [wŏt′ ər glăs′] **29** 6

waterfall [wŏt′ər föl] **80** 11, **89** 18

water-skier [wŏt′ər skē′ ər] **59** 10

watercress [wŏt′ər krĕs′] **6** 5

watering can [wŏt′ər ĭng kăn′] **27** 16

watermelon [wŏt′ər mĕl′ ən] **9** 26

wave [wāv] **91** 24

weapon [wĕp′ənz] **48**

weather [wĕdh′ər] **25**

weather forecaster
  [wĕdh′ər för′ kăst ər] **86** 1

weather satellite [wĕdh′ər săt′ ə līt]
  75 3

weaving [wē′ vĭng] **101** 30

web [wĕb] **63** 15

wedding ring [wĕd′ĭng rĭng′] **23** 4

weights [wāts] **78** 5

west [wĕst] **71** 74

West Virginia [wĕst′ vər jĭn′ yə] **73** 48

wet [wĕt] **25** 15

wet suit [wĕt′ soot′] **91** 38

whale [wāl] **68** 9

wheat [wēt] **60** 22

wheat farm [wēt′ färm′] **81**

(wheat) field [wēt′ fēld′] **81** 16

wheel [wēl] **52** 4

wheelbarrow [wēl′ băr′ ō] **27** 32,
  82 23

wheelchair [wēl′ chër′] **39** 2

whistle [wĭs′ əl] **90** 5

whole [hōl] **11** 27, **79** 29

whole (chicken) [hōl′ chĭk′ ən] **11** 16

width [wĭdth] **79** 35

wife [wīf] **2** 4

willow [wĭl′ ō] **61** 31

wind [wĭnd] **80** 4

windbreaker [wĭnd′ brā′ kər] **19** 5

windlass [wĭnd′ ləs] **58** 23

windmill [wĭnd′ mĭl′] **80** 19

window [wĭn′ dō] **27** 7, **46** 15

window cleaner [wĭn′ dō klē′ nər]
  35 10

windpipe [wĭnd′ pīp′] **5** 60

windshield [wĭnd′ shēld′] **51** 45

windshield wiper [wĭnd′ shēld wī′ pər]
  50 6

windsurfer [wĭnd′ sür′ fər] **59** 14

windy [wĭn′ dē] **25** 13

wine [wīn] **16** 19

wine glass [wīn′ glăs′] **29** 5

wing [wĭng] **11** 22, **57** 9, **63** 4a,
  64 1a

Winter [wĭn′ tər] **26**

wipe [wīp] **38** 5

wire [wīr] **37** 35

wire mesh screen [wīr′ mĕsh skrēn′]
  78 6

Wisconsin [wĭs kŏn′ sən] **73** 49

witness [wĭt′ nəs] **43** 13

witness stand [wĭt′ nəs stănd′] **43** 18

wolf [woolf] **69** 29

woman [woom′ən] **2** 1

wood [wood] **36** 4

wood plane [wood′ plān′] **37** 32

woodpecker [wood′ pĕk′ ər] **64** 17

woods [woodz] **89** 32

woodwinds [wood′ wĭndz′] **98**

wool [wool] **101** 23

word processor [würd′ prŏ′ sĕs ər]
  83 7

work gloves [würk′ glŭvz′] **27** 26

workbench [würk′ bĕnch′] **36** 22

workshop [würk′ shŏp′] **36**

world [würld] **70**

worm [würm] **62** 11

wrench [rĕnch] **36** 10

wrist [rĭst] **4** 21

write [rīt] **77** 7

writer [rī′ tər] **86** 7

Wyoming [wī ō′ mĭng] **73** 50

X ray [ĕks′ rā′] **39** 1

X ray screener [ĕks′ rā skrē′ nər] **56** 11

xylophone [zī′ lə fōn′] **98** 31

yam [yăm] **7** 24

Yangtze River [yăng′ sē rĭv′ ər] **71** 69

yarn [yärn] **101** 31

Yellow Sea [yĕl′ ō sē′] **70** 37

Yenisey River [yĕn′ ə sā′ rĭv′ ər]
  71 65

Yukon River [yoo′ kŏn rĭv′ ər] **71** 56

zebra [zē′ brə] **66** 18

zinnia [zĭn′ ē ə] **60** 13

zip code [zĭp′ kōd′] **46** 12

zipper [zĭp′ ər] **101** 16

zoo [zoo] **87** 1

zucchini [zoo kē′ nē] **7** 27

アーカンソー州 72 4

アースつきプラグ 36 7

アーム 100 20

アーモンド 9 31

アイオワ州 72 15

アイシャドー 23 30

アイス：クリームコーン 18 35; スケ
　　ート 94; ボックス 91 41;
　　ホッケー 92

アイダホ州 72 12

アイライン入れ 23 33

アイロン 35 12; 台 35 13;
　　を掛ける 38 11

間に／で 102 4

青 104; 痣 40 17; 懸巣 64 8; 写真
　　82 6; 虫 63 1; 物屋 84 7; 焼き 82
　　6

赤 104 ; 鱒／鯥 65 6; 子／児 2 5; 杉
　　61 25;なす［茄子］ 7 19; 帽 56 5;
　　ん坊 2 5

明かりを点ける／ 灯 す 17 13

秋 26

アクセル 50 27

悪路用自転車 52 8

開ける 31 3

挙げる 77 1

揚げる 31 15

顎：(全体) 4 38; 先 4 3; 鬚 4 39

アコーデ(ィ)オン 98 28

あざらし［海豹］ 68 12

足 5E, 69 29a; 板 32 24; 親指 5
　　53; 小指 5 55; の甲 5 51; の爪 5
　　56; 場(組)み 82 7; 鰭 91 36; の
　　拇指 5 53; の拇指球 5 52; 指 5 54

脚 4 17; 肉 10 14, 11 20

アジア大陸 70 5

あしか［海驢］ 68 12

アスパラガス 6 18

遊び場 87 15

暖かい 25 8

アタカマ砂漠 71 50

頭 37 42a;板 32 14; 受け／支え 50
　　35

新しい 24 13

暑い 25 7

厚：板 82 16; 皮 8 8b; 切り 10 9, 10

15, 11 29; (手の)カーテン 28 23

宛先 46 11

後脚／後足 66 3b

穴を掘る 26 3

兄 3 9

姉 3 10

アパート 45 23

アパラチア山脈 71 41

あひる［家鴨］ 64 25; の池 87 8; の
　　肉 11 25

アフターシェーブローション 23 21

油を点す 38 12

炙：皿 30 17; 焼用肉 10 3, 10 8

アフリカ大陸 70 4

アボカド 9 33

雨靴 19 25

アマゾン川 71 59

網：戸 27 19; 焼き器 27 22; 焼き炉
　　88 12

編み：棒 101 25; 物 101 22

雨の降る 25 1

アメリカ：合衆国 72; 杉 61 25; 蔦漆
　　61 45; の典型的本通り 84; 篦鹿
　　67 35; 鰐 65 8; 野牛 67 19

アメリカンフットボール 92;
　　競技場 93B

洗熊 68 7

洗う 38 16

アラスカ：州 72 2; 湾 70 17

洗った 24 6

アラバマ州 72 1

アラビア海 70 30

蟻 63 13

ありくい［食蟻獣］ 66 5

アリゾナ州 72 3

歩く 77 8

アルコール 39 22

アルプス山脈 71 44

アルマジロ 66 2

淡い 24 9

杏(子) 9 25

安静 41 1

安全：検査官 56 9; ピン 33 11; 帽
　　21 28, 82 4

アンデス山脈 71 43

案内：係 99 16; 所 47 22

アンパイアー／アンパイヤー 92 1, 93 17

家鼠 66 9

凧　［紙鳶］ 91 22

胎貝 11 34, 62 3

錨 58 24

イグアナ 65 13

育児室 33

イグニッション 50 14

池 87 8

石 88 11

医師／医者 39 11

移植鏝 27 27

椅子 102 9

伊勢えび［海老］ 11 30, 62 13

板：材 82 16; 敷き遊歩道 90 1; (状
　　の)塊 13 18

痛みおよび傷病 40

炒める 31 15

一 104

一月 104 8

苺 ／ 莓 ／ストロベリー 8 15; の
　　ショートケーキ 18 25

いちじく［無花果］ 9 21

一尾 11 27

市松模様の 24 18

(一輪)手押し車 82 23

一塁手 93 8

一羽 11 16

一階正面席 99 12

1セント貨 13 27

一匹 11 27

糸(一巻き) 101 2

移動ベルト 15 23, 56 12

いとこ［従兄弟／従姉妹］ 3 7

犬 69

稲 60 21; 科植物と穀類 60

棘 ／ 荊 ／ 茨 60 18c

衣服に関する表現 24

胃(袋) 5 66

居間 28

妹 3 9

芋虫 63 1

医薬品 41

イヤフォーン型送受話器 83 2

イヤリング 23 1

入口 53 21

索 引

イリノイ州 **72** 13
医療および歯科医療 **39**
射る **97** 16
いるか[海豚] **68** 13
入れ物 **12** 2
色の名称 **104**
岩 **88** 11
隠元(豆) **6** 13
インジアナ州 **72** 14
飲食物販売店 **90** 2
印字機 **83** 4
インド洋 **70** 13
ヴァイオリン **98** 7
ヴィオラ **98** 8
ウイスコンシン州 **73** 49
ウインカー **51** 50
ウインド: サーファー **59** 14; サーフ
　ボード **59** 15; ブレーカー **19** 5
上: に/で **102** 2; に乗って **102** 5
ウエーター **16** 5
ウエーダー **88** 10
ウエートレス **16** 2, **16** 32
ウエスト **4** 13; スリップ **22** 8; バー
　ジニア州 **73** 48
ウエットスーツ **91** 38
植える **26** 4
ウオークマン **100** 30
(魚)釣り **88**
浮き袋 **90** 9
ウクレレ **98** 3
受け具 **23** 19
受け皿 **29** 21
受(け)取(り) **15** 20, **55** 24
受付係 **86** 17
動きを表わす前置詞 **103**
　兎（うさぎ） **66** 13
牛(の群れ) **81** 20
後ろ: 脚/足 **66** 3b; に/で **102** 9
薄い **24** 9
薄: 皮 **9** 37b; 切り **13** 21; にする **31**
　10; (手の)カーテン **32** 10
　鶉豆（うずら） **6** 13
　獺（うそ） **68** 10
打ち: 上げ台 **75** 15; 身 **40** 17
宇宙: 開発 **75**; 空間 **74A**; ステー
　ション **75** 1; 船 **75A**; 探査機 **75**

4; 飛行士 **75** 5; 服 **75** 6
打つ **96** 1
鬱金香（うっこんこう） **60** 1
器 **12** 2
腕 **4** 6; 時計 **23** 10; 輪 **23** 9
鰻（うなぎ） **65** 4
畝/畦（うね　うね） **81** 18
乳母車 **33** 14, **45** 27
馬 **67** 21, **81** 23
海: 亀（がめ） **65** 12; 狸（だぬき） **66** 12;
　辺の光景 **90**
海、湾、入り江 **70**
羽毛 **64** 7a; チョッキ **19** 12
右翼手 **93** 3
ウラニウム棒 **80** 15
裏庭 **27** 10
ウラル山脈 **71** 46
ウラン棒 **80** 15
上着 **21** 33
運送員 **49** 10
運転: 士 **55** 15; する **97** 15
運動靴 **20** 11
運搬車 **49**
絵 **28** 5; 葉書 **46** 17; を描く **77** 11
柄 **8** 2a
エアコン **32** 11
鱏/鱝（えい　えい） **65** 6
映画 **100C**; カメラ/撮影機 **100** 15
鋭角 **79** 8
曳(航)船（えいこうせん） **58** 13
映写機 **100** 16
営繕維持 **85A**
映像録画 **100A**
駅 **55** 18
刳り鉋（えぐ　かんな） **37** 37
枝 **61** 35a; 角（つの） **67** 35a
X線看視装置 **56** 11
閲覧請求票 **47** 12
エニセイ川 **71** 65
エネルギー **80**
エプロン **16** 6
衣紋掛け（えもん） **32** 2
鰓（えら） **65** 3c
襟 **20** 20; 巻き **19** 19
エレキ(ギター) **99** 26
円 **79** 11

エレベーター **45** 17, **80** 9
遠隔装作器 **28** 17
鉛管屋 **85** 1
(円)弧 **79** 16
エンジン **51F**, **52** 32; オイル **80** 33
円周 **79** 17
円錐（すい） **79** 28; 標識 **82** 19
縁石 **45** 26
円柱/円筒 **79** 26
延長コード（えんどう） **36** 5
豌豆 **6** 17
エンドゾーン **93** 23
煙突 **27** 9, **58** 18, **80** 22
燕麦（えんばく） **60** 23
鉛筆 **76** 24; 削り **76** 20, **83** 30
遠洋定期船 **58** 27
尾（おい） **65** 3a, **66** 3a
甥 **3** 13
応援団（お） **93** 20
雄牛/牡牛（お） **67** 34
欧州 **70** 3
横断歩道 **44** 4
鸚鵡（おうむ） **64** 16
大型海ざりがに[蝲蛄] **11** 30, **62** 13
　狼（おおかみ） **69** 29
大きい **24** 8
大皿 **29** 13
オーストラリア大陸 **70** 6
オートバイ **52** 30, **53** 19
オート麦 **60** 23
オーバー **19** 20; ヘッドプロジェク
　ター **76** 27
大鳩（ばと） **64** 1
オーブン **30** 32
オーボエ/オーボー **98** 15
オール **59** 22; 留め **59** 21
小川 **88** 6
悪寒 **40** 4
屋外テラス **27** 17
奥行き **79** 33
オクラホマ州 **73** 36
桶（おけ） **12** 6
おじ[伯父/叔父] **3** 3
押し: 入れ **32** 3; ピン **76** 25
おしゃぶり **33** 22
押す **26** 12

お玉杓子[蝌蚪] **65** 16
落ちる **96** 7
夫 **2** 3, **3** 12
おっとせい[膃肭獣] **68** 12
お抓み **15** 18
おでこ **4** 32
弟 **3** 9
男の子 **2** 8
踊り手 **99** 3
斧 **42** 14
おば[伯母/叔母] **3** 6
オハイオ州 **73** 35
お針 **101A**
オビ川 **71** 64
オフィスビル **44** 1
オホーツク海 **70** 35
おまる[御虎子] **33** 33
おもちゃ[玩具] 箱 **33** 29
錘 **78** 5
お八 **15** 18
親指 **4** 24
泳いでいる人 **91** 28
オランウータン **69** 18
オランダ:芥子 **6** 5; 三葉 **6** 10
織(り):糸 **101** 31; 物 **101** 30
折り:襟 **20** 1; 尺 **36** 1
折り畳み(式):スーツケース **56** 1; テーブル **56** 22; 乳母車 **33** 14
下りて **103** 3
折る **38** 1
オルガン **98** 29
オレゴン州 **73** 37
オレンジ **8** 8
下ろす **31** 2
音楽喜劇 **99B**
音楽、舞踊および観劇 **99**
音響製品 **100D**
温水器 **80** 17
温度 **25** 6; 計 **25** 5, **78** 22
雄鶏 **64** 21
女の子 **2** 9
(温)熱 **80** 27
音盤 **100** 23

蚊 **63** 13
蛾 **63** 21

ガーゼの:包帯 **39** 24; 傷当て **39** 25
カーデガン **21** 26
カーテン **28** 23, **32** 10, **99** 1; リング **34** 2; レール **34** 1
ガーター:蛇 **65** 9; ベルト **22** 14
ガードル **22** 15
カーラジオ **50** 18; アンテナ **51** 46
カウンター **16** 24; 椅子 **16** 25
貝 **91** 40; 殻 **62** 1a, **91** 40; 類と甲殻類 **11D**
櫂 **59**
海王星 **74** 18
絵画 **28** 5
介殻/外殻 **62** 1a, **90** 40
会計伝票 **16** 14
海軍 **48** 13; 兵 **48** 14
外出着 **19**
海水 **91** 30; 着 **90** 18; パンツ **91** 33
介添え人 **39** 8
階段:(の枠) **28** 12; (の)段 **28** 13
懐中電灯 **35** 3
回転:式改札口 **54** 12; 式検索簿 **83** 14; 木馬 **87** 5; 翼 **57** 2a
外套 **19** 20
街灯 **45** 29
飼葉桶 **81** 25
海兵隊 **48** 17; 員 **48** 18
解剖用具 **78** 33
買物:籠 **20** 18; 客 **15** 17; (用手押)車 **15** 19
外洋航路船 **58** 27
海狸 **66** 12
街路 **45** 31; 標識 **44** 8
返し **27** 22; てもらう **17** 10
返す **96** 1
楓 **61** 38
蛙 **65** 17
火炎菜 **7** 33
顔 **4** 1; 拭きタオル **34** 23
画家 **86** 3
かかし[案山子] **81** 19
踵 **5** 50, **20** 5
鏡 **32** 5
かき[牡蠣] **11** 33, **62** 2
かきつばた[杜若/燕子花] **60** 11
鉤:爪 **68** 2a; 針 **101** 29;

ホック **101** 14
垣根 **81** 9
掻き回す **31** 1
家禽肉 **11B**
書く **77** 7
核 **8** 2b, **9** 37a
角錐 **79** 25
拡声器 **76** 3
拡大鏡 **78** 15
楽団員 **99** 10
カクテルラウンジ **16B**
格納庫 **57** 17
攪拌する **31** 8
楽譜 **98** 2
額縁 **28** 4
崖/厓 **89** 21
掛け:鉤 **36** 16; 暦 **83** 9; 時計 **76** 2; 布団 **32** 22
駆け足/駈足をしている人 **91** 23
かけら **7** 25a
陰に/で **102** 9
下弦(の月) **74** 25
囲い **81** 24
傘 **20** 24
火災 **42** 5
下肢 **4** 17
樫 **61** 33
家事 **85B**; 室 **35**; と修繕に関する動作 **38**
火事 **42** 5
舵 **59** 5
梶木[旗魚](鮪) **65** 3
貸し出し:カード **47** 3; 口 **47** 2
果実:酒 **16** 19; 類 **8**
歌手 **99** 24
果樹 **81** 2; 園 **81** 1
カシューナッツ **9** 27
菓子類 **15** 18
槲 **61** 33
数の言い方 **104**
カスピ海 **70** 27
桛/束 **101** 24
風邪 **40** 11
火星 **74** 14
カセット **100** 26; デッキ **100** 22
家政婦 **85** 8

索 引

風の強い **25** 13

河川 **70**

家族の成長 **2**

加速ペダル **50** 27

ガソリン **80** 28; タンク **50** 34; ポンプ **53** 14; メーター **50** 9

肩 **4** 5; 肉 **10** 3, **10** 8

ガター **94** 3

型紙 **101** 6; セット **101** 7

片付ける **17** 6

かたつむり[蝸牛] **62** 1

塊 **12** 5, **12** 7, **13** 18

固め焼き: する **31** 14; 製品 **14** 11

家畜 **81** 12

課長 **83** 18

鷲鳥 **64** 26

楽器 **98**

滑空機 **57** 4

学校での動作 **77**

合唱団/合唱隊 **99** 18

滑走路 **57** 19

カップ **13** 19, **29** 20

家庭用品 **15** 15

角 **44** 3

下等動物 **62**

金: 網 **78** 6; 鎚 **36** 13;　鋸 **36** 18

カナリア/カナリヤ[金糸雀] **64** 14

蟹 **11** 36, **62** 9

カヌー **59** 2

加熱する **17** 4

化膿 **40** 14

河馬 **66** 14

樺 **61** 32

画鋲 **76** 25

花瓶 **28** 6

蕪 [蕪菁] **7** 34

カフカス山脈 **71** 45

カフスボタン **23** 12

カプセル **41** 5

壁 **28** 3

貨幣 **13**

花弁 **60** 18b

かぼちゃ[南瓜] **7** 26

髪(の毛) **4** 30

かまきり **63** 7

鎌倉えび[海老] **11** 30, **62** 13

カミソール **22** 9

かみそり[剃刀] **23** 20; の刃 **23** 23

紙: タオル **35** 23; 箱 **12** 1; 袋 **15** 25; (巻き)莨[煙草] **16** 31; マッチ **16** 28; 焼き **100** 11; 鑢 **37** 27

ガムテープ **46** 22

亀 **65** 12

カメラ **100** 8; マン **86** 10

鴨 **64** 25; 肉 **11** 25

貨物: 運搬車 **53** 25; 室 **57** 12; 自動車 **53** 26; 船 **58** 9; 搬入口 **57** 13; 容器 **58** 7

海鴎 **64** 4

カヤック **59** 17

火曜日 **104**

から **103** 10

カラー **20** 20

カラ海 **70** 31

芥子 **18** 1

烏 / 鴉 **64** 3; 麦 **60** 23

がらがら **33** 21; 蛇 **65** 10

雁/鴈 **64** 26

刈り: 込み 鋏 **27** 29; 込む **26** 8

カリフォルニア州 **72** 5

カリブ海 **70** 20

カリフラワー **6** 1

カルテ **39** 10

鰈 **65** 7

カレンダー **83** 9

乾いた **25** 14

皮 **8** 8b, **9** 20a, **9** 37b; を剥く **31** 5

川: 獺 **68** 10; 下り **89**

雁/鴈 **64** 26

簡易カート **56** 6

眼科医 **84** 9

カンガルー **66** 3

鉗橘類 **8**

観客 **99** 15; 席 **93** 10

缶切り **30** 4

間欠泉/間歇泉 **80** 5

管弦楽団 **99** 6

看護婦/看護士 **39** 19

カンザス州 **72** 16

銅子 **78** 28

ガンジス川 **71** 67

患者 **39** 20

緩衝: 器 **52** 31; 材 **33** 5

勘定書き **16** 14

管制塔 **57** 20

岩石 **88** 11

関節 **4** 22

乾燥: 果実 **9**; 機 **35** 24

肝臓 **5** 65

カンタループメロン **9** 36

寒暖計 **25** 5

缶詰 **12** 10, **14** 13

鉋 **37** 32

監督 **93** 21

甲板 **58** 22

灌木 **61** 41

顔面保護マスク **92** 15

丸薬 **41** 7

甘藍 **6** 3

甘露メロン **9** 35

木苺 **8** 16

キーボード **100** 33; 奏者 **99** 22

黄(色) **104**

気温 **25** 6

幾可図形 **79B**

機械糸鋸 **36** 3

気管 **5** 60

機関: 士 **55** 15; 銃 **48** 25

菊 **60** 4; ぢしゃ[萵苣] **6** 7

聴く **77** 6

器具 **39** 13

義兄 **3** 11

刻む **31** 11

雉(子) **64** 19

義姉 **3** 8

機首 **57** 8

騎手 **94** 21

起重機 **58** 6

徽章 **43** 5

気象衛星 **75** 3

着せ替え台 **33** 9

基礎 **82** 11

北 **71** 71; アメリカ大陸 **70** 1; 大西洋 **70** 11; 太平洋 **70** 9

ギター **98** 11

機体 **57** 14

機長 **56** 15

きつい **24** 3

キック: スタンド **52** 9; する **96** 3
木槌 **36** 11
きつつき[啄木鳥] **64** 17
切手 **46** 10
狐 **68** 6
切符 **55** 16, **56** 4; 売り場 **55** 19
義弟 **3** 11
軌道 **74** 21
機内持ち込み手荷物 **56** 2
ギニア湾 **70** 25
木の実 **9**
牙 **66** 17b
揮発油 **80** 28
ギプス／ギブス **39** 5
ギボン **69** 15
義妹 **3** 8
客室 **56** 19; 乗務員 **56** 20
逆の方向に **103** 5
脚本家 **86** 7
ギヤシフト **50** 17
脚立／脚榻 **35** 1
キャッチャー **92** 2, **93** 16; マスク
　92 3; ミット **92** 4
キャベツ **6** 3
スカンク **68** 8
キャンピングカー **53** 16
キャンプ **89**; ファイヤー **89** 31; 用
　焜炉 **89** 25
九 **104**
吸引棒 **35** 14
球果／毬果 **61** 34b
球技場 **93**
救急車 **42** 6
窮屈な **24** 3
休憩椅子 **27** 24
救護員 **42** 7
球根 **60** 8a
給士 **16** 5; する **17** 3
九十 **104**
救助員 **90** 6
牛: 肉 **10** 1; 乳 **14** 5; 挽肉 **10** 2
臼砲 **48** 28
救命: 具 **90** 9; 胴衣 **59** 1; 艇 **90** 10;
　ボート **58** 19, **90** 10
きゅうり[胡瓜] **7** 20
急流 **89** 17

教員 **76** 4
教科書 **76** 26
競技用トラック **94** 32
教室 **76**
鏡台 **32** 9
響尾蛇 **65** 10
喬木 **61, 60** 35
業務関係者 **86C**
魚貝類 **11C**
曲線 **79** 3
居室 **28**; つきモーターボート **59** 16
居住区 **75** 11
漁船 **58** 1; 員 **58** 2
魚類 **65A**; および爬行動物 **65**
切り: 傷 **40** 16; 揃える **26** 8; 身 **11**
　28; 分ける **31** 6
霧の立籠めた **25** 12
きりん **67** 29
切る **31** 9
キルティング **101** 32
綺麗にする **26** 2
銀河(系) **74** 1
金管楽器 **98**
銀行 **86B**
金星 **74** 12
金盞花 **60** 6
金銭登録機 **15** 21
金属探知機 **56** 10
筋肉 **5** 62
金鳳花[毛茛] **60** 17
銀幕 **100** 14
金曜日 **104**
九 **104**
抗／杙 **89** 30
空気: 入れ **52** 21; 調(製)機 **32** 11;
　フィルター **51** 52; 吹き出し口 **50**
　21; 弁 **52** 27; ポンプ **53** 13; マッ
　ト **91** 26; 濾過器 **51** 52
空軍 **48** 19; 兵 **48** 20
グーズベリー **8** 11
クォーターバック **93** 32
区画 **13** 22, **16** 9
九月 **104**
茎 **60** 1a
釘 **37** 41; 差し盤 **36** 15
矩形 **79** 19

草: 刈りをする **26** 6; 花および
　樹木 **60**
鎖／鏈 **23** 5; 歯車 **52** 20
櫛 **32** 6
孔雀 **64** 18
鯨 **68** 9
屑: 入れ **87** 11; 籠 **44** 15
薬: 屋 **45** 22; 指 **4** 27
下って **103** 3
口 **4** 2; 髭 **4** 40; 風琴 **98** 30; 紅 **23** 30
くちなし[梔子／山梔] **60** 14
喙／嘴 **64** 3a, **64** 24a
唇／脣 **4** 43
靴 **21** 49; 下 **22** 6, **22** 17; 下留めつ
　きベルト **22** 14; 底 **20** 6; 紐 **20** 7
クッキー **18** 22
掘削機／掘鑿機 **89** 4
クッション **28** 24
櫟 **60** 33
首 **4** 4; 飾り **23** 6
熊 **69**; 手 **27** 30; 手を掛ける **26** 10;
　の人形 **33** 3
くも[蜘蛛] **63** 16; の巣 **63** 15
曇った **25** 2
鞍 **94** 20
グライダー **57** 4
クラクション **50** 12
くらげ[水母／海月] **62** 12
グラス **13** 20
クラッチペダル **50** 25
クラブ **95** 5
グラブ **92** 12, **94** 11, **94** 15
グラフ用紙 **78** 11
クラリ(オ)ネット **98** 16
クランプ **78** 7
クランベリー **8** 13
栗 **9** 32
クリーマー **29** 24
クリームサンデー **18** 22
グリーン **95** 10
グリズリー **69** 23
クリップ **83** 28
グリル **27** 22, **88** 12
踝 **5** 49
車椅子 **39** 2
くるみ[胡桃] **9** 29

索 引

周を/に/で **103** 2
グレートサンジー砂漠 **71** 55
グレープフルーツ **8** 7
クレーン **58** 6
黒 **104**; 熊 **69** 21; 猩 猩 **69** 16; 猫 **102** 2; 豆 **6** 14
グローブ **92** 12
クロスカントリースキー **94**
クロセ: 編み **101** 28; 針 **101** 29
クロッカス **60** 9
軍隊 **48**
計器 **56** 14; 盤 **50** 19
渓谷/谿谷 **88** 3
警察: 官 **43** 6; 署 **43A**
計算器 **83** 19, **100** 34
刑事 **43** 2
掲示板 **76** 7
軽食販売車 **49** 8
繋船: 縄 **58** 25; 柱 **58** 26
毛糸 **101** 23
警笛 **50** 12, **52** 5
競馬 **94**; 場 **95D**
警備員 **86** 14
警棒 **43** 9
軽油 **80** 34
経理担当者 **86** 18
繋留場 **59** 19
計量: 器 **14** 7, **78** 25; 棒 **51** 58
ケーキパン **18** 26
ゲート **95** 20
ケーブルカー **55** 32
外科手術 **41** 2
消し: 印 **46** 9; ゴム **76** 21
消す **77** 3
ケチャップ **16** 4
結婚指輪 **23** 4
齧歯動物 **66**
決勝線 **95** 21
月食/月蝕 **74** 6
蜥蜴 **65** 15
月面着陸 **75B**
月曜日 **104**
ケトルドラム **98** 21
毛虫 **63** 1
煙 **42** 15; 感知器 **33** 15
蹴る **96** 3

弦 **98** 10a
牽引車 **49** 2, **81** 15
弦楽器 **98**
玄関番 **85** 11
検鏡板 **78** 31
検査官 **56** 9
剣先いか[烏賊] **62** 5
検索カード **47** 6
検札係 **54** 7
検察官 **43** 17
拳銃 **43** 7; サック **43** 8
原子炉 **80** 13
建設: 業者 **82** 5; 現場 **82A**; 工事 **82**; 作業員 **82** 14
舷窓 **58** 21
ケンタッキー州 **72** 17
建築家 **86** 8
拳闘 **94**
研磨紙 **37** 27
件名 **47** 10
現場監督/主任 **85** 13
鍵盤 **98** 1a
顕微鏡 **78** 30
弧 **79** 16
五 **104**
コアラ **66** 1
濃い **24** 10
子: 犬 **69** 27; 牛 **67** 31; 馬 **67** 22; 鹿 **67** 27; 猫 **68** 5; 羊 **67** 24; 羊肉 **10** 13; 持ち玉菜 **6** 4
コイン売り場 **54** 13
高圧線 **80** 24; 鉄塔 **80** 23
工員 **85** 12
硬貨 **13** 26
黄河 **71** 68
黄海 **70** 37
紅海 **70** 29
光学技師 **84** 9
高架路 **53** 3
交換: 器 **83** 3; 手 **83** 1
紅冠鳥 **64** 11
公共: 図書館 **47**; 輸送 **54**
航空: 機 **57**; 機関士 **56** 17; 機の種類 **57A**; 券 **56** 4; 母艦 **48** 4; (郵便用) 封筒 **46** 16
高血圧 **40** 10

口腔衛生士 **39** 14
虹彩 **5** 47
工作場 **36**
交差点/交叉点 **44** 11
格子縞の **24** 22
豪州 **70** 6
公衆電話器 **44** 7
工場作業 **85C**
高所作業用クレーン **82** 18
香水 **23** 27
恒星 **74** 4
高速道路 **53**
紅茶 **16** 15
甲虫 **63** 10
交通: 巡査 **44** 10; 信号 **45** 21
(公転)軌道 **74** 21
鸛 **64** 30
後部: 座席 **50** 32; バンパー **51** 42
高木 **61,60** 35
こうもり[蝙蝠] **66** 4; 傘 **20** 24
甲羅 **65** 18a
行楽用船舶 **59**
高路交差/高路交叉 **53** 3
港湾施設 **58**
小枝 **61** 33a
越えて **103** 6, **103** 8
小蝦/鰕[海老] **11** 31, **62** 8
ゴーグル **91** 35
コースター **16** 27
コーチ **93** 21
凍った **25** 16
コート **19** 24, **94** 13
コード **32** 26a
コーヒー **18** 34; ポット **29** 18; メーカー **30** 31
ゴール **92** 25; キーパー **92** 24; ポスト **93** 35
(コール天の)ズボン **21** 27
こおろぎ[蟋蟀] **63** 6
小型: いんこ[鸚哥] **64** 15; 貨物乗用車 **49** 4; ジェット機 **57** 3; の馬 **67** 20; (の)猿 **69** 14; (の)陸亀 **65** 12; 飛行船 **57** 5; ビデオ **100** 2; ボート **59** 18; 有蓋車 **49** 9
五月 **104**
小切手 **15** 27

漕ぎ船 **59** 23

ごきぶり［蜚蠊］ **63** 9

黒板 **76** 5; 消し／拭き **76** 11

固形燃料 **27** 23

柿（板） **82** 2

（ココ）椰子 **8** 3, **61** 26

ココナッツ **8** 3

心付け **55** 22

小匙 **29** 8

腰: 掛け **16** 25, **78** 34; （の括れ） **4** 13

濾し: 紙 **78** 16; 器 **30** 7

五色砂漠 **71** 49

個室 **83** 5

五十 **104**

胡椒入れ **29** 9

個人スポーツ **94**

擦る **38** 2

5 セント貨 **13** 28

小太鼓 **98** 19

黒海 **70** 6

国旗 **76** 1

コック **16** 1

コックピット **56** 13

骨折 **40** 15

小槌 **43** 12

小包 **46** 19

コップ **13** 20

鏝 **27** 21

子供: 椅子 **16** 8; たち **2** 7; 用座席 **50** 33

コネチカット州 **72** 7

木端 **82** 2

小箱 **13** 16

コピー機 **47** 18, **83** 24

ゴビ砂漠 **71** 54

五百 **104**

瘤 **67** 33a

コブラ **65** 11

駒 **64** 9

芥: 収集車／蒐集車 **49** 6; 箱 **87** 11; 容器 **35** 31

小麦 **60** 22; 農場 **81B**; 畑／畠 **81** 16

ゴム: ホース／管 **78** 18; 製円盤 **92** 17; ボート **89** 16; マット **50** 22

米 **60** 21

小物入れ **50** 20

小山 **88** 4

小指 **4** 28

コラムシャフト **50** 13

ゴリラ **69** 17

コルク栓 **16** 18; 抜き **16** 17

ゴルフ **94**; カート **95** 8; コース **95B**; バッグ **95** 7; ボール **94** 7; をして いる人 **94** 10

ゴルファー **94** 10

コロニアル様式の家屋 **27B**

転ぶ **96** 7

コロラド州 **72** 6

コロンビア特別区 **73** 51

コンガ **98** 20

コンクリートミキサー **49** 13, **82** 25

コンゴ川 **71** 62

コンセント **32** 26b, **36** 6

昆虫類 **63**

コンテナ **58** 7; 船 **58** 9

コントラバス **98** 10

コンバイン **81** 17

コンパクトディスク **100** 27

コンピューター **100E** ; （の端末） **76** 8, **83** 16

婚約指輪 **23** 3

コンロ **30** 30

サード **93** 4

サービス: エリア **53** 11; コート **95** 1; ライン **95** 3

サーブする **96** 2

サーフボード **91** 25

犀 **66** 16

サイド: テーブル **28** 29, **32** 27; ボード **29** 29; ミラー **50** 2

裁判: 官 **43** 10; 官席 **43** 16; 所 **43B**

財布 **20** 9

裁縫 **101A**

サイホン **16** 20

サイロ **81** 4

サウス: カロライナ州 **73** 40; ダコタ 州 **73** 41

魚 **11** 26

座金 **37** 40

サキソフォン／サキソホン **98** 24

砂丘 **90** 12

作業: 靴 **21** 32; ズボン **21** 30; 台 **36** 22, **78** 24; 手袋 **27** 26

柵 **81** 9, **82** 21

裂く **77** 9

索引カード: 箱 **47** 5; 類 **47** 4

削岩ドリル **82** 22

桜ん坊［桜桃］ **9** 19

酒（瓶） **16** 22

桟敷 **99** 14

刺し子（縫い） **101** 32

差し込み **32** 26b, **36** 6; （式）ネクタイ ピン **23** 13; 式レコード針 **100** 19

差出人住所氏名 **46** 8

差し針 **23** 18

座席 **54** 2

蠍 **63** 8

札入れ **20** 9

撮影: 係 **86** 4; 班 **86** 10

作家 **86** 7

サッカー **92**; ボール **92** 26

雑貨屋 **45** 22

サックス **98** 24

冊子 **13** 17

雑誌 **47** 16

薩摩芋 **7** 24

雑用係 **16** 3

砂糖 **16** 13; 入れ **29** 23; 黍 **60** 20

サドル **52** 16

砂漠／沙漠 **71**

サハラ砂漠 **71** 51

サポーター **22** 4

サボテン［仙人掌／覇王樹］ **61** 40

寒い **25** 10

寒け **40** 4

鮫 **65** 5

莢 **6** 17a; 隠元 **6** 15

鞘長 **62** 5

左翼手 **93** 1

サラダボール **29** 25

猿 **69** 14

砂楼 **91** 32

触る **77** 2

サン: グラス **90** 14; ルーフ **51** 44

三 **104**

三角: 巾 **39** 3; 形 **79** 6

索 引

三月 **104**
三脚 **100** 9
参考図書: 司書 **47** 23; 部 **47** 21
三十 **104**
山椒魚 **65** 14
三色菫 **60** 2
撒水: 器 **27** 13; バケツ[馬穴] **27** 16
酸素ボンベ **91** 37
サンダル **20** 19
山頂 **89** 20
サンド: イッチ **16** 16; ペーパー **37** 27
散髪屋 **84** 3
三分袖 **20** 21
三分の一 **79** 32
山脈 **71**
三輪車 **52** 6
三塁手 **93** 4
四 **104**
椎 **61** 33
Ｃ字形締め具 **36** 2
シーソー **87** 18
シーツ **32** 19; (を)取り替える **38** 13
CD **100** 27; プレーヤー **100** 28
シート **54** 2; ベルト **50** 23
ジープ **48** 9
ジェット: エンジン **57** 11; 機 **57** 18; 燃料 **80** 31
シェパード **69** 28
シェフ **16** 1
シエラマドレ山脈 **71** 42
鹿 **66** 26
歯科医 **39** 17
四月 **104**
直: 火で焼く **31** 13; 焼炉 **30** 33
敷(き): 皿 **16** 27; 布 **32** 19; 物 **32** 28
指揮/指麾: 者 **99** 8; 台 **99** 7; 棒 **99** 9
四季に関する動作 **26**
仕切り席 **16** 9
軸 **8** 2a
舳 **58** 5
(ジグソー)パズル **33** 31
字消し **76** 21
試験管 **78** 9; 立て **78** 8; 挟み **78** 29
時刻表 **55** 20

自在スパナ **36** 12
獅子 **68** 3
磁石 **78** 27
刺繍 **101** 27
四十 **104**
司書 **47** 23
辞書 **47** 24
舌 **4** 41
下着および夜着 **22**
下に／で **102** 3, **102** 8
仕立屋 **84** 6
七 **104**
七月 **104**
七十 **104**
七面鳥 **64** 20; (の肉) **11** 23
シチュー: 鍋 **30** 8; 用肉 **10** 4
市中の景観 **44**
七曜表 **83** 9
室内用鉢植え **61** 39
尻尾 **65** 3a, **66** 3a
辞典 **47** 24
自転車 **52** 15; 立て **52** 14; に乗っている人 **90** 4
自動: 二輪車 **52** 30, **53** 19; ぶらんこ[鞦韆] **33** 24; 変速伝動装置 **50A**
自動車: 運搬車 **49** 17; 修理工 **84** 2
市内電車 **55** 30
品書き **16** 7
芝: 刈り機 **27** 12; 生 **27** 15
支払う **17** 7
縛る **77** 12
絞り出し容器 **13** 15
縞: 馬 **66** 18; 模様の **24** 17; りす[栗鼠] **66** 6
シミーズ **22** 10
事務: 所 **83**; 机 **83** 13
締め: 具 **78** 7, **95** 16; 釘 **37** 38; (付け)る **38** 4
閉める **77** 5
指紋 **43** 24
ジャイアントパンダ **69** 20
じゃがいも **7** 23; のホイル焼き **18** 20
車庫 **27** 2
車掌 **54** 7
写真: 家 **86** 4; 機 **100** 8; 術 **100B**

ジャッキ **51** 38
シャベル **27** 31; **82** 15
斜辺 **79** 24
シャボテン[仙人掌／覇王樹] **61** 40
車輌 **54** 9; 出入道 **27** 1; と装備 **48A**
車輪 **52** 4, **57** 15
シャワー: カーテン **34** 5; ノズル **34** 4; 用キャップ **34** 3
ジャングルジム **87** 17
シャンデリア **29** 3
ジャンパー **19** 17
シャンピニオン **7** 30
シャンプー **34** 8
ジャンプする **96** 8
十 **104**; 一 **104**; 二 **104**; 三 **104**; 四 **104**; 五 **104**; 六 **104**; 七 **104**; 八 **104**; 九 **104**
銃: 剣 **48** 24; 身 **48** 23; 弾 **48** 26
十一月 **104**
十月 **104**
州間高速道路 **53** 1
蹴球 **92**
住居 **27**; 標示 **45** 24
従業員 **53** 12
ジュークボックス **16** 12
集合住宅 **45** 23
銃座 **48** 12
十字ドライバー **37** 25
鞦韆 **87** 16
絨毯／絨緞 **32** 28
(周転)軌道 **74** 21
シュートする **97** 16
十二月 **104**
獣肉 **10A**
獣肉、家禽肉および魚貝類 **10**
収納庫 **32** 3
重油 **80** 34
修理: する **38** 10; 工／屋 **84** 5
手芸 **101**
取材記者 **86** 11
主審 **92** 1, **93** 17
受信機 **100** 21
出札口 **55** 19
10セント **13** 29
手動: ブレーキ **52** 24; 変速伝動装置

50B

シュノーケル **91** 34

樹皮 **61** 35c

シュミーズ **22** 10

シュラーフザック **89** 26

主翼 **57** 9

手榴弾 **48** 29

巡航艇 **59** 16

乗員 **75** 12

消化器 **42** 11

消火: および救出活動 **42**; 栓 **42** 9

定規/定木 **76** 23

乗客 **54** 6, **55** 25

小球根 **7** 25a

上弦(の月) **74** 23

じょうご **78** 17

昇降機 **45** 17, **80** 9

錠剤 **41** 6

上肢 **4** 6

乗車券 **55** 16

猩猩 **69** 18

掌状木 **60** 15

乗船待合所 **58** 29

小腸 **5** 67

小児用: ウエットティッシュー **33**
　8; 洗浄剤 **33** 6

証人 **43** 13; 台 **43** 18

乗馬: している人 **87** 6; する **97** 13;
　(専用)道 **87** 7

消防: 兜 **42** 12; 士 **42** 10; 車 **42** 3

錠(前) **52** 13; 師 **85** 4

静脈 **5** 68

照明筒 **51** 41

小遊星 **74** 20

乗用車 **50**, **53** 15

(蒸留)酒(瓶) **16** 22

じょうろ[如雨露] **27** 16

小惑星 **74** 20

上腕 **4** 7

ジョージア州 **72** 10

ショート **93** 5

書架 **47** 11

女給 **16** 2

ジョギングコース **87** 9

食塩入れ **29** 10

職業 Ⅰ **84**; Ⅱ **85**; Ⅲ **86**

食指 **4** 25

食事: 室 **29**; に関する動作 **17**

触手 **62** 12a

燭台 **29** 28

食卓 **29** 7; 椅子 **29** 17; 用刃物 **29**
　22

食堂 **29**

食道 **5** 61

食パン **14** 12

食料品 **15** 24

女子用車体 **52** 3

女性 **2** 1

除雪車 **49** 5

書棚 **28** 22, **83** 20

食器 **29** 1; 洗い機 **30** 1; 戸棚 **29** 2,
　30 22; 用洗剤 **30** 10; 用布巾 **30** 18

ジョッキー **94** 21

ショベルカー **82** 26

書店 **45** 18

書名 **47** 9

女優 **99** 20

書類: 入れ **83** 12; 鞄 **21** 37; 綴じ
　83 22

ショルダーバッグ **21** 35

白樺 **61** 32

ジラフ **67** 29

尻 **4** 15; の側面 **4** 16

地りす[栗鼠] **66** 8

司令船 **75** 8

白 **104**; 蟻 **63** 11; 熊 **69** 22; 黒熊
　69 20; (猫) **102** 3

シロップ **18** 6

シロフォン/シロホン **98** 31

芯 **8** 2b, **9** 37a

人員 **48B**

新月 **74** 26

診察台 **39** 6

寝室 **32**

伸縮性: 繋 **33** 19; 包帯 **40** 13a

針状葉 **61** 34a

シンセサイザー **99** 21

心臓 **5** 64

腎臓 **5** 70

親族関係 **3**

身体 **4A**

人体各部 **4**

寝台 **32** 21; の足板 **32** 24; の頭板
　32 14

進入傾斜路 **53** 21

シンバル **98** 18

審判 **92** 1, **93** 17, **93** 22

新聞 **21** 48; 売店 **45** 30

診療補助者 **42** 7

森林警備隊員 **88** 5

巣 **64** 31

水泳: 着 **90** 18; パンツ **91** 33

西瓜/水瓜 **9** 26

垂下竜骨 **59** 6

水準器 **82** 3

水上スキーをしている人 **59** 10

推進装置 **75** 13

水星 **74** 11

水生/水棲哺乳動物 **68**

彗星 **74** 2

膵臓 **5** 71

垂直安定板 **57** 10

スイッチ **37** 43c

水中眼鏡 **91** 35

水道管 **35** 18

水兵 **48** 14

水平器 **82** 3

水曜日 **104**

スーツケース **56** 7

数学 **79**

スーパーマーケット **14**

スエットバンド **20** 12

スカート **21** 36

スカーフ **19** 19

スカンク **68** 8

スキー **94** 33; 板 **95** 17; 靴 **95** 15;
　斜面/場 **95C**; 帽 **19** 16; ヤー **94**
　35; リフト **95** 18; をしている人 **94**
　35

頭巾つきコート **19** 8

ずく[木菟] **64** 6

掬う **26** 13

スクーター **52** 29

スクリーン **100** 14

スケート: 靴 **19** 15, **94** 26; の刃 **94**
　27; リンク **94** 25

スコアボード **93** 19

スコップ **27** 31, **90** 17

索 引

スコーン **18** 27
頭上投影器 **76** 27
涼しい **25** 9
雀 **64** 10; 蜂 **63** 20
(スターティング)ゲート **95** 20
スタンド **52** 9, **93** 10
スチュワード **56** 70
頭痛 **40** 6
ズッキーニ **7** 27
ステーキ **18** 21; 用肉 **10** 5
ステレオ **28** 20; カセットプレー
　ヤー **100** 25
ストック **94** 34, **95** 14
ストップウォッチ **78** 13
ストレッチ **95** 19
ストロー **16** 10
ストロベリー **8** 15
砂 **91** 31; の城 **91** 32; 場 **87** 13; を
　撒く **26** 14
スナップ **101** 13
すばい桃 **8** 17
スパチュラ **40** 12a
スパゲッティー **18** 10
スパナ **36** 10
スパニエル犬 **69** 24
スピーカー **28** 21, **76** 3, **100** 24
スピードメーター **50** 10
スピットン **39** 16
スプーン **29** 8
スプリットエンド **93** 24
スプリングマットレス **32** 18
スプレー **13** 24
スペア: タイヤ **51** 39; リブ **10** 10
スペースシャトル **75C**, **75** 14
滑り台/辷台 **87** 12
滑る **97** 9
スポイト **78** 26
スポーク **52** 26
スポーツ: カー **53** 17; に関する動作
　96 ; 用ジャンパー **19** 5
スポットライト **99** 4
ズボン **20** 4, **21** 27
スポンジ **34** 7; モップ **35** 6
菫 **60** 16
李 **9** 22
スライド **100** 12; 映写機 **100** 13; ガ

ラス **78** 31
スリップ **22** 10
スリマー **22** 9
(鋭い) 喙 / 嘴 **64** 3a
寸法 **79E**
背: 板 **92** 19; (中) **4** 11; 肉 **10** 3,
　10 8; 中の痛み **40** 8; 鰭 **65**
セイウチ[海象] **68** 11
星雲 **74** 1
青果市場/青果店 **45** 28, **84** 7
清潔な **24** 6
星座 **74** 3
清浄剤 **35** 9
清掃(局)員 **49** 7
晴天の **25** 4
生徒 **76** 19
制動灯 **50** 29
製氷皿 **30** 21
制服 **21** 45
制帽 **21** 43
正方形 **79** 9
精油所 **80** 12
西洋: 芥子 **18** 1; 酸塊 **8** 11; 李 **9**
　34; 大根 **7** 29; 梨 **8** 18; 箱柳 **61**
　30; 柊 **61** 37; 松茸 **7** 30
清涼飲料 **16** 11
セーター **19** 13, **19** 23
世界地図 **70**
セカンド **93** 7
脊髄 **5** 58
石炭 **80** 7
赤道 **71** 70
石油輸送船 **58** 15
施条銃 **48** 21
舌圧子 **40** 12a
絶縁テープ **37** 34
石鹸 **34** 15; 台 **34** 6
接着剤 **37** 33; **76** 17
絶壁 **89** 21
瀬戸物 **29** 1
セパード **29** 28
(ゼム)クリップ/ゼムピン **83** 28
セメント **82** 10; 車 **49** 13, **82** 25
ゼリー **18** 30
セロ **98** 9
ゼロ **104**

セロリ **6** 10
千 **104**
栓 **34** 10, **78** 10; 抜き **16** 17, **30** 6
線 **79A**; 画を描く **77** 11; 分 **79A**
船外エンジン **59** 12
戦艦 **48** 5
扇形 **79** 15
閃光電球 **100** 7
潜水艦/潜水艇 **48** 7
戦車 **48** 10; 砲 **48** 11
船首 **58** 5
選手控え席 **93** 13
前照灯 **51** 48
先生 **76** 4
船倉 **58** 8
センター **93** 2, **93** 27
全体 **79** 29
洗濯: 籠 **35** 29; 機 **35** 30; する **38**
　16; 糊 **35** 21; 挟み **35** 20; 物 **35**
　28; 物入れ **34** 28; 用洗剤 **35** 25
蠕虫 **62** 11
剪定鋏 **27** 29
戦闘機 **48** 1
潜望鏡 **48** 8
船尾 **58** 11
前部バンパー **51** 51
洗面用: 品と化粧品 **23B** ; シンク **34**
　19
線路 **54** 10
前腕 **4** 9
象 **66** 17; 牙 **66** 17b; の鼻 **66** 17a
双眼鏡 **90** 7
臓器 **5F**
送球 **94**
惣菜売場 **14** 1
掃除: 機 **35** 16; 機を掛ける **38** 14;
　夫 **85** 9
走者 **94** 31
操縦: 士 **56** 15; 室 **56** 13, **75** 10; す
　る **97** 15
装身具 **23A** ; および化粧品 **23**
装帯 **89** 22
送電: 線 **80** 24; 塔 **80** 23
走塁する **96** 6
ソーセージ **10** 7
速記録 **43** 15

ソックス **22** 17
注ぐ **31** 4
速達便(小包) **46** 23
速度：計 **50** 10；制限標識 **53** 8
その他の：楽器 **98**；植物 **61**；針仕事
　101B；輸送手段 **55E**
祖父 **3** 2
ソファー **28** 25
ソフト：仕上げ剤 **35** 27；ボール **92**；
　ボールの球 **92** 10
祖父母 **2** 10
祖母 **3** 1
空の旅 **56**

ターミナルビル **57** 16
ターンテーブル **100** 18
大宇宙 **74**
対角線 **79** 20
大工 **85** 2
泰山木 **61** 29
体重計 **34** 32
退出：傾斜路 **53** 2；する **77** 13
　大猩猩 **69** 17
体操 **94**；選手 **94** 23
大腿 **4** 18
　橙色 **104**
台地 **88** 1
タイツ **19** 14
タイトエンド **93** 30
台所 **30**
大パンダ **69** 20
タイピスト **83** 6
タイプ：する **77** 10；ライター **83** 10；
　用椅子 **83** 17
大砲 **48** 11
タイマー **78** 13
タイヤ **50** 37, **52** 28
大洋 **70**
太陽 **74** 7, **80** 3；系 **74B**；熱収集器／
　蒐集器 **80** 17
大陸 **70**
タイル **34** 27
ダウンベスト **19** 12
楕円(形) **79** 18
タオル掛け **34** 25
鷹 **64** 7

高い **24** 11
高さ **79** 34
高高指 **4** 26
打楽器 **98**
滝 **80** 11；**89** 18
タクシー **55D**, **55** 27；運転士 **55**
　26；乗り場 **55** 28
(卓上)計算器 **83** 19, **100** 34
タグボート **58** 13
タクラマカン砂漠 **71** 53
凧[紙鳶] **91** 22
蛸 **62** 6
タコス **18** 23
打者 **92** 7, **93** 14
出す **17** 3
駝鳥 **64** 12
卓球 **94**
ダッグアウト **93** 13
ダッシュボード **50** 19
手綱 **94** 22
竜の落し子[海馬] **65** 1
縦／竪：抗 **80** 10；樋 **27** 18
　鬣／騣 **67** 21a；犬 **69** 30
炭団 **27** 24
棚 **47** 26
種 **8** 8c
ダブルベース **98** 10
食べる **17** 1
卵 **64** 13
玉子(の目玉焼き) **18** 31
玉菜 **6** 3
球拾い **93** 18
ダム **80** 18
タラップ **58** 20
垂木／榱 **82** 1
樽の栓 **16** 20
段 **82** 9
担架 **39** 12
タンカー **58** 15
断崖 **89** 21
タンクローリー **49** 3
炭鉱 **80** 6
ダンサー **99** 3
端子 **51** 55
単車 **52** 30, **53** 19
短銃 **43** 7

箪笥 **32** 30
男子用：車体 **52** 11；パンツ **22** 3
男性 **2** 2
タンバリン／タンブリン **98** 17
短パン **20** 14
ダンプカー **49** 14
暖房 **80** 27
男優 **99** 19
暖炉 **28** 8
チアリーダー **93** 20
地域住民の公園 **87**
小さい **24** 7
チームスポーツ **92**
チェーン **52** 18；ソー **27** 25
チェックイン **56**
チェロ **98** 9
チェンジレバー **52** 22
地下鉄 **54B**；駅 **44** 16
地球 **74** 8；**74** 13；儀 **47** 19
蓄電池 **51** 54
乳首 **3** 18
ちさ／ちしゃ[萵苣] **6** 6
地図帳 **47** 20
父 **3** 5
乳牛 **66** 32, **81** 11
地中海 **70** 24
チップ **55** 22
地方検事 **43** 17
茶色 **104**
チャック **101** 16
茶碗 **29** 20
中央：(走行)車線 **53** 6；分離壁 **53**
　18, **82** 24
中堅手 **93** 2
注射 **41** 8；器 **39** 27；針 **39** 26
駐車：場 **45** 19；灯 **51** 49
中心 **79** 13
チューナー **100** 21
チューバ **98** 27
チューブ **13** 15；の浮き袋 **91** 29
厨房 **30**
注文する **17** 5
注油する **38** 12
チューリップ **11** 20, **60** 1
蝶 **63** 3
長円(形) **79** 18

索 引

(長距離)バス **53** 20
長江 **71** 69
頂上 **89** 20
聴衆 **99** 15
長春花 **60** 6
聴診器 **39** 9
調整食品売場 **14** 1
朝鮮薊 **6** 11
腸詰め **10** 7
頂点 **79** 21
長方形 **79** 19
跳躍する **96** 8
調理: 済み食品 **18**; 台 **30** 27
鳥類 **64**
チョーク **76** 10; 受け **76** 9
直線 **79** 1; コース **95** 19
著者名 **47** 8
貯蔵・醸酵塔 **81** 4
直角 **79** 23; 形 **79** 19; 三角形 **79** 22
チョッキ **21** 39
直径 **79** 12
直交線 **79** 2
塵: 取り **35** 8; 箱 **34** 13; 叩き **35** 2
チンパンジー **69** 16
陳列: 棚 **14** 6, **47** 17; 冷蔵庫 **15** 16
通勤: 客 **55** 17; 列車 **55** 14
通信衛星 **75** 2
ツードアセダン車 **51D**
通風孔 **50** 21
ツーリングハンドル **52** 12
通路 **14** 10, **56** 23
柄 **37** 43b
使い捨て紙おむつ[御襁褓] **33** 12
月 **74** 9; 着陸船 **75** 7; の形相 **74C**; の名称 **104**
突き抜けて **103** 1
机 **28** 14, **76** 16, **83** 13
衝羽根朝顔 **60** 7
蔦漆 **61** 45
突っ掛け靴 **21** 42
筒先 **42** 17
綴り **13** 17
綱 **89** 23
繋ぎ **21** 30
角 **66** 16a
翼 **57** 9, **64** 1a

(鍔つき)帽子 **19** 18
唾吐き **39** 16
壺 **12** 6
蕾／萼 **60** 18a
妻 **2** 4
爪先 **5** 54
積み: 木 **33** 32; 荷 **58** ·10
摘む **26** 7
爪 **4** 23; 切り **23** 31; ブラシ **34** 20; 鑢 **23** 24
詰める **26** 9
釣り **88**; 糸 **88** 8; 竿 **88** 7; 用網 **88** 9
吊: 革 **54** 8; 床 **27** 11; 包帯 **39** 3
つるこけ桃 **8** 13
蔓状植物 **61** 42
吊す **38** 6
鶴嘴 **82** 13
橡 **61** 33b
手 **4B**; 斧 **36** 17; 首 **4** 21; 錠 **43** 4; 摺 **28** 11; に持つ **17** 12; 荷物 **56** 8; 荷物検査 **56**; 風琴 **98** 28; 拭きタオル **34** 23; 袋 **19** 1; 投げ弾 **48** 29; (指)の爪 **4** 23; (を)挙げる **77** 1
ティー **95** 13; シャツ **21** 29; ポット **29** 19
ディーゼルオイル **80** 34
庭園用ホース **27** 14
定期刊行物部 **47** 15
庭球 **94**
提琴 **98** 7
停車合図紐 **54** 1
ディスクジョッキー **86** 9
ディスプレー **100** 32
ティッシュペーパー **32** 13
底辺 **79** 7
低木 **61** 41
デージー **60** 5
テーブル: クロス **29** 16; (の上を)整える **17** 8
テールランプ **50** 31
手押し: 一輪車 **27** 32; 車 **82** 23, **87** 4
手紙 **46** 7
テキサス州 **73** 43
擲弾 **48** 29

出口 **53** 2; 標示板 **53** 24
デッキ **58** 22; チェアー **90** 20
鉄琴 **98** 31
天辺に／で **102** 10
手長猿 **69** 15
テニス **94**; コート **95A**; ボール **94** 1
テネシー州 **73** 42
掌 **4** 29
デパート **44** 5
手羽肉 **11** 22
デラウエア州 **72** 8
テリヤ **69** 25
出る **77** 13
テレビ: アンテナ **27** 3;(受像機) **28** 18, **100** 5
テレビジョン技術 **100** 5
店員 **86** 12
点火スイッチ **50** 14
天花粉 **33** 7
電気 **80** 32; ギター **99** 26; 工 **85** 6; 座布団 **41** 3; スタンド **28** 28; 洗濯機 **35** 30; 掃除機 **35** 16; ドリル **37** 43
天気予報官 **86** 1
電球 **35** 22
電極 **51** 55
天候に関する表現 **25**
甜菜 **7** 33
電算機 **100E**;(の端末) **76** 8, **83** 16
電子: 技術および写真術 **100**; レンジ **30** 23
天井 **28** 2; 扇風機 **28** 1
電信柱 **80** 26
電線工事作業員 **82** 17
(天体)望遠鏡 **74** 22
電柱 **80** 26
テント **89** 24
電動: 研磨機 **37** 26; 鋸 **27** 25
転倒する **96** 7
電灯の: 傘 **28** 27; スイッチ **32** 25
天道虫[瓢虫] **63** 14
店内籠 **14** 8
天然ガス **80** 29
天王星 **74** 17
天火 **30** 32;(で)固め焼きする **31** 14

天秤 **78** 4
臀部 **4** 15
天幕 **89** 24
電話:(器) **32** 26; **83** 15; 交換機 **83** 3; 交換手 **83** 1
ドア: 把手 **50** 4; ロック **50** 1
樋 **27** 11
トイレットペーパー **34** 30
トイレブラシ **34** 31
東海 **70** 36
唐: 辛子/芥子[蕃椒] **7** 22; 黍 **6** 12, **60** 24; なす[茄子] **7** 26
投函口 **46** 13
投球する **97** 10
道具: 置き場 **27** 28; 箱 **36** 23
瞳孔 **5** 48
投手 **93** 12
搭乗 **56**; カード **56** 18; 客 **56** 3; 桟橋 **58** 20; 手続き **56**
頭触角 **62** 1b
灯台 **58** 14
胴体 **57** 14
頭髪 **4** 30
頭部 **4** C
動物園 **87** 1
動脈 **5** 69
(とう)もろこし[(玉)蜀黍] **6** 12, **60** 24
動力源 **80A**
道路: 工事 **82b**; 清掃車 **49** 1; 標識 **53** 23
蟷螂/螳螂 **63** 7
遠ざかって **103** 5
トースター **30** 16
トースト **18** 33
通り **45** 31; 抜けて **103** 1
とかげ[石竜子] **65** 15
毒: 漆 **61** 44; オーク **61** 43; 針 **63** 8a
刺 **60** 18c
時計 **23** 10, **76** 2; のベルト **23** 11
床屋 **84** 3
ところに/で **102** 1
登山 **89**; 靴 **19** 9
綴じ **13** 17
閉じた **24** 16

図書: 館員 **47** 1; 司書 **47** 23
閉じる **77** 5
土星 **74** 16
塗装工 **85** 7
土台 **82** 11
(とっくり[徳利]襟の)セーター **19** 13
とど[胡獱] **68** 12
整える **17** 8, **38** 8
飛び: 込む **97** 14; 跳ねる **96** 8
溝鼠 **66** 7
トマト **7** 19
留め: 金 **23** 17, **78** 7; ねじ[螺子/捻子/捩子] **37** 39
艫 **58** 11
土曜日 **104** 7
虎 **68** 2
ドライバー **37** 24
トラクター **81** 15
トラック **53** 25; 運転士 **49** 16
ドラム **98** 19; 奏者 **99** 27
トランク **51** 40
トランス **80** 25
トランペット **98** 25
取り替える **38** 13
取り付け部品 **35** 17
鶏肉 **11** 24; 一羽 **11** 16
(鳥の)巣 **64** 31
ドリブルする **97** 11
塗料 **37** 31
ドリル **39** 15; (の)曲がり柄 **36** 9
取る **17** 10
捕る **96** 4
ドル紙幣 **13** 25
トレーナー: ズボン **20** 10; (の上着) **20** 8
トレーラー: 車 **49** 15; ハウス **53** 10
ドレッシング **18** 12
トレンチコート **21** 38
トロッコ **80** 8
ドロップハンドル **52** 2
泥除け **52** 10
トロンボーン **98** 23
鈍角 **79** 5
団栗/橡 **61** 33b; 形かぼちゃ[南瓜] **7** 28
緞帳 **99** 1

とんぼ[蜻蛉/蜻蜒] **63** 4
ナイフ **29** 15
ナイフ・フォーク・スプーン類 **29** 22
内部器官 **5F**
ナイル川 **71** 63
(ナイロン製)靴下 **22** 6
長い **24** 2
長椅子 **44** 14, **87** 10
長上着 **19** 24
中: から外へ **103** 7; に/で **102** 7; へ **103** 12; 指 **4** 26
長さ **79** 36
長袖 **20** 15
流れ星 **74** 5
なす(び)[茄子] **7** 21
投げる **97** 10
夏 **26**
ナット **37** 39
棗椰子 **9** 23
名無し指 **4** 27
七 **104**
ナプキン **29** 14
鍋掴み **30** 34
波 **91** 24; 乗り板 **91** 25; 乗りをする **97** 12
なめくじ(ら/り)[蛞蝓] **62** 4
納屋回り **81** 8
楢 **61** 33
南極: 海 **70** 14; 大陸 **70** 7
南京豆 **9** 28
軟膏 **41** 9
ナンバープレート **50** 28
南氷洋 **70** 14
南米 **70** 2
二 **104**; の腕 **4** 7
二階正面桟敷 **99** 13
二月 **104**
肉屋 **84** 13
煮込み隠元(豆)/鶉豆 **18** 3
西 **71** 74
ニジェール川 **71** 61
二十 **104**; 一 **104**
25セント貨 **13** 30
日曜日 **104**
日光浴をしている人 **90** 19

索 引

日食/日蝕 **74** 10

二分の一 **79** 30

日本海 **70** 36

荷物: 室 **51** 40, **75** 9; 棚 **56** 21

乳牛 **67** 32, **81** 11

ニュー: ジャージー州 **73** 30; ハンプシャー州 **73** 29; メキシコ州 **73** 31; ヨーク州 **73** 32

入室する **77** 14

ニュースキャスター **86** 2

乳製品 **14** 4

二輪車 **52**

煮る **17** 4

二塁手 **93** 7

楡 **61** 36

庭師 **85** 3

鶏 **64** 23

人形 **33** 28; の家 **33** 25

人参 **7** 32

葫[大蒜] **7** 25

縫(い): 包の動物人形 **33** 27; 針 **101** 18; 目 **101** 10, **101** 19; 物 **101A**

拭う **38** 5

布: おむつ[御襁褓] **33** 13; 切れ **35** 4; 地 **101** 4

濡れた **25** 15

根 **61** 35d

葱 **7** 31

ネクタイ **21** 47; 留め **23** 14; ピン **23** 13, **23** 14

ネクタリン **8** 17

ネグリジェ **22** 21

猫 **68** 4

ねじ[螺子/捻子/捩子]: 釘 **37** 42; 回し **37** 24; 山 **37** 42b

鼠取り器 **35** 32

熱 **40** 2, **80** 27; 気球 **57** 1

ネックレス **23** 6

ネット **92** 23, **95** 2

ネバダ州 **73** 28

根深 **7** 31

寝袋 **89** 26

ネブラスカ州 **73** 27

寝巻き **22** 19

練り: 歯磨き **34** 16; 焼き製品 **14** 11

ネルのシャツ **19** 3

捻挫 **40** 13

燃焼部 **30** 29

燃料: 運搬車 **49** 3; 計 **50** 9

脳 **5** 57

農家 **27A**

農業就労者 **81** 7

濃耕および牧畜 **81**

農産物 **14** 9

農場: 経営者 **81** 7; 内住居 **81** 3; 内物置 **81** 5

ノース: カロライナ州 **73** 33; ダコタ州 **73** 34

喉/咽 **5** 59; の痛み **40** 12

鋸 **36** 8

ノズル **42** 17

野鼠 **66** 7

延ばす **17** 11

上って **103** 11

飲み物 **14** 14

飲む **17** 2

糊 **37** 33, **76** 17

乗(り): 換え切符 **54** 4; 組員 **75** 12

乗る **97** 13

歯 **4** 42; 医者 **39** 17; 痛 **40** 9; ブラシ **34** 21

葉 **61** 36a

パーキングメーター **45** 20

バージニア州 **73** 46

バーテン **16** 21

ハードコピー **83** 8

バーナー **30** 29

ハーネス **89** 22

ハーブ **6** 9

ハープ **98** 6

ハーフバック **93** 33

ハーモニカ **98** 30

バーモント州 **73** 45

バイアステープ **101** 12

灰色 **104**; 熊 **69** 23

ハイエナ **69** 30

バイオリン **98** 7

ハイカー **88** 2

配管工 **85** 1

排気管 **52** 33

排球 **92**

バイク **52** 30, **53** 19

背景 **99** 2

灰皿 **16** 29

陪審員: 席 **43** 20; 団 **43** 21

肺(臓) **5** 63

ハイソックス **22** 16

バイソン **67** 19

排水: 管 **27** 18; 孔 **34** 9

配達員 **85** 10

売店 **90** 2

パイナップル **8** 4

ハイヒール **20** 25

パイプ **16** 26

バイヤステープ **101** 12

培養皿 **78** 3

入る **77** 14

バウンドする **97** 11

蠅 **63** 18

剝ぎ取り器 **36** 14

衡/秤 **14** 7, **34** 32, **78** 4

掃く **38** 7

爆撃機 **48** 2

麦酒 **16** 23

白鳥 **64** 28

爆弾 **48** 3

瀑布 **80** 11, **89** 18

白墨 **76** 10; 受け **76** 9

白楊 **61** 30

刷毛 **76** 18

バケツ[馬穴] **35** 15, **90** 16

バケットシート **50** 16

箱 **13** 12

運ぶ **26** 16

鰲 **62** 13a

鋏(一丁) **101** 17

挟み式イヤリング **23** 15

梯子 **42** 1, **82** 8; (の)段 **82** 9

榛の実 **9** 30

馬車 **55** 33

パジャマ **22** 19

場所を表わす前置詞 **102**

走る **96** 6

バス **53** 20, **54A**; 運転士 **54** 3; タオル **34** 24; 停留所 **44** 13; マット **34** 12; ローブ **22** 20

バスーン **98** 14

バスケット：ネット **92** 20; ボール **92**; ボールの球 **92** 21
バスする **96** 5
パズル **33** 31
パソコン **100** 31
櫨 [黄櫨] (漆) **61** 44
旗 **76** 1, **82** 20
バター **18** 18
パター **94** 9
ばた足練習ボード **91** 27
肌着 **22** 1
畑／畠 **81** 16; りす[栗鼠] **66** 8
八 **104**
鉢 **12** 6; 巻き **20** 12
撥 **98** 19a
パチオ **27** 17
蜂鳥 **64** 2
八月 **104**
八十 **104**
二十日：大根 **7** 29; 鼠 **66** 9
バック：ボード **92** 19; ミラー **50** 7; ライト **50** 30
パック **92** 17
バックル **20** 17
バッジ **43** 5
発射台 **75** 15
発疹 **40** 1
ばった[飛蝗／蝗虫] **63** 6
バッター **92** 7
ハッチバック **51** 43
バッテリー **51** 54
発電 **80B**; 機 **80** 21; 所 **80** 20
(8.5×14インチの)法律用箋 **83** 26
バット **92** 5; ボーイ **93** 18
発動機船 **59** 13
鳩 **64** 1
ハドソン湾 **70** 18
波止場 **58** 3, **58** 28
花 **60**; あやめ／菖蒲 **60** 11; サフラン [洞夫藍] **60** 9; 水木 **61** 28; 屋 **84** 11; 椰菜 **6** 1
鼻 **4** 36; の穴 **4** 37
放つ **97** 16
バナナ(一房) **9** 20
羽 **64** 7a
羽根 **63** 4a

翅 **64** 1a
幅 **79** 35
パパイヤ **8** 6
バフィン湾 **70** 16
蛤 **11** 32
母 **3** 4
ハム **10** 12
填め込み式レコード針 **100** 19
ハモニカ **98** 30
腹 **4** 14
ばら[薔薇] **60** 18
パラナ川 **71** 60
針 **66** 11a; 編みレース **101** 26; 金 **36** 35; 金綴じ器 **83** 27; 金剝し **83** 29; 刺し／立て／坊主／山 **101** 3; 目 **101** 19
バリケード **82** 21
貼り付け紙 **46** 21
春 **26**; 巻き **18** 25
バルチック海／バルト海 **70** 22
馬鈴薯 **7** 23
バレー／バレエ **99A**
バレーボール **92**; の球 **92** 22
バレンツ海 **70** 23
ハワイ州 **72** 11
半：径 **79** 14; 割／裂 **65** 14; 身 **11** 17; ズボン **20** 14; 袖 **20** 21; ダース **13** 13; 分 **79** 30
パン **49** 9, **53** 26
パン：ケーキ **18** 5; 職人 **84** 8; 屋 **44** 6, **84** 8; 用小皿 **29** 11
ハンガー **32** 2
バンカー **95** 11
ハンググライダー **57** 6
犯罪および刑罰 **43**
パンジー **60** 2
判事 **43** 10; 席 **43** 16
反射板 **52** 25
バンジョー **98** 5
帆船 **59** 4
パンダ **69** 20
パンツ **22** 12
帆底材 **59** 7
パンティー **22** 11; ストッキング **22** 5
ハンド：バッグ **20** 23; ボール **94**; ボールの球 **94** 12
バンドエイド **39** 4

ハンドル **50** 8
ハンバーガー：(の肉) **18** 9; (用)パン **18** 17
販売員 **86** 12
ハンモック **27** 12
火 **28** 9
ピアス **23** 16; (の)受け具 **23** 19; (の)差し針 **23** 18
ピアノ **98** 1
ビーカー **78** 23
ビーズ(紐) **23** 7
ビーチ：タオル **90** 15; パラソル **90** 21; ボール **90** 11
ビート **7** 33; 板 **91** 27
ピーナッツ **9** 28
ビーバー **66** 12
ビーフシチュー **18** 14
ビール **16** 23
ビオラ **98** 8
被疑者 **43** 3
東 **71** 73; シナ海 **70** 38
引き：金 **48** 22; 網 **59** 11
(引き出し[抽斗]つき)鏡台 **32** 9
(ビキニ)パンティー **22** 11
曳船 **58** 3
低い **24** 12
低テーブル **28** 26
ピクニック：籠 **88** 13; 場 **88**; テーブル **88** 15
ピクルス **18** 8
ひげ剃り：後化粧水 **23** 21; クリーム **23** 22
鼻孔 **4** 37
被告：側弁護官／弁護士 **43** 22; 人 **43** 23
膝 **4** 19
ピザ **18** 29
肘／肱 **4** 8; 掛け **50** 3
美術担当者 **86** 3
秘書 **83** 11
非常ブレーキ **50** 15
ピストル **43** 7
額 **4** 32
左(追い越し)車線 **53** 5
ピック **98** 11a
引っ越し：業者 **49** 12; 専用車 **49** 11

索　引

ピッコロ 98 12

羊 67 25, 81 10

ヒッチハイカー 53 9

ピッチャー 93 12; マウンド 93 11

ビット 37 43a

ヒップ 4 16

蹄 67 35b

ビデオ 100 4; カセット 100 3; カメ
　ラ 100 1

尾灯 50 31

ひと切れ 13 22

ひとで[海星] 62 7

人差し指 4 25

眸 5 48

雛 64 22; 菊 60 5

避難階段 42 4

狒狒 69 19

備品管理係 93 18

尾部 57 10

ピペット 78 14

ひまわり[向日葵] 60 19

ヒマラヤ山脈 71 47

姫貝 11 34, 62 3

紐 46 20

百 104

百日草 60 13

百万 104

日焼け止め化粧水 91 39

ヒヤシンス[風信子] 60 10

百科事典 47 25

百貨店 44 5

豹 68 1

氷点 25 11

美容師 84 10

氷嚢 41 4

漂白剤 35 26

日除け 27 8, 32 12, 33 1, 50 5; 眼
　鏡 90 14

雛 64 22

平: 槽 37 28; 底荷船 58 12; 台ト
　ラック 49 18; 土間席 99 12

開いた 24 15

開き身 11 28

(平たい) 喙 ／ 嘴 64 24a

鰭 65 3b; 足 68 12a

広口瓶 12 9

広げる 17 11

瓶/壜 12 3

ピン 23 8, 94 5

ピンキング 鋏 101 5

ピンク 104

ピンセット 78 32

ビンディング 95 16

ピンポン 94; ボール 94 19

ファースト 93 8

ファイブドア 51E

ファイル: 係 83 23; キャビネット
　83 21

ファウルライン 93 9

ファゴット 98 14

ファスナー 101 16

ファッションデザイナー 86 6

ファミリーレストラン 16A; および
　カクテルラウンジ 16

ファンベルト 51 53

ブイ 58 16

フィニッシュ 95 21

(Vネックの) セーター 19 23

フィルム: (一巻) 100 17; (一本)
　100 10

風琴 98 29

風車 80 19

封書 46 7

ブーツ 19 21

封筒 46 16, 83 31

ブーム 59 7

風力 80 4

フェアウエー 95 12

フェリー 58 17

笛 90 5

フォーク 29 12; リフト 58 4

鰭 65 5

深: 靴 19 21; 皿 13 23; 鍋 30 13

噴き上げ 87 14

武器と弾薬 48C

拭き取る 38 5

拭く 38 9

複式収穫機 81 17

複写機 47 18, 83 24

副操縦士 56 16

腹痛 40 7

脹ら脛 4 20

袋 8 8a, 12 8, 66 3c; (入り) 砂糖
　16 13; 熊 66 1

梟 64 6

節 4 22

付随車 53 10

蓋 30 9

豚 67 30; 肉 10 6; 肉の厚切り 18
　15

舞台 99 5

部隊 48B

(二瘤) 駱駝 67 33

二股手袋 19 11

普段着 20

縁縫い 101 11

部長 83 18

フットボールの球 92 13

筆 76 18

埠頭 58 3, 58 28

葡萄 (一房) 8 1

不動産仲介人 85 5

太腿 4 18

撫 61 33

船: 着き場 58 3, 58 28; 荷 58 10

父母 2 6

踏み台 35 1

浮標 58 16

冬 26

フライドチキン 18 28

フライパン 30 5

ブラインド 32 12, 33 1

ブラウス 21 34

プラグ 37 43d

ブラジャー 22 13

フラスコ 78 2

フラッグ 95 9

ブラックベリー 8 12

フラッシュ 100 7

プラットホーム 54 11

フラミンゴ 94 29

プラム 9 34

フランカー 93 31

ぶらんこ 87 16

ブリーフ 22 12

フリスビー 90 13

プリズム 78 1

フリッパー 91 36

フリュート **98** 13
プリンター **83** 4
プリント **100** 11; アウト **83** 8; 柄の **24** 21
古い **24** 14
ブルー: ジーンズ **19** 6; ベリー **8** 14
フルート **98** 13
ブルゾン **19** 17
プルーン **9** 22
ブルドーザー **82** 27
フルバック **93** 34
ブレーカー **35** 5
ブレーキ **52** 17; ペダル **50** 26; ランプ **50** 29
ブレザー **20** 2
ブレスレット **23** 9
触れる **77** 2
フレンチホルン **98** 26
フロアシフト **50** 24
ブローチ **23** 8
プログラマー **86** 16
プログラム **99** 17
ブロッコリ **6** 2
プロパンガス **80** 30
プロペラ機 **57** 7
フロリダ州 **72** 9
フロントガラス **51** 45
噴煙 **42** 15
分光器 **78** 1
噴射式: エンジン **57** 11; 推進機 **57** 18
噴水 **87** 14
分数 **79**
ブンゼン灯/ブンゼンバーナー **78** 20
分銅 **78** 5
噴霧器 **13** 24
分類番号 **47** 7
へ **103** 9
ヘア: ドライヤー **34** 26; ブラシ **32** 7
平均台 **94** 24
平行線 **79** 4
ベーコン **10** 11, **18** 32
ベース **93** 6, **98** 10; ギター奏者 **99** 23; ライン **95** 4
ベーリング海 **70** 34
壁面飾り棚 **28** 19

壁内テニス **94**
軸先 **58** 5
ベスト **21** 39
ペダル **39** 18, **52** 19
ペチュニア **60** 7
ヘッド: プロテクター **94** 14; フォーン/ホーン **100** 29; ライト **51** 48; レスト **50** 35
ベッド **32** 21; カバー **32** 23; (を)整える **38** 8
ペトリ皿 **78** 3
紅: 差し指 **4** 27; 鶴 **64** 29
蛇 **65** 9
ベビー: カー **33** 14; サークル **33** 30; パウダー **33** 7; ローション **33** 6
部屋: 着 **22** 21; 履き **22** 18
ベランダ **27** 5
ベリー類 **8**
ペリカン **64** 24
ヘリコプター **57** 2
ペルシャ湾 **70** 28
ベルト **20** 16, **89** 22; の留め金 **20** 17
ヘルメット **21** 28, **42** 12, **52** 7, **82** 4, **92** 6, **92** 14
ベレー帽 **19** 22
辺 **79** 10
変圧器 **80** 25
ベンガル湾 **70** 32
便器 **34** 29
ペンキ **37** 31; 皿 **37** 28; 刷毛 **37** 30; 屋 **85** 7; ローラー **37** 29; を塗る **26** 1
ペンギン **64** 27
ペンシルベニア州 **73** 38
返送用住所 **46** 8
変速レバー **50** 17, **50** 24
ベンチ **44** 14, **87** 10
ペンチ **36** 19
扁桃 **9** 31
弁当箱 **21** 31
帆 **59** 9
ホイールキャップ **50** 36
ポインセチヤ **60** 15
法衣 **43** 11
望遠鏡 **74** 22

防寒用下着 **22** 7
帚/箒 **35** 7; 星 **74** 22
膀胱 **5** 72
方向指示: 器レバー **50** 11; 灯 **51** 50
縫合部 **39** 21
帽子 **19** 2, **19** 8
(棒状の)塊 **12** 5
防水長靴 **88** 10
宝石: 商 **84** 12; 箱 **32** 4
包装 **12** 4
包帯 **39** 24
砲弾 **48** 27
膨脹式ゴムボート **59** 20
法廷 **43B**; 吏 **43** 19; 速記者 **43** 14
砲塔 **48** 12
法服 **43** 11
方に **103** 4
放牧場 **81** 6
法律用箋 **83** 26
ほうれんそう[菠薐草] **6** 8
頬 **4** 35; 紅 **23** 32
ポークチャップ **18** 15
ホース **42** 8, **51** 57
ポーチ **27** 6
ボート **59** 23
ボーフォート海 **70** 15
ホームプレート **93** 15
ボーリング **94**; のボール **94** 6
ホール **94** 8
ボール **13** 23, **30** 24; 箱 **12** 1; ペン **76** 22
保温瓶 **88** 14
捕球する **96** 4
ボクシング **94**
牧畜: 業者(女子) **81** 22; 業者(男子) **81** 21; 場 **81C**
牧童 **81** 21, **81** 22
(北斗七星の)星座 **74** 3
北米 **70** 1
牧羊犬 **69** 28
ポケット **21** 41
歩行: 器 **33** 23; 者 **44** 12
保護: ゴーグル **94** 28; 帽 **82** 4; 眼鏡 **78** 12
埃を払う **38** 15
穂先 **37** 43a

索 引

拇指 4 24; 球 5 52
穂軸 6 12a
乾し草(の梱) 81 13
乾し草·家畜·農器具置場 81 5
乾し/干し葡萄 9 24
捕手 92 2, 93 16
補助輪 52 1
帆: つきボード 59 15; 柱 59 8; 船 59 4
帆立貝[海扇] 62 10; (の柱) 11 35
蛍 63 17
ボタン 20 3, 101 9; 孔 101 8
北海 70 21
北極: 海 70 8; 熊 69 22
ホック 101 13
ホッケーのスティック 92 18
ボックス席 99 11
発疹 40 1
ホッチキス 83 27
ホット: ケーキ 18 5; ドッグ 18 2
北氷洋 70 8
ポテト: チップ 18 4; フライ 18 27
歩道 45 25
ポニー 67 20
哺乳: 動物Ⅰ 66; 動物Ⅱ 68; 瓶 33 17; (瓶の)乳首 33 18
骨つき肋肉 10 10
炎/焰 36 39, 78 21
ポプラ 61 30
ボラード 58 26
ホルスター 43 8
ボルト 37 38
本: 箱 28 22, 80 23; 屋 45 18; 塁 93 15
盆 16 33
ボンゴ 98 22
ボンネット 51 47
ポンプ 13 14; 車 42 2

マイクロフィルム 47 13; リーダー 47 14
(真)後ろに/で 102 9
前: 脚/足 66 3d; 掛け 16 6; に/で 102 6; ベランダ 27 6
曲がり柄 36 9

薪 28 10; を割る 26 11
巻き 12 11; 揚げ機 58 23; 尺 36 21, 101 15
幕 99 1
枕 32 16; カバー 32 15
孫: 息子 2 12; 娘 2 11
マサチューセッツ州 72 21
(真)下に/で 102 8
鱒 65 2
マスカラ 23 28
マスコミと芸能 86A
マスト 59 8
(混ぜ物)ボール 30 24
待ち針 101 20
松 61 34; 笠/ふぐり[陰嚢]/ぼっくり[毬] 61 34b; 葉杖 39 7
睫 5 46
マッシュ: ポテト 18 17; ルーム 7 30
マットレス 32 17
窓 27 7, 102 1; 口 46 15; 口係員 86 15; 用洗剤 35 10
俎板/真魚板 30 26
マニキュア 23 25
マフィン 18 27
瞼 5 45
マフラー 19 19
魔法瓶 88 14
繭 63 2
眉: (毛) 5 44; 書き/墨 23 26
マリーゴールド 60 6
丸: 木船 59 2; 首セーター 19 7; ごと 11 16, 11 27; 酸塊 8 11; 鋸 36 20; 窓 58 21
周りを/に/で 103 2
満月 74 24
マンゴー 8 5
マンション 45 23
マントルピース 28 7
マンドリン 98 4
マンホール 45 32
(真ん)前に/で 102 6
万力 37 36
ミートボール 18 11
磨き: 粉 35 9; たわし[束子] 30 11
磨く 38 3

幹 61 35b
ミキサー 30 12
右(出口専用)車線 53 7
未決箱 83 12
短い 24 1
ミシガン州 72 22
ミシシッピー: 川 71 58; 州 72 24
ミシン 101 1
氷 42 16; 着 90 18; 切り 30 2; グラス 29 6; 差し 29 4, 78 2; 栓 34 18; 玉模様の 24 19; 飲み場 81 25, 87 19; を遣る 26 5
ミズーリ州 73 25
道走り 64 32
三揃(スーツ) 21 40
ミット 27 20
蜜蜂 63 19
密閉容器 30 15
三叉 81 14
緑(色) 104
ミトン 19 11
南 71 72; アメリカ大陸 70 2; シナ海 70 39; 大西洋 70 12; 太平洋 70 10
ミニカム 100 2
ミネソタ州 72 23
見張り台 90 8
耳 4 34; 当て 19 10; 飾り 23 1
みみず[蚯蚓] 62 11
みみずく[木菟] 64 6
ミュージカルコメディー 99B
舳 58 5
ミルク入れ 29 24
ムース 67 35
向って 103 4
むかで[百足/蜈蚣] 63 22
蒸し: 器 30 3; 焼き鍋 30 14
虫: 螫され 40 3; 眼鏡 78 15
無地の 24 20
蒸す 31 12
息子 3 16
結ぶ 77 12
娘 3 15
胸 4 12; 肉 11 21
無名指 4 27

紫(色) **104**
目/眼 **5D**; 隠し **27** 8, **32** 12, **33** 1; 薬 **41** 10; 覚し時計 **32** 8; の回りの痣 **40** 5
姪 **3** 14
冥王星 **74** 19
雌牛/牝牛 **67** 32
メーター **55** 23
メーン州 **72** 19
メキシコ湾 **70** 19
眼鏡 **21** 44; 蛇 **65** 11
芽キャベツ **6** 4
メジャー **101** 15
メッセンジャー **86** 19
メニュー **16** 7
目盛りつきシリンダー **78** 25
メモ用紙 **83** 25
メリーランド州 **72** 20
綿: 玉 **39** 23; 棒 **33** 10
麺棒 **30** 25
毛布 **32** 20
モーターボート **59** 13
モーテル **90** 3
木材 **36** 4; (用)鉋 **37** 32
木星 **74** 15
木曜日 **104**
潜る **97** 14
木蓮 **61** 29
凭れ椅子 **28** 16
木管楽器 **98**
木琴 **98** 31
モップ **35** 6
モデル **86** 5
モトクロス用自転車 **52** 8
物: 売り **87** 3; 置き **27** 28; 掛け **32** 1; 差/指 **76** 23; 干し紐 **35** 19
モノレール **55** 29
モハーベ砂漠 **71** 48
モビール **33** 2
揉上 **4** 33
桃 **9** 37; 色 **104**
腿 **4** 18; 肉 **11** 19; 肉の塩漬け薫製 **10** 12
舫綱 **58** 25
森 **89** 32

もろこし[蜀黍] **6** 12, **60** 24
門衛 **85** 11
モンキーレンチ **36** 12
モンタナ州 **73** 26

八百屋 **84** 7
野営 **88**
野外: 音楽堂 **87** 2; 活動 **88**; 競技場 **95**; 生活用具 **89** 27
薬罐/薬鑵 **30** 28
やぎ[山羊] **67** 28
(焼肉用)直焼炉 **30** 33
野球 **92**; のダイヤモンド **93A**; 帽 **92** 11
薬: 剤士 **84** 1; 草 **6** 9; 品戸棚 **34** 14
役職者 **86** 13
やけど[火傷] **40** 18; する **17** 14
野菜: サラダ **18** 13; ミックス **18** 16; 類 **6**
椰子 **61** 26
鋏 **36** 19
柳 **61** 31
屋根 **27** 4
破る **77** 9
山 **89** 19; 荒らし **66** 11; (状の)塊 **12** 7; 鳥 **64** 19
槍いか[烏賊] **62** 5
湯: 上がり着 **22** 20; 栓 **34** 17
遊泳者 **91** 28
ユーカリ[有加利](樹) **61** 27
遊戯用囲い **33** 30
遊撃手 **93** 5
ユーコン川 **71** 56
遊星 **74**
郵袋 **46** 4
有袋類、貧歯類、飛行哺乳動物 **66**
有蹄動物 **66**
有毒植物 **61**
郵便: 受け **46** 1; 為替 **46** 18; 局 **44** 9, **46B**; 局員 **46** 14; 車 **46** 5; 集配員 **46** 3; 制度 **46**; 配達 **46A**; 番号 **46** 12; 袋 **46** 4; 物 **46** 2; 物の種別 **46C**; ポスト **46** 6
床 **32** 29; に敷きつめたカーペット **28** 15

雪: (を)掻き落とす **26** 15; の降る **25** 3
油井 **80** 1; 櫓 **80** 2
ユタ州 **73** 44
茹でる **31** 16
ユニフォーム **92** 9
指: 挿し/貫き **101** 21; 輪 **23** 2
湯舟 **34** 11
弓 **98** 7a
油面ゲージ **51** 58
ゆり[百合] **60** 3
揺り籃 **33** 26
緩い **24** 4
洋傘 **20** 24
容器、量および貨幣の単位 **12**
用紙 **76** 13
幼児用ベッド **33** 4
揚子江 **71** 69
洋灯 **89** 29
用途と製品 **80C**
曜日の名称 **104**
洋服: 掛け **32** 2; 屋 **84** 6
用務員 **85** 9
ヨーロッパ大陸 **70** 3
浴室兼手洗い **34**
浴槽 **34** 11
浴用タオル **34** 22
横切って **103** 6
汚れた **24** 5
涎 掛け **33** 20
ヨット **59** 4
予備: タイヤ **51** 39; モップ **35** 11
読む **77** 4
四 **104**
四十 **104**
四分の一 **11** 18, **79** 31

ライオン **68** 3
ライター **16** 30
ライト **93** 3; ガード **93** 28; タックル **93** 29; バン **50C**
ライフル **48** 21
ライム **8** 10
駱駝 **67** 33
酪農場 **81A**

索 引

ラクロス **92**; のスティック **92** 16
ラケット **94** 2, **94** 18, **94** 29; ボール **94**; ボールの球 **94** 30
ラジエーター **51** 56
ラズベリー **8** 16
螺旋ノート **76** 15
落下: 傘 **48** 6; する **96** 7
落花生 **9** 28
らっこ[海獺/猟虎] **68** 10
喇叭 **52** 5; 水仙 **60** 8
ラバーカップ **35** 14
ラフ **95** 6
ラプテフ海 **70** 33
ラベル **46** 21
ラマ **66** 15
蘭 **60** 12
ランニング **20** 13
ランプ **89** 29; ウエー **53** 2
リードギター奏者 **99** 25
リオグランデ川 **71** 57
理科実験室 **78**
陸: 亀 **65** 12; 軍 **48** 15; 軍兵 **48** 16; 上競技 **94**; (上・淡水の)亀 **65** 18
りす[栗鼠] **66** 10
立体: 音響装置 **28** 20; 交差十字路/交叉十字路 **53** 4; 図形 **79C**
立方体 **79** 27
リトルリーグ **92**; の選手 **92** 8
理髪師 **84** 3, **84** 10
リモコン **28** 17
流星(体) **74** 5
留置場 **43** 1
リュックサック **19** 4
料金 **55** 21; (徴集)所 **53** 27; 箱 **54** 5; (表示)メーター **55** 23
領収書 **55** 24; **15** 20
両親 **2** 6
両生類/両棲類および爬行動物 **65B**
療養および治療法 **41**
料理: に関する動作 **31**; 人 **16** 1
旅行: 業務取扱者 **84** 4; 者 **56** 3
リラ豆 **6** 16
離陸 **57B**

リング **94** 17; スタンド/立て **78** 19; バインダー **76** 14
林檎 **8** 2
塁 **93** 6
ルイジアナ州 **72** 18
(ルーズリーフ)用紙 **76** 13
ルーペ **78** 15
ルブアルハーリー砂漠 **71** 52
零 **104**
冷却: 器 **51** 56; 塔 **80** 16
冷蔵: 庫 **30** 19; 箱 **91** 41
霊長類 **69**
冷凍: 庫 **14** 3, **30** 20; 食品 **14** 2
レース編み **101** 28
レーン **94** 4; コート **21** 38; シューズ **19** 25
レコード **100** 23
レジ **15** 21; カウンター **15** 26; 係 **15** 22
レシート **15** 20, **55** 24
レタス **6** 6
レッカー車 **49** 2
列車 **55C**
レトレーバー **69** 26
レナ川 **71** 66
レフ(ェ)リー **94** 16
レフト **93** 1; ガード **93** 26; タックル **93** 25
レポーター **86** 11
レモン[檸檬] **8** 9
煉瓦 **82** 12
レンジ **30** 30
レンズ **100** 6
レントゲン写真 **39** 1
連絡: 係 **86** 19; 船 **58** 17; 票 **83** 25
艫 **58** 11
炉: 柵 **28** 7; 心 **80** 14; (で燃える)火 **28** 9
廊下 **76** 12
籠球 **92**
蠟燭 **29** 27
漏斗 **78** 17
露営 **88**

ロードアイランド州 **73** 39
ロープ **89** 23; ウエー **55** 31
ロールパン **18** 19
ローロデックス **83** 14
濾過紙 **78** 16
六 **104**
六月 **104**
録画・再生装置 **100** 4
六十 **104**
路肩 **53** 22
ロケット **75** 13
ロッカー **76** 6
六缶入り **13** 13
ロッキー山脈 **71** 40
ロッキングチェアー **33** 16
ロックバンド **99C**
六百二十一 **104**
驢馬 **67** 23
ロビー **44** 2
路面電車 **55** 30
ロンパス **33** 19

環 **74** 16a
ワープロ/ワードプロセッサー **83** 7
ワイオミング州 **73** 50
ワイシャツ **21** 46
ワイパー **50** 6
ワイヤー **52** 23
ワイン **16** 19; グラス **29** 5
脇に/で **102** 11
腋(の下) **4** 10
惑星 **74**
枠つきリュックサック **89** 28
分け目 **4** 31
ワゴン車 **49** 9; **50C**
鷲 **64** 5
ワシントン州 **73** 47
渡す **17** 9
渡って **103** 8
渡り鶫 **64** 9
ワッシャー **37** 40
割る **31** 7
ワンピース(ドレス) **20** 22

1